Dayanna

Performance Coach™ 4

English Language Arts

CONTENTS

DEAR STUDENT

Welcome to *Performance Coach*!

We made this book to help you strengthen your reading, writing, and language skills. These skills are important to have for every subject you study this year, not just English Language Arts.

Each lesson in this book has three parts:

GETTING THE IDEA ①

Review some of the basic concepts and skills you've already learned.

② COACHED EXAMPLE

Answer a set of questions. Don't worry—the questions have hints that will help you!

LESSON PRACTICE ③

Now you're on your own! Answer more questions to show what you know.

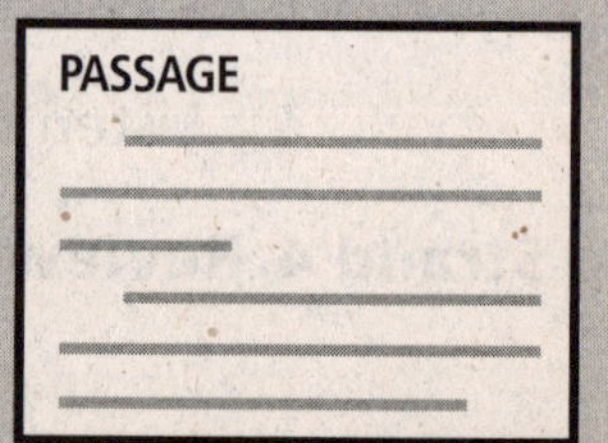

There are a few different types of questions in *Performance Coach*. For some, you will have to choose the best answer. For others, you will write out your answer. You will also see questions that have more than one part. There may be more than one correct answer for you to select. Be sure to read the directions carefully so you know how to answer each item.

HAVE A GREAT YEAR!

Sincerely,
TRIUMPH LEARNING

STRAND 1

Working with Literature

Fiction

1 GETTING THE IDEA

Fiction is a type of writing about made-up people and events. There are many types of fiction. You have probably read fiction in the form of a short story or a novel with chapters.

Type of Fiction	Description
realistic fiction	has characters, events, and a setting that could exist in the real world
historical fiction	takes place in the past and may involve important people or events from history; details are made up by the author
science fiction	tells about science and technology of the future; may be set in the future, space, or an unusual place
folktale	a story from long ago that has been repeated for many years
myth	a traditional story that explains how something was created or how it works
legend	a type of folktale about heroes and their brave actions

Every work of fiction has characters, a setting, a plot, a point of view, and a theme.

Characters

Characters are the people, animals, or magical creatures who take part in the action of a story. Authors show what characters in a story are like by including details about how they look; what they do, say, and think; how they react to others; and how others react to them. What do you learn about Mia's character in the passage on the next page? How does the author use details to show it?

Mia was busy preparing for Dora's arrival. Dora would be staying with Mia's family because her mother was ill. Mia knew Dora was worried, so she thought of ideas to take her mind off things. Dora liked to draw, so Mia sharpened her colored pencils and put them on Dora's desk. She also made a list of Dora's favorite foods for her dad to buy at the grocery store.

Setting

The **setting** of a story is where and when the story takes place. The setting can affect the characters, theme, or plot. An author may directly state the setting or just include details that give clues about it. Read the passage below. Underline details about the setting.

After weeks in a covered wagon, Benjamin could finally see the misty Oregon coast. He had traveled for miles over dusty plains, with the clip-clop of horses' hooves in his ears, and he couldn't wait for his first glimpse of the ocean.

Plot

The **plot** is what happens in a story. It is made up of a series of events. The plot has a **conflict**, or a problem the characters try to solve. An interesting plot makes the reader want to find out what will happen next and how the story will end. When you **summarize** a story, you tell in your own words the most important plot events from the beginning, middle, and end of the story. Your summary should be brief.

Point of View

The **point of view** is the perspective from which a story is told. The **narrator** is the person or character who tells the story. A story with a **first-person point of view** is told by a narrator who is a character in the story and who uses the pronoun *I*. The reader hears how only the narrator thinks and feels. In a story with a **third-person point of view,** the narrator is not a character in the story and does not use the pronoun *I*. A third-person narrator may be able to tell the thoughts and feelings of some or all of the characters.

Illustrations

Illustrations help readers understand and enjoy the text of a story. They can show details from the text more clearly. They can show what characters and settings look like. Illustrations can add to the humorous or serious mood of a story.

Theme

The **theme** of a story is the lesson or message that the author wants readers to understand. An author usually does not state the theme of the story. The reader has to figure it out by making an **inference**, or a guess based on evidence. Read the story summary below.

> Tara wanted the lead role in the school play, but she was afraid to try out. Even though she felt nervous, she found courage and auditioned for the role. To her surprise, she performed better than anyone else and got the part.

One way to find the theme of a story is to look at the challenges the characters face and how they overcome—or don't overcome—these challenges. In the story summarized above, the author is suggesting a message about facing fear. Here's how you might use text evidence to find the theme of this story.

Text Evidence	Inference about Theme
• Tara was afraid to try out but found the courage to audition. • She performed well and got the role.	People should try to reach their goals even if they feel afraid.

Language Spotlight • Context Clues

Context clues are words and phrases that help you understand the meaning of a word you do not know. Read the following sentences. The words with two underlines are clues to the meaning of *agriculture*.

> For hundreds of years, agriculture was the way most people earned a living. Farmers grew crops such as wheat, barley, potatoes, turnips, beets, and other vegetables.

What do the clue words tell you about the meaning of the word *agriculture*? Use a dictionary to check the meaning of the word.

Read the passage.

The Giant Turnip

adapted from a Russian folktale

Long, long ago, in a small village in Russia, there lived a farmer and his family.

The farmer was a big, strong old man whom everyone called Grandfather. His big, strong wife was called Grandmother. Their grandson was a big, strong young man named Ivan who had a big, strong wife named Galina.

The family grew many kinds of vegetables on their land, but Grandfather loved turnips most of all. He loved roasted turnips, turnip stew, pickled turnips—anything with turnips in it. One day, he decided to grow the biggest turnip anyone had ever seen. He planted seeds in the rich, black soil and watered them. In a month, leaves began to push through the soil into the sunlight. A month later, the leaves were huge.

Grandfather was sure he had grown the biggest turnip ever. He grabbed the leaves and tried to pull the turnip out of the ground. He pulled as hard as he could, but the turnip wouldn't move.

So he called Grandmother for help. She grabbed Grandfather's waist, and they pulled and pulled until their strength was gone. The turnip did not move.

So Grandmother called Ivan to help. Ivan grabbed Grandmother's waist, and Grandmother grabbed Grandfather's waist. The three of them pulled and pulled and pulled until their strength was gone. But the turnip wouldn't move.

So Ivan called his wife, Galina, for help. Galina grabbed Ivan's waist, and Ivan grabbed Grandmother's waist, and Grandmother grabbed Grandfather's waist. The four of them pulled and pulled and pulled and pulled until their strength was gone. The turnip wouldn't move.

So Galina whistled for her big, strong dog. The dog grabbed Galina's belt in his mouth, and Galina grabbed Ivan's waist, and Ivan grabbed Grandmother's waist, and Grandmother grabbed Grandfather's waist. The five of them pulled and pulled and pulled and pulled and pulled some more until their strength was gone. But the turnip was still stuck in the ground.

Finally, a little mouse came by and offered to help. Everyone laughed when they saw the mouse and said, "What can she do to help? She's too small and weak!" That didn't stop the mouse. She jumped right up and grabbed the dog's tail, and the dog grabbed Galina's belt in his mouth, and Galina grabbed Ivan's waist, and Ivan grabbed Grandmother's waist, and Grandmother grabbed Grandfather's waist. All six of them pulled with all their strength. . . .

The turnip popped out of the ground!

Everyone thanked the little mouse because it was her bit of strength that made the difference. Then, they all sat down to eat the giant turnip.

Answer the following questions.

1 Read the sentences from the passage.

Everyone laughed when they saw the mouse and said, "What can she do to help? She's too small and weak!" That didn't stop the mouse.

What does the last sentence reveal about the mouse?

Write your answer on the lines below.

Hint Authors use a character's words, actions, and reactions to others to show what the character is like. How does the mouse react to the family members' view of her? What qualities does she reveal through her actions?

2 Which of the following sentences would you include in a summary of this passage? Select **all** that apply.

A. Grandfather loves turnip stew.

B. Grandfather grows a giant turnip.

C. The turnip won't come out of the ground.

D. Galina is wearing a belt.

E. The whole family and some animals pitch in to pull up the turnip.

Hint Remember that a summary includes only the most important events from the beginning, middle, and end of a text. Summaries need to retell what happens in the story, but they don't have to include all the details.

3 The following question has two parts. First, answer Part A. Then, answer Part B.

Part A

Which of these sentences could be a theme for the passage? Circle **all** that apply.

A. Working together is a good way to solve a problem.

B. Only strong young people should work on a farm.

C. Don't look down on someone based solely on size; he or she may surprise you.

D. Don't start a project that you can't do all by yourself.

Part B

Which excerpt from the story **best** supports your answers to Part A? Circle **all** that apply.

A. Grandfather was sure he had grown the biggest turnip ever.

B. The five of them pulled and pulled and pulled and pulled and pulled some more until their strength was gone. But the turnip was still stuck in the ground.

C. All six of them pulled with all their strength. . . . The turnip popped out of the ground!

D. Everyone thanked the little mouse because it was her bit of strength that made the difference.

E. Then, they all sat down to eat the giant turnip.

Hint The theme is the lesson or message that the author wants the reader to understand. Think about what lessons readers could learn from this story.

4 How does the illustration relate to specific descriptions in the passage?

Write your answer on the lines below.

Hint Look closely at the illustration and compare what's shown to the descriptions in the passage. Think about what the illustration helps you visualize. Then, find that scene in the passage.

Use the Reading Guide to help you understand the passage.

An Earth Day Group Effort

Reading Guide

What is Jasmine's role in the Earth Day celebration?

What does Jasmine's mom suggest she do? Why does Jasmine decide her mom is right?

How would you describe Jasmine's personality? How do you know?

Whose thoughts and feelings does the reader hear in this story?

On Tuesday morning, I was up for hours before my alarm clock rang. I had a whole list in my head, and I just knew I wouldn't rest until everything on the list was crossed off. This year, I was supervising the planning for the fourth grade Earth Day celebration. My teacher had made me the leader, and I needed to do a good job because everyone was counting on me!

That morning, Mom noticed that I was inhaling my breakfast. "Are you going for a world record in cereal eating?" she asked.

"Nope," I said, "but I have to get to school early. I have so much Earth Day work to do!"

"Jasmine, are you sure you aren't doing too much?" Mom asked. "Why don't you give some tasks away?"

I scanned the list in my head again, and I decided Mom was right.

That day, I gave everyone a job to do. Sophie was in charge of selling tickets to the celebration, Josh's job was to make and post flyers around the school, and Manuel would write an Earth Day speech. I would still oversee everything, but I had also kept the biggest job of painting a "Save Our Earth" banner. It would be twenty feet long and ten feet high, with letters big enough to be read from the entire schoolyard. I was a little worried about finding the time to actually make it.

The thing is, as soon as I gave all the jobs away, I suddenly had a new job: answering everyone's questions. After school, I had just tracked down some fabric in the art room when Manuel stopped by and found me.

"Do you think my speech should focus on recycling or not littering?" he asked. "I think both are important."

"Hmm," I said, my banner completely forgotten. Before I knew it, Manuel and I had spent an hour talking about speech ideas, and it was time to go home.

Reading Guide

What do Jasmine's actions in this passage show about her?

Why do Manuel, Sophie, and Josh want to help Jasmine?

What lesson do Jasmine and her friends learn from the events in this story?

The next morning, I got to school early again, and Sophie was already waiting for me.

"I have the tickets," Sophie said, "but I don't know the school rules for collecting money."

I didn't either. "Let's go ask the principal," I said. By the time we were done, it was time to start social studies class.

That afternoon wasn't any better. I had just sat down in the art room to sketch out my banner when Josh appeared.

"Hey, Jasmine. Can I borrow your markers?" he asked. "I need to make the flyer, but all the markers in here are dried up."

Inside, I groaned, but I knew I had to give Josh the markers. The flyers had to go up soon. After all, no one would show up to our celebration if they didn't know about it.

I looked down at the sketch for my banner. I'd drawn one hand holding up Earth to show that our planet needs people to take care of it.

The day before the celebration, I finally had time to start painting. But after two hours, my eyes were blurry, and I still wasn't done. I was starting to worry. How would I finish in time? I walked outside to get some fresh air and think about it.

When I got back to the art room, I saw Sophie, Manuel, and Josh standing around the unfinished banner.

"You've been helping us all week," Manuel said. "It's time for us to help you."

Josh grabbed some blue paint and painted the oceans while Sophie painted the continents green. Manuel started stenciling the letters for the words.

Now that everyone was helping, my brain suddenly felt a lot less crowded. A new idea for the banner design came to me.

"Let's add more hands holding up the planet," I said, "to show that everyone can work together to save Earth!"

Answer the following questions.

1 Reread these sentences from the passage.

This year, I was <u>supervising</u> the planning for the fourth grade Earth Day celebration. My teacher had made me the leader, and I needed to do a good job because everyone was counting on me!

Based on context clues, what does <u>supervising</u> mean?

A. planning a celebration

B. being in charge of something

C. being first in line for a celebration

D. failing at an important job

2 The following question has two parts. First, answer Part A. Then, answer Part B.

Part A

Which word **best** describes Jasmine?

A. angry

B. responsible

C. strong

D. forgetful

Part B

Which sentence from the story **best** supports your answer to Part A?

A. My teacher had made me the leader, and I needed to do a good job because everyone was counting on me!

B. I scanned the list in my head again, and I decided Mom was right.

C. Inside, I groaned, but I knew I had to give Josh the markers.

D. "Let's add more hands holding up the planet," I said, "to show that everyone can work together to save Earth!"

3 Who is the narrator of the passage? Is the narrator telling the story from a first-person point of view or a third-person point of view? Explain how you know.

Write your answer on the lines below.

4 Circle the statements that describe possible themes of this story. Circle **all** that apply.

A. Many workers speed up the work.

B. Don't do other people's work for them.

C. Working with others leads to disagreements.

D. A person who helps others will likely get help in return.

E. You can get more done when you work alone.

5 How does the illustration help you understand the story's events?

Write your answer on the lines below.

6 "The Giant Turnip" and "An Earth Day Group Effort" explore a similar theme, but they use different points of view to do it. Explain how the stories' different points of view affect how each story is told and how the theme is shown. Describe an event from each story that supports the theme.

Write your response on the lines below.

Poetry

1 GETTING THE IDEA

Poetry is a special type of writing that uses words to create a strong feeling, image, or message through meaning, sound, and rhythm.

Structure

Poetry has a special structure. It is usually made up of **lines**, which are rows of text. Lines may or may not be complete sentences. The poem may be broken into groups of lines called **stanzas**. In most poetry, stanzas are used the way paragraphs are used in stories or articles. The stanzas fit together to provide a poem's overall structure.

Read the following excerpt from Lord Alfred Douglas's "In Winter." How many lines does it have? How many stanzas are shown?

> Oh! for a day of burning noon
> And a sun like a glowing ember,
>
> Oh! for one hour of golden June,
> In the heart of this chill November.

The Sounds of Poetry

Poems are meant to be read aloud. Poets think carefully about the sounds of the words they choose and how the words work together to create rhythm, rhyme, and meaning.

Rhythm is the pattern of stressed and unstressed syllables in a line. It creates the "beat," or **meter**, of a poem. To hear a stressed and an unstressed syllable, say the word *poem* aloud. You can hear that the first syllable is stressed, or said more strongly, and the second syllable is unstressed: ***PO**-em*.

On the following page, read aloud Edward Lear's "There Was a Young Lady Whose Chin." Can you hear its rhythm? Read it again, using your finger to tap along to the rhythm. You tend to tap on the stressed, or stronger, syllables.

> There was a Young Lady whose chin
> Resembled the point of a pin;
> So she had it made sharp,
> And purchased a harp,
> And played several tunes with her chin.

Rhyme describes words with the same ending sound. Many poems have lines that end with words that rhyme. Poems that rhyme may have a rhyme scheme in which the last words of certain lines follow a clear pattern. A **rhyme scheme** is shown by a sequence of letters, such as *aabb*. For example, the letters *aabb* stand for a four-line stanza in which line 1 and line 2 rhyme (*a*) and line 3 and line 4 rhyme (*b*).

Reread "There Was a Young Lady Whose Chin." Underline the words that rhyme. Write the letter *a* or *b* at the end of each line to show the poem's rhyme scheme.

Repetition is the repeating of words or lines in poetry. Poets often use repetition to show important ideas in a poem or to reveal the meaning or theme. Read this excerpt from Walt Whitman's poem "Song of Myself." Circle the words that are repeated.

> I celebrate myself, and sing myself,
> And what I assume you shall assume,
> For every atom belonging to me as good belongs to you.
>
> I loafe and invite my soul,
> I lean and loafe at my ease observing a spear of summer
>   grass.

Alliteration is the repetition of a consonant sound. Poets use it to draw attention to certain words or to make the poem sound nice. Reread the excerpt from "Song of Myself" above. Circle the initial consonants whose sounds are repeated.

Figurative Language

Poets choose words to create pictures in the reader's mind. They use both literal language and figurative language. **Literal language** is language that means exactly what the words say. **Figurative language** does not always mean what the words say. It has a deeper meaning. Four kinds of figurative language are similes, metaphors, allusions, and personification.

A **simile** is a comparison that uses the words *like* or *as*. Read the simile. What two things are being compared?

> Kris got caught in the rain and looked like a wet rat.

A **metaphor** is a comparison that does not use the words *like* or *as*. It says that one thing *is* another. Read the metaphor. What two things are being compared?

> I can always depend on Patel. He is a rock.

An **allusion** is a reference to a person, place, event, or work of literature, such as a myth. Knowing what an allusion refers to can help you understand its meaning. Often, some words in an allusion are capitalized. This can help you spot the allusion. Then, you can use context clues or look it up to find its meaning. What is the allusion in this sentence? What does it mean?

> People said that the millionaire had the Midas touch because every business she started made money.

Personification is the giving of human qualities to nonhuman things. What human quality is the wind given in this sentence?

> The wind whistled through the trees.

Point of View and Theme

In poetry, **point of view** refers to the speaker of the poem. The **speaker** is the voice of the poem and acts like a narrator does in a story. The point of view in the poem may reflect the poet's thoughts and feelings or those of another person or character.

Often, the speaker in a poem reflects on a topic, revealing the poem's theme. The **theme** is the message the poet wants to share with the reader. A theme may be about human nature or society. Read the excerpt from Emily Dickinson's poem "Hope Is the Thing with Feathers." Which lines reveal its theme?

> "Hope" is the thing with feathers
> That perches in the soul,
> And sings the tune without the words,
> And never stops at all.

Kinds of Poems

The chart shows some kinds of poetry. What other kinds do you know?

Kind of Poem	Definition
lyric poem	a short poem that is like a song and usually deals with the speaker's thoughts or feelings
epic poem	a long poem that tells about the adventures of a hero or a historic event, such as a great military victory
narrative poem	a poem that tells a story
limerick	a humorous five-line poem that rhymes
free verse	a poem that does not follow any fixed rules of rhythm, rhyme, or structure
haiku	a very short poem with three lines and just seventeen syllables; does not rhyme and is usually about nature
ode	a poem that includes two or more stanzas with similar structures; each line must rhyme with another line in the same stanza; usually a serious poem about a meaningful topic

Language Spotlight • Greek and Latin Roots

Many words in English come from Greek or Latin. These word parts are called **roots**. Knowing the meanings of Greek and Latin roots can help you figure out the meanings of some words in English. Look at these examples.

autograph = *auto* + *graph*

auto = self
graph = write

autograph: a person's handwritten signature

thermometer = *thermo* + *meter*

thermo = heat
meter = to measure

thermometer: a tool used to measure heat

What other words can you think of with the roots *auto* and *meter*? How can you use what you know about roots to understand the meanings of those words?

2 COACHED EXAMPLE

Read the poem.

Escape at Bedtime

by Robert Louis Stevenson

The lights from the parlor and kitchen shone out
    Through the blinds and the windows and bars;
And high over head and all moving about,
    There were thousands of millions of stars.
There ne'er[1] were such thousands of leaves on a tree,
    Nor of people in church or the Park,
As the crowds of the stars that looked down upon me,
    And that glittered and winked in the dark.

The Dog, and the Plough,[2] and the Hunter, and all,
    And the star of the sailor, and Mars,
These shone in the sky, and the pail by the wall
    Would be half full of water and stars.
They saw me at last, and they chased me with cries,
    And they soon had me packed into bed;
But the glory kept shining and bright in my eyes,
    And the stars going round in my head.

[1] **ne'er**: short for *never*

[2] **Plough**: the British spelling of *plow*; also the British name for the constellation called the Big Dipper in the United States

Answer the following questions.

1. The poem mentions the Dog, the Hunter, and Mars in the night sky. These names relate to characters in Greek and Roman myths.

   Based on this information, what is the **best** conclusion you can draw?

   A. The Dog, the Hunter, and Mars are constellations.

   B. The Greeks and Romans saw the same objects in the sky.

   C. Many planets and constellations got their names from characters in myths.

   D. The words *dog*, *hunter*, and *Mars* are from the Greek and Roman languages.

Hint Recognizing references to myths and mythological characters can help you better understand the meaning of the poem.

2. Read this line from the poem.

   They saw me at last, and they chased me with cries,

   Explain what this line reveals about the speaker of the poem.

   Write your answer on the lines below.

Hint Notice the pronouns the speaker uses. Does it seem like he is an outsider describing events that happen to someone else?

3 Which of the following is true about the first stanza? Choose **all** that apply.

A. Lines 1 and 3 rhyme. Lines 2 and 4 rhyme.

B. All the lines have the same number of stressed syllables.

C. The first stanza has 8 lines.

D. Lines 1 and 2 rhyme. Lines 3 and 4 rhyme.

E. Lines 2, 4, and 6 have the same number of stressed syllables.

F. The first stanza has 5 lines.

Hint First, count the lines in the first stanza. Next, say the words at the ends of the lines. Which ones rhyme? Finally, read the first stanza aloud and clap when you hear a stressed syllable. Think about ways that stressed syllables add to the rhythm of the poem.

4 The following question has two parts. First, answer Part A. Then, answer Part B.

Part A

Read the lines from the poem and the question that follows.

> **As the crowds of the stars that looked down upon me,**
> **And that glittered and winked in the dark.**

What kind of figurative language is this?

A. allusion

B. metaphor

C. personification

D. simile

Part B

Which choice explains your answer to Part A?

A. The speaker says the stars are like people dressed in glittering party clothes.

B. The stars do not just look like crowds of people—they *are* crowds of people.

C. The stars "look down" and "wink" at the speaker—this makes them seem human.

D. The poet uses the phrase "looked down upon me" to allude to Greek gods and goddesses.

Hint Notice how the stars are described in these lines. Look for the action words that tell you what the stars are doing. Would stars really be able to do all of these things?

Use the Reading Guide to help you understand the poem.

The Spider and the Fly

by Mary Howitt

Reading Guide

How does the spider use figurative language to describe its web?

Look at the word *vain* in the first stanza. How can you use context clues to figure out the meaning of this word?

"Will you walk into my parlor?" said the spider to the fly,—
"'Tis the prettiest little parlor that ever you did spy.
The way into my parlor is up a winding stair;
And I have many curious things to show you when you're there."
"Oh no, no," said the little fly; "to ask me is in vain;
For who goes up your winding stair can ne'er come down again."

"I'm sure you must be weary, dear, with soaring up so high;
Will you rest upon my little bed?" said the spider to the fly.
"There are pretty curtains drawn around; the sheets are fine and thin;
And if you like to rest awhile, I'll snugly tuck you in!"
"Oh no, no," said the little fly; "for I've often heard it said,
They never, never wake again, who sleep upon your bed!"

Said the cunning spider to the fly—"Dear friend, what can I do
To prove the warm affection I've always felt for you?
I have within my pantry good store of all that's nice;
I'm sure you're very welcome—will you please to take a slice?"
"Oh no, no," said the little fly, "kind sir, that cannot be;
I've heard what's in your pantry, and I do not wish to see."

Reading Guide

How is this poem like stories you've read? How is it different?

Look at the second stanza on this page, and find the figures of speech that make comparisons. How does the poet use these figures of speech for effect?

"Sweet creature," said the spider, "you're witty and you're wise;
How handsome are your gauzy[1] wings, how brilliant are your eyes!
I have a little looking-glass[2] upon my parlor shelf,
If you'll step in one moment, dear, you shall behold yourself."
"I thank you, gentle sir," she said, "for what you're pleased to say,
And bidding you good-morning now, I'll call another day."

The spider turned him round about, and went into his den,
For well he knew the silly fly would soon come back again;
So he wove a subtle web in a little corner sly,
And set his table ready, to dine upon the fly.
Then he came out to his door again, and merrily did sing,—
Come hither,[3] hither, pretty fly, with the pearl and silver wing;
Your robes are green and purple—there's a crest upon your head!
Your eyes are like the diamond bright, but mine are dull as lead!"

Alas! alas! how very soon this silly little fly,
Hearing his wily,[4] flattering words, came slowly flitting by.
With buzzing wings she hung aloft, then near and nearer drew,
Thinking only of her brilliant eyes, her green and purple hue—

[1] **gauzy**: thin and transparent

[2] **looking-glass**: mirror

[3] **hither**: here

[4] **wily**: tricky, sneaky

Reading Guide

Reread the last stanza. What is the message of this poem? How do you know?

Thinking only of her crested head—poor foolish thing! At last,
Up jumped the cunning spider, and fiercely held her fast!
He dragged her up his winding stair, into his dismal den,
Within his little parlor—but she ne'er came out again!

And now, dear little children, who may this story read,
To idle, silly flattering words, I pray you, ne'er give heed;[5]
Unto an evil counselor[6] close heart, and ear, and eye.
And take a lesson from this tale of the Spider and the Fly.

[5] **heed**: listen to

[6] **counselor**: a person who gives advice

Answer the following questions.

1. This question has two parts. First, answer Part A. Then, answer Part B.

Part A

In the poem, the spider calls his web "a winding stair." What kind of figurative language is this?

A. simile

B. metaphor

C. allusion

D. personification

Part B

Which choice explains your answer to Part A?

A. The spider says its web is like a winding stair, because the fly can climb up the web to the spider's "parlor."

B. The poet says the spider's web *is* a winding stair, even though she is just comparing its web to a winding stair.

C. The poet is alluding to one song about a "stairway to heaven" and another song about a "stairway to the stars."

D. In this poem, both the spider and the fly have human qualities: the spider is evil and the fly is conceited.

2 The following question has two parts. First, answer Part A. Then, answer Part B.

Part A

Read the lines from the poem and the question that follows.

> **Said the cunning spider to the fly—"Dear friend, what can I do**
> **To prove the warm affection I've always felt for you?"**

Which of the following is the **best** definition for affection?

A. love

B. scorn

C. hunger

D. laughter

Part B

Which Latin root below would **best** help you figure out the meaning of the word affection?

A. *echo*, meaning "sound"

B. *fact,* meaning "action"

C. *affect,* meaning "feeling"

D. *effect*, meaning "accomplishment"

3 What kind of poem is "The Spider and the Fly"?

A. lyric poem

B. narrative poem

C. limerick

D. free verse

4 The following question has two parts. First, answer Part A. Then, answer Part B.

Part A

Which sentence **best** sums up the theme of this poem?

A. Spiders can be very dangerous creatures.

B. Being too vain can make others dislike you.

C. By flattering others, you can trick them.

D. It can be dangerous to listen to others' flattery.

Part B

Which lines from the poem **best** support your answer to Part A?

A. So he wove a subtle web in a little corner sly, / And set his table ready, to dine upon the fly.

B. Alas! alas! how very soon this silly little fly, / Hearing his wily, flattering words, came slowly flitting by.

C. He dragged her up his winding stair, into his dismal den, / Within his little parlor—but she ne'er came out again!

D. Unto an evil counselor close heart, and ear, and eye. / And take a lesson from this tale of the Spider and the Fly.

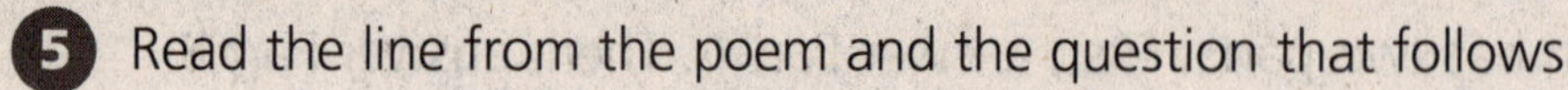

5 Read the line from the poem and the question that follows.

Your eyes are like the diamond bright,

What kind of figurative language is this?

A. allusion

B. metaphor

C. personification

D. simile

6 How does the poet use structure and figurative language to tell a story in "The Spider and the Fly"? Give specific examples of rhyme, rhythm, and figurative language. Be sure to use details from the poem in your response.

Write your response on the lines below.

LESSON 3

Drama

1 GETTING THE IDEA

A **drama** is a story written to be performed by actors. Movies, television shows, and plays are dramas. Like other types of fiction, dramas have a setting, characters, plot, and theme. In a drama, however, most of the story is told through the characters' words.

To understand a drama, it is important to understand its parts and how they work together.

Elements of Drama	Definition
act	the main section of a drama
scene	a smaller section of an act
setting	where and when the action takes place
cast of characters	the people in a drama
dialogue	the words the characters speak
stage directions	actions to be performed by the actors

Acts and Scenes

A drama is divided into sections called **acts**. A **scene** is a smaller part of an act. Each new act or scene shows a change in the setting, plot, or characters.

Setting

In most fiction stories, authors include many details about the **setting**. In a drama, setting is revealed with short descriptions at the beginning of the play and the beginning of each scene. Sometimes, the actors' costumes or props give clues about the setting.

Read the following description of setting and underline words that show where and when the drama takes place.

> *A summer evening in present-day Philadelphia. A teenage girl stands on the stoop of a row house. She is looking up and down the street.*

Characters

The **cast of characters** appears at the beginning of a drama. It lists all the characters in the play. The characters may be listed in the order in which they appear in the play, or they may be listed in order of importance. Sometimes, there is a brief description after a character's name.

Dialogue and Stage Directions

The words the characters speak are **dialogue**. In stories, dialogue appears within quotation marks. In dramas, dialogue does not have quotation marks and comes directly after a character's name. In addition, authors of dramas do not describe how characters think and feel. Instead, the audience must figure out how the characters think and feel through their words and actions.

The **stage directions** tell characters how to speak their lines, where to go onstage, or how to move. They also give information about sound, lighting, props, and costumes. Stage directions appear in italics inside parentheses.

Look at this part of a play. Which words do the characters speak? What do you learn about the characters from the dialogue and the stage directions?

> (*Bruno enters, bouncing a basketball.*)
> NORA: (*sternly*) Bruno, you're an hour late. You're trying my patience!
> BRUNO: (*shrugs*) I'm sorry. I had practice. (*smiles*) You know, Nora, you sound just like Mom.
> NORA: (*laughs*) I can't help it. I'm responsible until Mom gets home. I was worried about you.

Theme

A drama, just like a story, has a theme. The **theme** is the message the author wants to share, such as "Good deeds are rewarded." To find the theme, think about what the characters do and say, and how they respond to one another.

Figurative Language

Dialogue in drama, just as in real-life conversation, contains idioms. An **idiom** is a word or phrase that has a different meaning from the meaning of the individual words. Here are some common idioms.

Idiom (used in a sentence)	Meaning
Sometimes you try my patience.	frustrate me
It totally slipped my mind.	became something I forgot
We're going to be late. Shake a leg!	Hurry up!
Take an umbrella. It's raining cats and dogs.	raining heavily

To understand what an idiom means, pay attention to the words and sentences around it. Use context clues to figure out the meaning. You can also use context clues to figure out the meaning of old-fashioned words and phrases that might appear in plays that are set in the past or were written in the past.

Language Spotlight • Affixes

An **affix** is a word part added to the beginning or end of a word to make a new word. An affix added to the beginning of a word is a **prefix**. An affix added to the end of a word is a **suffix**.

Circle the prefixes and underline the suffixes in the words below.

preheat **unfairness** **review** **amusement** **motherhood**

In each example above, how does the prefix and/or suffix affect the meaning of the root?

Read the play.

The First Labor of Hercules

Cast of Characters

KING EURYSTHEUS, a mythical king of Greece
SOLDIER, the king's guard
HERCULES, a mythical Greek hero

Act I

In the age of the Greek myths, in a palace. The king sits on a throne. A soldier with a spear stands guard. Hercules, wearing a tunic and sandals, stands before the throne.

KING EURYSTHEUS: (*boldly*) Hercules, the Lion of Nemea terrorizes the valley. Your first challenge is to bring me its hide.

SOLDIER: (*to King*) But, sire, arrows and spears merely bounce off the beast. It's an impossible task.

KING EURYSTHEUS: (*sneers*) Yes, but I am told Hercules is a hero of amazing strength. Let's see if our hero can live up to his reputation.

HERCULES: I accept your challenge. (*bows to king and exits*)

Act II, Scene 1

Afternoon of the same day. Hercules is crouched outside a mountain cave.

HERCULES: (*whispers*) I have found the lion's subterranean lair. The lion is within. When it comes out, I shall be ready. (*A roar is heard offstage.*) What's this? How did the beast exit the cave without my knowledge? (*exits stage, reappears on other side*) Of course, there are two ways in and out. I have blocked the first one. Now I will wait inside for the lion. But to prove my courage and strength, I will wrestle him with my bare hands. (*throws down club and shield, enters cave*)

Act II, Scene 2

The lights fade as night falls. A shadowy shape crosses the stage and enters the cave.

HERCULES: (*shouting*) Beware, beast! Hercules has come to put an end to you!

(*Shouts and roars follow, then silence.*)

Act III

Evening of the next day, outside the palace gates. Hercules approaches, wrapped in the lion's hide.

SOLDIER: Halt! Who goes there? (*Lights rise to show Hercules in disguise.*) Sire, Sire! Come quickly. It's the Lion of Nemea!

KING EURYSTHEUS: (*wails*) All is lost! We are doomed!

HERCULES: (*throws off pelt*) It is I, Hercules! I have defeated the beast and brought the pelt as commanded.

KING: (*amazed*) Perhaps you *are* a hero. Surely, a true hero will accept another challenge. Can you kill the Hydra of Lerna?

SOLDIER: (*to king*) But, sire, the Hydra is an enormous water serpent with nine heads. And its venom is poisonous!

KING EURYSTHEUS: (*sneers*) Yes, but Hercules is a hero of amazing strength. I'm sure he will take another challenge.

HERCULES: I accept your second challenge. (*bows to king and exits, curtain closes*)

Answer the following questions.

1 Read the sentences from the play and the question that follows.

> **KING EURYSTHEUS: (*sneers*) Yes, but I am told Hercules is a hero of amazing strength. Let's see if our hero can live up to his reputation.**

What does the idiom live up to mean?

A. to be as good as people say

B. to stay alive

C. to accept a challenge

D. to fight a lion

Hint Think about what the king says about Hercules and his strength. People who have great skill or talent often become well known.

2 The following question has two parts. First, answer Part A. Then, answer Part B.

Part A

Read the sentences from the play.

> **HERCULES: I have found the lion's subterranean lair. The lion is within. When it comes out, I shall be ready.**

What does the word subterranean mean?

A. over the mountain

B. below the earth

C. under the water

D. a large cave

Part B

Which **two** word parts can help you figure out the meaning of subterranean?

A. the prefix *sub-*, meaning "below"

B. the root *trans*, meaning "across"

C. the suffix *-ion*, meaning "process"

D. the root *terra,* meaning "earth"

E. the prefix *super-*, meaning "above"

Hint Remember that an affix is a word part added to the beginning or end of a word or a root. Your answer to Part B should support your answer to Part A.

3 *The First Labor of Hercules* is a play that has three acts. Explain how the setting changes from act to act and how the changes in setting develop the plot.

Write your answer on the lines below.

____

____

____

____

____

Hint The plot is the series of events in a story. How do the different settings in the play affect the events that take place?

4 Read the parts of a drama in the box below. Then, follow the directions that follow.

setting	dialogue	cast of characters	stage directions

The chart below shows examples of different parts of a play. Complete the chart by writing the name of each part next to the correct example.

Parts of a Play	**Examples**
	KING EURYSTHEUS, a mythical king of Greece SOLDIER, the king's guard HERCULES, a mythical Greek hero
	(A roar is heard offstage.)
	Afternoon of the same day. Hercules is crouched outside a mountain cave.
	SOLDIER: Halt! Who goes there?

Hint Think about the ways a drama's different parts fit together in a play.

Use the Reading Guide to help you understand the play.

Snake on a Bus: A One-Act Play

Reading Guide

Who are the characters in the play?

What do the characters do to show the bus is moving?

What happens that causes all the characters to react?

Cast of Characters

MRS. PINTO, school bus driver
AKEEM, boy, 9
OLIVIA, girl, 8
JAMIE, girl, 9
JONAH, boy, 10
LEAH, girl, 10

Modern day. School bus on city street. Chairs arranged as seats on the bus. A seat for the driver is at the front. Mrs. Pinto bounces in her seat as she drives the bus. Akeem, Olivia, Jamie, and Jonah are lined up at a bus stop with their backpacks.

MRS. PINTO: (*stops bouncing*) Here we are, first stop of the morning. (*opens door*) Hi, gang! All aboard!

(*Students enter bus, greeting the driver. They take seats near the front. Leah arrives, carrying an aquarium with a wire lid.*)

LEAH: Sorry I'm late, Mrs. Pinto! (*climbs on and sits at back of bus*)

MRS. PINTO: Okay, everyone sitting? We're off.

(*The bus continues. Mrs. Pinto and students bounce slightly in their seats.*)

AKEEM: (*looking back at Leah*) Hey, Leah, what's in the aquarium?

MRS. PINTO: Oh, my! Hold on, kids!

(*Mrs. Pinto steers and leans hard to the right; students lean hard to the right, too. Some of the students cry out in surprise.*)

Reading Guide

How would you describe Mrs. Pinto? Explain your description.

What happens in the play to complicate the plot?

Are you able to picture what is happening? How?

MRS. PINTO: (*shaken*) I can't believe that car just ran a red light! It almost plowed right into us! Is everyone all right? Hold on, kids. I'll pull over.

(*Mrs. Pinto mimes pulling over and stopping bus; stands to check on students.*)

AKEEM: (*holding head*) Wow! That hurt!

MRS. PINTO: Is everyone all right?

OLIVIA: I'm fine, Mrs. Pinto. You warned us just in time!

JAMIE: Me, too, Mrs. Pinto! That was some fancy driving!

JONAH: (*worried*) I'm okay, but I think Akeem hurt his head.

AKEEM: (*rubs forehead*) Nah, it's okay. I just banged it on the window.

MRS. PINTO: Let me see. (*examines Akeem's forehead*) I think it's just a bump, but check with the school nurse just to be on the safe side.

LEAH: (*bends down to pick up aquarium lid from floor*) Oh, no. (*looks around*)

MRS. PINTO: Are you okay, Leah?

LEAH: *I* am, but I think Louis has escaped. I'm bringing him in for science—

JAMIE: (*interrupts*) Louis? Who's Louis?

LEAH: My pet snake. I'm bringing him in for science and—

OLIVIA: (*shrieks*) Snake? There's a serpent on the bus! (*jumps on seat*)

LEAH: (*calmly*) Olivia, screaming is unnecessary. Louis is a harmless garter snake. You're probably scaring *him*.

JONAH: Here, I'll help look for him. (*crawls around, looking for snake*)

AKEEM: (*pulls feet onto seat*) Sorry. I'm sure Louis is a fine snake, but snakes and I just don't get along.

Reading Guide

How is the problem solved?

How do the actors know what they should do to show the characters' feelings?

The rubber snake that Leah holds is a prop. A prop is an object that helps the actors in a play tell the story. Why is a prop used instead of a real snake?

JAMIE: I'll help, Leah. What does Louis look like? (*begins searching*)

OLIVIA: (*whimpers*) It's a s-s-s-snake! It's long and slithery—with poisonous fangs!

LEAH: (*kindly*) Honestly, Olivia. No poisonous venom, no fangs. (*to Jamie*) Louis is about two feet long, dark green with three yellow stripes that run down his body.

JAMIE: I thought so. Is that him over by Olivia's backpack?

OLIVIA: (*screeches*) That's not funny, Jamie!

MRS. PINTO: Jamie, please. Don't scare her.

JAMIE: I'm sorry, Liv. I was just teasing.

LEAH: There you are, Louis! (*stands, holding rubber snake*) I've found him!

OLIVIA: (*embarrassed*) That's Louis! Now I feel silly. He looks so . . . harmless.

LEAH: That's okay, Olivia. (*smiles*) My mom only likes Louis when he's in his tank. (*to Louis*) Back into the tank you go. (*puts snake in aquarium; replaces lid*)

MRS. PINTO: (*sighs*) Okay, children. Louis has been found. Everyone get back in your seats. It will be a Herculean effort, but let's see if we can get this bus and you to school on time!

(*All return to seats. Mrs. Pinto starts driving, and all bounce slightly. The curtain closes.*)

Answer the following questions.

1. Read these sentences from the play.

   MRS. PINTO: (*sighs*) Okay, children. Louis has been found. Everyone get back in your seats. It will be a Herculean effort, but let's see if we can get this bus and you to school on time!

   What do the words a Herculean effort mean?

   A. a myth about Hercules

   B. an attempt at an impossible task

   C. a battle against a serpent

   D. a way to jeer at or insult Hercules

2. The following question has two parts. First, answer Part A. Then, answer Part B.

   Part A

   Read these sentences from the play and the question that follows.

   MRS. PINTO: Let me see. (*examines Akeem's forehead*) I think it's just a bump, but check with the school nurse just to be on the safe side.

   What is the meaning of just to be on the safe side?

   A. to find a safe place to hide

   B. to run away from a dangerous situation; to flee

   C. to be overly afraid of taking risks

   D. to do something in case it is necessary; to be cautious

   Part B

   What other action does Mrs. Pinto take to be on the safe side?

   A. says hello to the students

   B. bounces in her seat

   C. pulls over to check on the students

   D. gets the bus to school on time

3 These events are from the play, but they are out of order. Write the numbers 2, 3, 4, and 5 to put the events in the correct order.

1	Mrs. Pinto stops the bus to pick up the students.
	Leah discovers that Louis is missing.
	Mrs. Pinto checks to see that the students are okay.
	After a search, Louis is found and returned to his tank.
	Mrs. Pinto swerves to avoid a car.
6	Mrs. Pinto asks the students to get back in their seats.

4 Read the sentences from the play and answer the question that follows.

LEAH: (*calmly*) Olivia, screaming is unnecessary. Louis is a harmless garter snake. You're probably scaring *him*.

What does the word unnecessary mean?

A. not important

B. more important

C. not needed

D. needed again

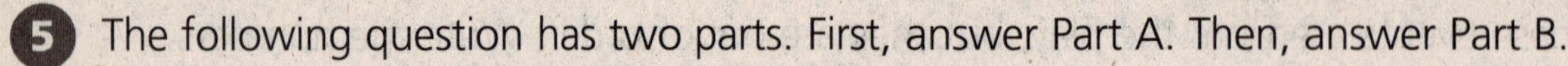

5 The following question has two parts. First, answer Part A. Then, answer Part B.

Part A

Which word **best** describes Leah?

A. creative

B. unfriendly

C. nervous

D. easygoing

Part B

Which dialogue line **best** supports your answer to Part A?

A. **LEAH:** (*bends down to pick up aquarium lid from floor*) Oh, no. (looks around)

B. **LEAH:** *I* am, but I think Louis has escaped. I'm bringing him in for science—

C. **LEAH:** (*calmly*) Olivia, screaming is unnecessary. Louis is a harmless garter snake.

D. **LEAH:** There you are, Louis! (*stands, holding rubber snake*) I've found him!

6 Think about the settings of *The First Labor of Hercules* and *Snake on a Bus: A One-Act Play*. Explain how the settings of each play affect the plots. Use details from the plays in your response.

Write your response on the lines below.

Analyze Literature

1 GETTING THE IDEA

One way to analyze literature is to think about how a particular story is like or unlike another one you know. Comparing and contrasting helps you better understand both stories. When you **compare** and **contrast**, you tell how things are similar and different. In fiction, you can compare and contrast story elements, including characters, setting, plot, point of view, and theme.

Compare and Contrast Characters

Story characters are a lot like real people. Characters in different types of fiction may have much in common. Or, two characters in stories about the same topic may be very different. You can compare and contrast how characters look, how they act, what they say, how they treat others, and how others react to them.

Compare and Contrast Settings

Two stories may be set in the same place or time, or in different places and times. To compare and contrast settings, first look for details about setting in each story. These details may tell you the weather, the location, and the time of day. The way characters dress and speak may give clues to the time period.

Compare and Contrast Plots

Plot structure is how the events of the story are put together. Here is how you can analyze plot structure.

- Determine what happens in the beginning, the middle, and the end of the story.
- Determine what problem the main character or characters must solve.
- Look for details about how the characters solve the problem.

Compare and Contrast Themes

Theme is the message an author wants readers to take away from a story. Two stories might have the same theme—such as the importance of remaining true to oneself—but the characters may discover this lesson in different ways.

Compare and Contrast Points of View

To analyze stories for point of view, think about who is narrating, or telling, each story. A story might be told in first-person point of view by one of its characters or in third-person point of view by an outside narrator. **First-person point of view** uses pronouns such as *I* and *my*, and gives readers a look into one character's thoughts. **Third-person point of view** uses pronouns such as *he*, *she*, and *they*, and often tells readers the thoughts and feelings of more than one character. Think about how the choice of point of view affects each story. Ask yourself: If this had a different point of view, how would the story be different?

Read the following passages. They have different plots, settings, and points of view, but a similar theme: A safe, simple life is better than one that is fancy, but dangerous.

I was visiting my cousin Caroline in the city. What an amazing place! Museums, theater, restaurants . . . and the shopping! Oakville has nothing like this. But as I was chattering to Caroline, crossing the street, a taxi came about an inch from hitting me! Maybe I should go home. There I know a taxi won't run me over.

City Mouse invited his country cousin to dine with him. Every tasty item in the kitchen cupboard was laid out, to Country Mouse's delight. Suddenly, they heard a thump. The cupboard door opened. The cat! The mice ran and hid. Then the Country Mouse packed his bags and returned to his cornfield where he could be safe.

Compare and Contrast Checklist

This checklist of questions can help you compare and contrast stories.

- Who are the main characters, and what are they like?
- Who is telling the story? Whose thoughts and feelings does the author reveal?
- What is the setting?
- What is the plot? What happens in the beginning, middle, and end of the story?
- What problem do the characters have? How do they solve it?
- What is the theme or central message?

After analyzing both texts, use your answers to compare and contrast them.

Language Spotlight • Multiple-Meaning Words

A **multiple-meaning word** is a word that has more than one meaning. Read the following sentence.

Dad bought flour, sugar, and other kitchen staples.

You may know that *staples* are small wire fasteners that hold papers together. But in the sentence above, that meaning of *staples* does not make sense. To figure out the correct meaning, try these strategies:

- Use clues from the context of the sentence.
- Identify a meaning or meanings of the word based on the clues.
- Say each meaning in the sentence to see which makes sense.
- Confirm the meaning by looking up the word in a dictionary.

Now try each strategy. What is the meaning of *staples* in the sentence above?

Read the passage.

Suan's Good Luck

a Filipino folktale

My name is Suan, and I was born clever and lucky. My story begins a long time ago when I was young. I lived with my mother in a small hut in the rain forest. One day, instead of going to school, I climbed a tree that stood by the roadside and watched my mother return from market. Then, I hurried home before her and cried, "Mother, I know what you bought in the market today." I told her everything she had purchased. I did this day after day, and my mother began to believe that I had special powers.

One day when I was a young man, a ring belonging to the prince's daughter disappeared. Everyone searched for it, but in vain. The prince offered his daughter's hand in marriage to the one who could find the lost ring. My mother took me to the palace and presented me to the prince.

"Well, Suan, tomorrow tell me where the ring is," said the prince.

"Yes, my lord, I will if you give your soldiers over to me for tonight," I replied.

The prince agreed, and that evening, I ordered the soldiers to stand around me. I pointed at each one and said, "The ring is here." It so happened that I fixed my eyes on the guilty soldier who trembled and became pale. "I know who has it," I said. Then, I ordered the soldiers to retire.

Later, the guilty soldier came to me and begged, "I will give you the ring. But please don't turn me over to the prince!"

"Give it to me, and you shall be safe," I said.

The next morning, I came to the palace with a turkey. "Where is the ring?" the prince demanded.

"This turkey has swallowed it," I replied. The turkey was cooked, and when it was cut open, the ring was found inside.

"You have done well, Suan. You shall have my daughter's hand," said the prince. And that is how I became the princess's husband. But my story does not end there.

A few years later, there was a bet to prove my skill. A prince from another land bet a riverboat full of treasure that I could not tell the number of seeds in his orange. I had no idea and did not know what to do. At midnight, I went secretly to the prince's riverboat and eavesdropped. That is how I learned the number of seeds.

In the morning I told him, "Your orange has nine seeds," and thus I won his treasure.

Hoping to recover his loss, the same prince came again to test me. This time he brought fourteen riverboats full of gold. He asked me to tell him what was inside his golden ball. That night I sneaked out to the riverboats, but I learned nothing. The next morning, I was called into the presence of the prince. I still had no idea what was in the ball, so I said scornfully, "Nonsense!"

"That is right!" shouted the prince. "The ball contains *nine cents*." Consequently, I won the fourteen riverboats full of gold. From that time on, nobody doubted me.

Answer the following questions.

1 Suan said that he was born lucky. Which event from the passage is the **best** example of his luck?

A. Suan said, "Nonsense," and the prince thought he said *nine cents*.

B. Suan learned the number of orange seeds by eavesdropping.

C. Suan told his mother what she bought at the market.

D. Suan's mother believed he had special powers.

Hint A lucky character has good things happen to him or her. The character does not cause these good things to happen. Which event describes a misunderstanding that helps Suan?

2. The following plot events are out of order. Write the numbers 1 through 6 in the boxes to put the events in the correct order.

- [ ] Instead of going to school, Suan watches his mother return from market.
- [ ] By chance, Suan stares at the guilty soldier, which causes the soldier to confess.
- [ ] Suan tells his mother what she has purchased at the market.
- [ ] Suan hides the ring in a turkey. The ring is found when the turkey is cut open.
- [ ] Suan marries the princess.
- [ ] Suan's mother takes Suan to the prince because she thinks Suan has powers to find the ring.

Hint How does one event in the story lead to the next? What is the final result?

3 Read the following excerpt from the passage.

One day, instead of going to school, I climbed a tree that stood by the roadside and watched my mother return from market. Then, I hurried home before her and cried, "Mother, I know what you bought in the market today." I told her everything she had purchased. I did this day after day, and my mother began to believe that I had special powers.

What does this passage tell you about Suan's character?

____

____

____

____

Hint What do Suan's actions show about his character? Think about what Suan did and why. Why was Suan's mother fooled?

4 Reread these paragraphs from the passage.

Later, the guilty soldier came to me and begged, "I will give you the ring. But please don't turn me over to the prince!"

"Give it to me, and you shall be safe," I said.

The next morning, I came to the palace with a turkey. "Where is the ring?" the prince demanded.

"This turkey has swallowed it," I replied. The turkey was cooked, and when it was cut open, the ring was found inside.

Based on these paragraphs, what is the **best** conclusion you can draw about the ring?

A. The turkey ate the ring accidentally.

B. Suan fed the ring to the turkey to protect the soldier.

C. The soldier hid the ring by feeding it to the turkey.

D. Suan told the prince that the soldier hid the ring in the turkey.

Hint Consider what the soldier asked Suan for in exchange for the ring and what Suan promised the soldier. How did he keep that promise?

Use the Reading Guide to help you understand the passage.

Doctor Know-All

adapted from a folktale by the Brothers Grimm

Reading Guide

What is the point of view in this story? Think about who is telling it and the pronouns the narrator uses.

What is the setting of this story? Look for descriptive words and phrases.

Why did Crab ask the doctor how he could become a doctor himself?

Once upon a time there was a poor peasant by the name of Crab. One day, Crab drove two oxen with a load of wood into town, where he sold the wood to a doctor. He received his money just as the doctor was sitting down to eat. When the peasant saw how well the doctor ate and drank, his heart longed for the same things. He asked if he, too, could become a doctor.

"Certainly," said the doctor, "in no time at all."

"What do I have to do?" asked Crab.

"First, buy an ABC book that has a picture of a rooster in it. Second, sell your wagon and your two oxen and buy some clothing and other things that doctors use. Third, have a sign painted with the words 'I am Doctor Know-All' and nail it above the door to your house."

Crab did everything he was told to do. After he had doctored a little—but not very much—some money was stolen from a great and wealthy nobleman. Someone told the nobleman about Doctor Know-All. Because his name was Doctor Know-All, people believed that he must know where the money had gone. So the nobleman had his carriage hitched up, rode out to the village, and asked Crab if he was Doctor Know-All.

"Yes, I am."

"Then you must come with me and recover my stolen money."

"Yes, but my wife, Greta, must come along, too."

The nobleman agreed, and they all rode away together. They arrived at the nobleman's court just at mealtime, and the nobleman invited Doctor Know-All to eat.

Reading Guide

How are Crab's words misunderstood?

What is the effect of each misunderstanding? Look at the way the nobleman reacts.

What do Crab's actions show about his character?

"Yes, but include my wife, Greta," he replied, and the two of them sat down behind the table. Crab and his wife had never dined with a nobleman at his court, but the peasant knew there would be many different courses of food.

When the first servant brought out a platter of fine food, Crab nudged his wife and said, "Greta, that's the first one," meaning to tell her it was the meal's first course.

However, the servant thought that he meant, "That's the first thief," and because the servant was indeed a thief, he took fright. Outside he said to his fellow servants, "The doctor knows everything. He said that I'm the first one."

The second servant did not want to go inside at all, but finally he had to, and when he entered with the next course, Crab nudged his wife and said, "Greta, that's the second one."

This servant took fright as well and ran outside. It did not go any better for the third servant. When he delivered the third course, Crab said, "Greta, that's the third one."

The fourth servant brought in a covered platter, and the nobleman said that Doctor Know-All should demonstrate his skills by guessing what it contained. Crab looked at the platter, and seeing no way out of his dilemma, he said to himself, "Oh, poor Crab!"

The fourth servant took the cover off the platter, and it contained crab.

Seeing this, the nobleman called out, "If Doctor Know-All knows that, then he must know who has the money as well!"

Reading Guide

Why did Crab not tell the nobleman who had stolen the money?

Is there a lesson in this tale? Why or why not?

The fourth servant grew very fearful and motioned to Crab to go outside. There, all four of the servants confessed that they had stolen the money. They offered to give it all to Crab—plus some extra—if he would not tell the nobleman that they stole his money. If the nobleman found out they were thieves, they would all be punished. They showed Crab where the money was hidden. Crab was satisfied with this, and he went back inside and sat down again at the table.

"My lord," he said, "Now I will look in my book to see where the money is hidden." Crab flipped through the book that the doctor had told him to buy. He was looking for the picture of the rooster.

However, the fifth servant—who was also a thief—hid behind the door in order to hear if Doctor Know-All knew anything else. Crab leafed back and forth in his book searching for the picture of the rooster. Not finding it, he said, "I know that you are in there. Come on out."

The man behind the door thought that Doctor Know-All was talking to him and, terrified, he jumped out, saying, "The man really does know everything!"

Then Doctor Know-All showed the nobleman where the money was, but he did not tell who had stolen it. Thus, he received a large reward from the nobleman and from the servants who had not been caught. His "powers" to find the money made Doctor Know-All a famous—and wealthy—man.

Answer the following question.

1 This question has two parts. First, answer Part A. Then, answer Part B.

Part A

Read these sentences from the passage.

When the peasant saw how well the doctor ate and drank, his heart longed for the same things. He asked if he, too, could become a doctor.

Based on the passage, what does the phrase longed for mean?

A. wanted very much

B. lasted longer because of

C. grew longer because of

D. did not want

Part B

Which phrase from the story's first paragraph **best** supports your answer to Part A?

A. by the name of Crab

B. sold the wood to a doctor

C. received his money

D. how well the doctor ate

Answer the following questions about both stories in this lesson.

2 Which of these are true statements about **both** "Suan's Good Luck" and "Doctor Know-All"? Select **all** that apply.

A. They are traditional folktales.

B. They take place in the Philippines.

C. They take place a long time ago.

D. They take place in Europe.

3 Write a paragraph that compares and contrasts Suan and Dr. Know-All. Describe each character's main actions. Tell how each man's life changes as a result of his actions.

4 This question has two parts. First, answer Part A. Then, answer Part B.

Part A

Which of these makes sense as a theme for **both** passages?

A. Kindness is always best.

B. Persistence and hard work will be rewarded.

C. People who are dishonest will always be punished.

D. Success is sometimes a matter of being in the right place at the right time.

Part B

Which details from the passages provide evidence for your answer to Part A?

A. Suan tricks his mother into believing that he has special powers. Crab calls himself Doctor Know-All so people think that he knows all.

B. Suan won fourteen boats of gold when his words were misunderstood for the right answer. Crab received a reward for accidentally getting a thief to confess.

C. Suan's mother presents Suan to the prince. The doctor gives Crab advice.

D. The prince asks Suan to guess what is in the golden ball. The nobleman asks Crab to guess what is on the covered platter.

5 Reread the following excerpts from "Suan's Good Luck" and "Doctor Know-All" below.

from "Suan's Good Luck"

My name is Suan, and I was born clever and lucky. My story begins a long time ago when I was young. I lived with my mother in a small hut in the rain forest. One day, instead of going to school, I climbed a tree that stood by the roadside and watched my mother return from market. Then, I hurried home before her and cried, "Mother, I know what you bought in the market today."

from "Doctor Know-All"

Once upon a time there was a poor peasant by the name of Crab. One day, Crab drove two oxen with a load of wood into town, where he sold the wood to a doctor. He received his money just as the doctor was sitting down to eat. When the peasant saw how well the doctor ate and drank, his heart longed for the same things. He asked if he, too, could become a doctor.

Compare and contrast the points of view from which the two stories are narrated. Explain how each point of view affects the story. How do the different points of view help your understanding of the stories' elements?

Write your response on the lines below.

6 Both of these passages are folktales. Write a paragraph that compares and contrasts the themes of the passages. Include text evidence about each passage's plot, characters, and setting to support your ideas.

Write your response on the lines below.

Read the play.

The Death of King Arthur

Cast of Characters

KING ARTHUR
SIR BEDIVERE
THREE QUEENS

Act I

A lonely grove of trees just out of sight of a lake. It is night, the moon is out, and King Arthur lies mortally wounded from combat. Sir Bedivere kneels nearby, having carried Arthur from the battlefield.

KING ARTHUR: (*weakly*) The time is near, Bedivere. The wound is deep and there is nothing that can be done about it. Yet there still remains one task for you to perform.

SIR BEDIVERE: Anything, my king.

KING ARTHUR: (*He offers his sword to Bedivere.*) Take Excalibur, my sword. It has served me since I became king. Carry it to the lake and fling it far into the water. Watch carefully. Then return to me and tell me what you see.

SIR BEDIVERE: I will do as you desire, but it seems wrong to throw such a famous and glorious sword into the water. It will forever be a symbol of your reign.

KING ARTHUR: Long ago, as a young man, I stood beside this lake. A hand rose from the water holding the sword aloft. I took it and have used it to guard and protect my kingdom since that moment. It is right to return it to the lake. Go and do as I asked.

As Sir Bedivere carries Excalibur to the lake, he admires the famous sword.

SIR BEDIVERE: (*to himself*) What an extraordinary and beautiful sword, a legend the world over. The most costly jewels embellish its handle. It would be terrible to throw it in the lake. I cannot do it.

Sir Bedivere conceals the sword in the bushes beside the lake and returns to King Arthur.

SIR BEDIVERE: I have done as you requested, my lord.

KING ARTHUR: Thank you, my knight. What did you see or hear?

SIR BEDIVERE: The clouds blown by the wind and the crash of waves on the rocks.

KING ARTHUR: (*with a weak, faint voice*) My noble knight, it is beneath you to lie to your king. Go once more and throw the sword into the lake.

Sir Bedivere goes once more to the lake. He takes up Excalibur and admires it once more and then again conceals it in the weeds and returns to Arthur.

SIR BEDIVERE: My lord, I did as you commanded and threw Excalibur into the lake.

KING ARTHUR: What did you see?

SIR BEDIVERE: I saw the waves on the lake and heard them smashing on the shore.

KING ARTHUR: It is not well that you try to deceive me when I count on you in my dying moments. Go once more and throw Excalibur with all your might into the lake.

Sir Bedivere goes a third time to the lake, and without looking more at Excalibur, he heaves it as far into the lake as he can. He watches and then returns to Arthur.

SIR BEDIVERE: Truly I have done what you asked, my king.

KING ARTHUR: What did you see?

SIR BEDIVERE: I saw an arm reach up from the lake and grasp the sword as it fell. Three times the arm raised the sword and brandished it proudly, and then it drew Excalibur into the water.

KING ARTHUR: You have done all I asked and now I have but one last request. Help me to the shore of the lake.

Act II

Sir Bedivere helps King Arthur stand and gently assists him in reaching the shore, where a ship carrying three queens awaits them.

KING ARTHUR: Place me on the ship, Sir Bedivere. It will bear me home.

Bedivere places King Arthur on the ship, where he is received by the three queens.

KING ARTHUR: I now say goodbye to you, Sir Bedivere. You have been my most courageous and trustworthy knight. Now, go and live as you can and tell the tale of King Arthur and his knights. Let not the story of our time be forgotten.

The ship leaves the shore and sails into the distance. Sir Bedivere watches as it takes his king away. When it at last disappears beyond the horizon, he turns slowly and walks away into the night.

Answer the questions.

1. Read each excerpt from the play. Write the excerpt in the row of the chart that **best** describes what part of the play it is.

A lonely grove of trees just out of sight of a lake.
THREE QUEENS
KING ARTHUR: Thank you, my knight.
(*with a weak, faint voice*)

Cast of characters	
Setting	
Stage direction	
Dialogue	

2 Read the sentences from the play.

KING ARTHUR: Place me on the ship, Sir Bedivere. It will bear me home.

Which definition **best** describes how the word bear is used in this sentence?

A. to give birth
B. to produce fruit
C. to carry
D. to endure

3 This question has two parts. First, answer Part A. Then, answer Part B.

Part A

Which event does the illustration show?

A. the first time Bedivere goes to the lake

B. the second time Bedivere goes to the lake

C. the third time Bedivere goes to the lake

D. the fourth time Bedivere goes to the lake

Part B

Which of the following statements **best** explains what the illustration helps you understand?

A. Bedivere is finally able to throw Excalibur into the lake.

B. Bedivere regrets throwing Excalibur into the lake.

C. Bedivere thinks Excalibur is too beautiful to throw away.

D. Bedivere wants to keep Excalibur for himself.

4 Which **two** statements **best** explain why—the first time Bedivere returns—Arthur says Bedivere is lying and tells him to "go once more and throw the sword into the lake"?

A. Arthur can see where Bedivere has hidden Excalibur.

B. Bedivere's description of what he saw at the lake does not match what Arthur was expecting to hear.

C. Bedivere has a suspicious look on his face.

D. Earlier, Bedivere asks Arthur whether it is wise to return Excalibur.

E. Arthur really doesn't want to return Excalibur to the lake.

5 The events below are from the play, but they are out of order. Write the numbers 2, 3, 4, and 5 to put the events in the correct order.

1	Arthur and Bedivere return from battle.
	Bedivere admires the sword's beautiful jewels.
	Bedivere finally returns Excalibur to the lake.
	Arthur asks Bedivere to return Excalibur to the lake.
	Bedivere twice lies to Arthur about returning the sword.
6	Arthur sails away with the three queens.

Read the passage.

Returning a Treasure

Ana sighed as she walked into the Beachport Public Library. Her family had just moved to this sleepy coastal town, and because it was summer vacation, she hadn't had many opportunities to meet anyone. As Ana browsed the **Fiction: Adventure Stories** section, Ms. Albertson, the librarian, asked if she had heard the local legend about pirate's treasure. "It was supposedly buried somewhere near here in the eighteenth century," Ms. Albertson said. "People search for it all the time." She went on to tell Ana all about it.

Ana was intrigued by the story and decided she'd try to find the hidden treasure. The next morning, she borrowed her mother's metal detector and started the search. Over the next few weeks, Ana found more than fifteen dollars in coins buried in the sand. She also found eyeglasses, a crushed watch, aluminum cans, parts from old cars, kitchen utensils, a rusted typewriter, and a number of items she couldn't identify. The one thing she didn't find was treasure.

Then one day, Ana dug into the sand and let out a gasp: It was a ruby ring! "A real treasure!" she exclaimed.

Ana hurried home to show it to her mother and then rushed down to the library to show Ms. Albertson, who'd become her one friend in town.

"That's a valuable ring," Ms. Albertson said approvingly. "Lots of people have looked for treasure, but you're the first one I know who actually found her own Excalibur!"

Ana loved the ring and wore it all the time. Then one day at the library, a notice on the community bulletin board caught her eye. "Lost! One ruby ring. Lost on the beach outside of town. If you find it, notify Margaret Sputner at 555-0659."

Ana's jaw dropped. She had heard about Ms. Sputner. "She's dreadful," Ms. Albertson had warned. "She thinks she owns the beach, and she's liable to sic her dog on you if she thinks you're trespassing. She's done it before."

At first, Ana was determined to keep the ring. Besides, she reasoned, if anyone did find out that she had found Ms. Sputner's ring, they might not blame her for keeping it.

But over the next few days, Ana began to feel guilty. By the weekend, she knew she had to return the ring to its rightful owner.

Ana looked up Ms. Sputner's address. She lived in an old mansion on the edge of town near the beach. As Ana slowly walked up the marble steps to the front door, she began to feel uneasy. *What if she really does sic her dog on me?* she wondered. Nevertheless, Ana continued climbing, knocked on the door, and waited. An elderly woman opened the door. She was dressed all in black, and her face was deeply lined—and scowling. Ms. Sputner peered suspiciously at Ana through a narrowly opened doorway.

"I read your note," Ana squeaked nervously. "Did you lose a ring?"

Ms. Sputner's eyebrows went up. "If you've found a ring, you give it to me right now!"

Ana hesitated, but then said, "I won't give it to you unless you describe it for me, please."

Ms. Sputner's scowl deepened, but she described the ring she had lost. The description matched the ring that Ana had found, and Ana reluctantly handed it over. Ms. Sputner grabbed the ring, glanced at it quickly, turned, and slammed the door in Ana's face without so much as a thank you.

Ana felt stunned and then confused. The next day, she told Ms. Albertson what she had done and how Ms. Sputner had acted. The librarian raised her eyebrows, pursed her lips, and sympathized.

"It doesn't surprise me," she said. "Ms. Sputner has behaved like that as long as anyone can remember. I'm sorry it happened to you when you were just being kind."

"I almost didn't give it back," Ana said thoughtfully, "but I'm glad I did. It was hers. Maybe it meant something special to her." Ana smiled. "It's okay. I'll find my own Excalibur!"

Answer the questions.

6 This question has two parts. First, answer Part A. Then, answer Part B.

Part A

Which phrase from "Returning a Treasure" is an allusion to the play "The Death of King Arthur"?

A. a valuable ring

B. said approvingly

C. looked for treasure

D. her own Excalibur

Part B

Think about the allusion you identified in Part A. Which statement **best** explains what this allusion reveals about "Returning a Treasure"?

A. Like King Arthur's buried treasure, the ruby ring is worth a lot of money.

B. Like King Arthur's beautiful sword, the ruby ring is precious and meaningful.

C. Bedivere lies to noble King Arthur, but Ana tells mean Ms. Sputner the truth.

D. Bedivere values King Arthur's approval, and Ana values Ms. Albertson's approval.

7 This question has two parts. First, answer Part A. Then, answer Part B.

Part A

Which of the following describes the narrator in "Returning a Treasure"?

A. Ana, a first-person narrator

B. Ms. Sputner, a first-person narrator

C. a third-person narrator who shares Ana's thoughts

D. a third-person narrator who shares Ana's and Ms. Sputner's thoughts

Part B

Which sentence from the story **best** supports your answer to Part A?

A. Over the next few weeks, Ana found more than fifteen dollars in coins buried in the sand.

B. "She thinks she owns the beach, and she's liable to sic her dog on you if she thinks you're trespassing."

C. As Ana slowly walked up the marble steps to the front door, she began to feel uneasy.

D. The librarian raised her eyebrows, pursed her lips, and sympathized.

8 Skim the story to find details that describe the setting. Then identify **two** ways that the story's setting affects the plot events or the characters.

9 Read each statement in the box. Decide whether it could be a theme for "The Death of King Arthur," for "Returning a Treasure," or for both passages. Write the statement in the correct area on the diagram.

Doing the right thing can be hard.
Being a good person is rewarding.
The value of loyalty cannot be measured.
Your conscience will tell you the right thing to do.

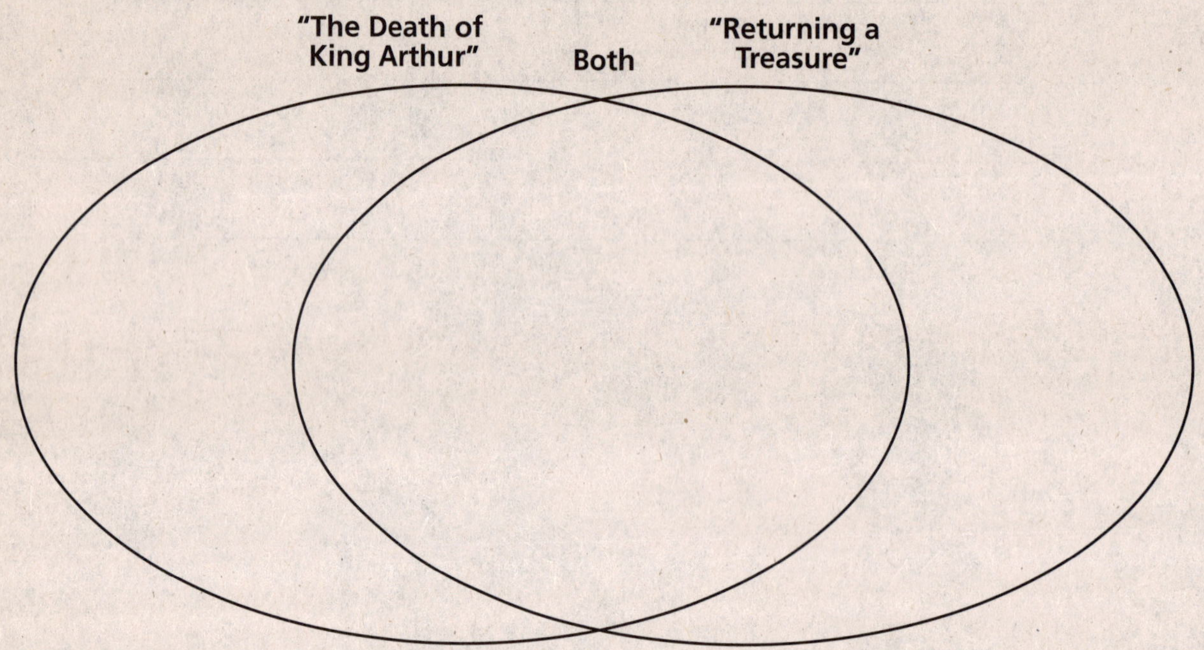

10 Think about the characters of Sir Bedivere in "The Death of King Arthur" and Ana in "Returning a Treasure." Describe how these two characters are alike and different. Include answers to these questions in your response:

- What problem does each character face?
- What difficult choices must each character make?
- How does each character respond to the plot events and to the problem?
- What does each character learn from his or her experience?

Remember to include text evidence from both passages to support your ideas.

Write your comparison on the lines provided.

STRAND

2

Working with Informational Texts

LESSON 5

Articles

1 GETTING THE IDEA

Nonfiction texts, also called **informational texts**, tell about the real world. They give information, or facts, about real people, places, events, or things. This chart shows some types of nonfiction.

Type of Nonfiction	Purpose
biography	tells the true story of a person's life
essay	shares the author's outlook or point of view
speech	presents a topic that is shared orally
textbook	gives factual information about a topic

Main Idea and Details

The most common type of nonfiction is an **article**. You can find nonfiction articles in a newspaper or magazine and online. Every article has a **main idea** that tells what the text is mostly about. The facts that support the main idea are called **evidence**. Types of evidence include dates, names, facts, examples, and quotes. Each paragraph in the article also has a main idea and supporting details. The main idea is often stated toward the beginning of the paragraph. Read the paragraph and underline the main idea.

> The Founder's Day parade was cancelled. After three days of severe storms, the day started out sunny. However, a wave of cool air moved in by mid-morning. When dark clouds rolled across the sky, the mayor cancelled the parade.

When you read nonfiction, you can also use the available facts and details to make inferences. An **inference** is a guess based on text evidence and your own knowledge and experience. What inference can you make about why the mayor cancelled the parade? Circle the details that support that inference.

Text Structure

Authors share information in a way readers can understand. The way an author organizes information is called **text structure**. Here are some common text structures that authors use.

Sequence A **sequence structure** puts events, steps, or facts in time order. Dates, ages, numbers, and time-order words, such as *first* and *last*, show sequence.

Read the paragraph. Circle words that help show the sequence.

> Thomas Edison began working when he was twelve. He sold newspapers, candy, and fruit on a train. At fifteen, he learned how to use a telegraph machine. He did this job for seven years. In 1869, at the age of twenty-two, Edison became a full-time inventor.

Compare and Contrast When authors **compare and contrast,** they tell how two or more things are alike and different. Often, one paragraph tells how the subjects are alike, and another paragraph tells how they are different. Sometimes, sentences alternate telling how the subjects are alike and different.

Read the paragraphs. Circle the sentences that tell how dolphins and porpoises are alike. Underline the sentences that tell how they are different.

> Many people confuse dolphins and porpoises. Both are playful, warm-blooded mammals. Both breathe air and use sound waves to help them move underwater.
>
> A closer look shows that dolphins have long snouts, while porpoises have shorter ones. Dolphins have a curved dorsal fin, but porpoise fins are triangular. Dolphin teeth are shaped like cones; however, porpoise teeth are shaped like spades.

Cause and Effect A **cause-and-effect structure** explains what happens and why. The **cause** is why an event happens. The **effect** is what happens as a result. Sometimes, there can be more than one cause for an effect or more than one effect of a cause.

Problem and Solution In a text structure organized by **problem and solution**, the author states a problem and suggests a way to solve the problem.

Read the following paragraph. Underline the problem once and the solution twice. How are the problem and solution ordered?

> People who own tropical fish sometimes find that the fish jump out of the tank. If no one is around to scoop up the fish and return them to the tank, they will die. What can fish owners do to prevent this from happening? They can put a lid on the fish tank.

Text Features

Authors also use **text features** to organize information. These tools help readers find and follow facts and ideas.

- **Headings** and **subheadings** tell what a section of an article is about. They help readers find information quickly.
- **Bulleted lists** summarize a lot of information. Each bulleted item tells about one new idea.
- A **caption** appears above or below a photograph or graphic. It explains what the photograph or graphic is about.
- A **sidebar** is a separate section of text, often shown in a box, that relates to the main article. It may give additional interesting facts or share a different point of view.

Language Spotlight • Synonyms and Antonyms

Synonyms are words with the same or almost the same meaning. *Happy* and *glad* are synonyms. **Antonyms** are words with opposite meanings, such as *good* and *bad*. Read these sentences. Are the underlined words in each sentence synonyms or antonyms? How do you know?

The lake was calm, so we floated on the peaceful waters all day.

I thought the science quiz would be easy, but it was difficult.

Read the passage.

Tornado Safety

It might have looked fun when a tornado took Dorothy to Oz, but there is nothing fun about tornadoes. These severe storms are funnel-shaped clouds with dangerous, twisting winds. The winds average thirty miles per hour, but don't be fooled. They can reach 300 miles per hour. They carry some of the fastest winds on Earth. Tornadoes have picked up houses. One even plucked the feathers right off a chicken.

Tornadoes can move in any direction and can change directions quickly. They form at any time of day and all year long. The United States has more tornadoes than any other country in the world—more than 1,000 of them touch down each year. They injure more than 1,500 people annually. Given how frequent and dangerous tornadoes are, it is important to practice tornado safety. That means making a safety plan, practicing it, and following that plan if a tornado ever comes along.

Did You Know?
Three of every four tornadoes on Earth touch down in the United States.

In parts of the country where tornadoes are common, emergency sirens alert people to possible danger.

Be Alert and Make a Plan

Warm, humid air; winds; and dark, threatening skies are signs of a possible tornado. When these conditions exist, listen to weather reports. If the weather service announces a tornado watch or warning, take it seriously. Follow any directions you hear. Find out about your community's warning system and listen for signals.

If you live in an area where tornadoes occur, it is especially important to have an emergency plan in place. Follow these steps when making your plan.

- **Supplies** First, prepare emergency kits. A kit should have supplies for three days. It should include food, water, flashlights, radios, batteries, and a first-aid kit. The American Red Cross can provide a full list of the supplies you need.
- **Shelter** Next, talk to your family and decide on a meeting place, such as a basement, a safe room, or a tornado shelter. If none of these options exist, plan to meet in a room or hallway without windows, preferably on the ground floor.
- **Contacts** Be sure to choose a contact person. This person should not live too close to you. Family members can check in with this person in an emergency of if they become separated from one another. Post all emergency numbers close to house phones and save them in cell phones.

Practice Your Plan

Once you have your plan in place, practice it every six months. You should also replace the food and water supplies in the emergency kits at the same time. Check and replace the batteries in your smoke alarms, flashlights, and radios as needed. Make sure all fire extinguishers are working.

Follow Your Plan

During a tornado, follow the plan. Stay calm and move to a safe place. If you are indoors, sit facing a wall with your elbows to your knees. Cover the back of your head with your hands. If you are outdoors, go inside as quickly as possible. If you are at school, follow the school safety plan and all instructions from your teachers.

Tornadoes are dangerous. Preparation and practice can go a long way, though, toward keeping you safe.

Answer the following questions.

1 Read the paragraph from the passage and the question that follows.

> **During a tornado, follow the plan. Stay calm and move to a safe place. If you are indoors, sit facing a wall with your elbows to your knees. Cover the back of your head with your hands. If you are outdoors, go inside as quickly as possible. If you are at school, follow the school safety plan and all instructions from your teachers.**

Which **two** sentences from the paragraph tell what you should do if you are indoors?

A. During a tornado, follow the plan.

B. Stay calm and move to a safe place.

C. If you are indoors, sit facing a wall with your elbows to your knees.

D. Cover the back of your head with your hands.

E. If you are outdoors, go inside as quickly as possible.

F. If you are at school, follow the school safety plan and all instructions from your teachers..

Hint The first correct answer contains a very good clue. The second correct answer also tells what to do if you are indoors.

2 Which choice **best** summarizes the passage?

A. Most tornadoes happen in the United States.

B. Tornadoes are dangerous storms, with twisting winds.

C. A family needs to set aside supplies.

D. A safety plan can help your family stay safe during a tornado.

Hint What is the article mostly about? Reread the headings. What do they tell you?

3 The following question has two parts. First, answer Part A. Then, answer Part B.

Part A

Which **three** phrases or sentences are headings in the article?

A. In parts of the country where tornadoes are common, emergency sirens alert people to possible danger.

B. Three of every four tornados on Earth touch down in the United States.

C. Be Alert and Make a Plan

D. First, prepare emergency kits.

E. Practice Your Plan

F. Follow Your Plan

Part B

Based on the headings, what text structure does the author use to organize the passage?

A. sequence

B. compare and contrast

C. problem and solution

D. cause and effect

Hint Remember that headings help an author organize information in a passage. Think about how the author of "Tornado Safety" uses headings in the passage.

4 The following question has two parts. First, answer Part A. Then, answer Part B.

Part A

Read this sentence from the passage.

> **These severe storms are funnel-shaped clouds with dangerous, twisting winds.**

Which word is a synonym of severe?

A. light

B. violent

C. famous

D. delicate

Part B

Which word from the sentence **best** supports your answer to Part A?

A. storms

B. clouds

C. dangerous

D. twisting

Hint For Part A, use the other words in the sentence to help you understand the meaning of *severe*. Remember that synonyms have similar meanings. For Part B, find the best context clue to the meaning of *severe*.

Use the Reading Guide to help you understand the passage.

Storm Spotters and Storm Chasers

Reading Guide

Why do members of the NWS sometimes run toward storms?

Which text structure organizes the information in paragraph 2?

What is Skywarn? How does it work?

Most people run away from storms. Some members of the National Weather Service (NWS), though, run *toward* tornadoes. That seems a little crazy, but it is for a good reason. The NWS wants to keep people safe. They study how tornadoes form and behave, and then they try to better predict them.

Many people and programs contribute to this effort. There are storm spotters and storm chasers. The two are different. Spotters stay close to home. They report on weather in their area. Chasers are on the move. They will travel hundreds of miles to find storms as they form. Although the NWS appreciates help from storm spotters, it discourages storm chasing. Tornadoes are dangerous, so storm chasers are highly trained people with special equipment.

Skywarn

Skywarn is an important storm-spotting program. It started in the 1960s. The NWS runs training programs for spotters across the United States. The 290,000 trained volunteers observe and measure the weather. They report wind speeds, hail size, rainfall, and clouds in an area. These weather conditions can help show when a tornado is developing. Skywarn volunteers pass the information on to emergency services or their local NWS Forecast Center.

Skywarn spotters take pictures like this to pass on to the National Weather Service.

Reading Guide

What were the goals of the VORTEX 2 project?

What are some of the key details in paragraph 3? How do they support the main idea of the paragraph?

Why do you think the author included the sidebar?

The VORTEX Projects

VORTEX was a storm-chasing project that took place in the springs of 1994 and 1995. VORTEX stands for Verification of the Origins of Rotation Tornadoes Experiment. During the VORTEX project, scientists were able to collect data on the entire lifecycle of a tornado for the first time. VORTEX 2 took place in the spring of 2009 and 2010.

VORTEX 2 had several goals. NWS scientists wanted to learn more about how tornadoes form. They also wanted to know why some tornadoes are strong but others are weak. This information could help the NWS issue more accurate and faster warnings. At the start of the program, warnings came about thirteen minutes before the storm. About 70 percent of them were false alarms. The NWS wanted to improve that record because early, accurate warnings save lives.

The project was a major effort. One hundred twenty-five scientists and crew members manned the VORTEX 2 team. They traveled thousands of miles across the Southern Plains. Their equipment included fifty special vehicles. Among the different trucks used was the Tornado Intercept Vehicle (TIV). A TIV weighs about eight tons, or 16,000 pounds. It has to be heavy so strong winds cannot get underneath and lift it up. The vehicles hold many of the same tools that would also be found in a weather station. Their radar systems track storms. They launch weather balloons, which record air pressure, wind speed and direction, and air temperature.

> A tornado warning means a tornado was seen by a spotter or by radar.

Reading Guide

Why was TOTO left in the path of a tornado? What can you infer about TOTO's failure to work?

Why is VORTEX 2 still important to the NWS?

New Technology

Many tornado-chasing vehicles carry amazing instruments that can go *into* a tornado to gather data. It has taken decades to develop some of these tools. One of the earliest models came out in 1981. Called TOTO (TOtable Tornado Observatory), it was a metal drum filled with weather tools. Scientists left the drum in the path of a tornado. They hoped that a tornado would scoop it up on its way by. Then, TOTO could collect information. Unfortunately, this never happened.

Scientists also tried shooting rockets into a tornado from an airplane. This idea didn't work either, but the scientists learned from these failures. VORTEX 2 carried new tools called StickNet probes and Tornado Pods. They can successfully enter tornadoes to gather data.

Research Continues

Though the VORTEX projects have ended, scientists are still studying the data the storm-chasing teams collected. The NWS expects the information will help them better protect people and property in the future.

Answer the following questions.

1. Which detail from the text identifies how storm spotters are different from storm chasers?

   A. The NWS runs training programs for spotters across the United States.

   B. Skywarn started in the 1960s.

   C. Spotters stay close to home.

   D. Many people and programs contribute to this effort.

2. Read these sentences from the passage and the directions that follow.

   Many people and programs contribute to this effort. There are storm spotters and storm chasers. The two are different. Spotters stay close to home. They report on weather in their area. Chasers are on the move. They will travel hundreds of miles to find storms as they form.

   Name the structure the author uses to organize this section of the passage, and write one to two sentences to explain your answer.

   Write your answer on the lines below.

3 Read this sentence from the passage and the directions that follow.

They study how tornadoes form and behave, and then they try to better predict them.

Which is the **best** synonym for the word behave in this sentence?

A. act

B. operate

C. perform

D. react

4 Which sentences support the main idea that the NWS wants to keep people safe from tornadoes? Check **all** that apply.

A. The NWS runs training programs for spotters across the United States.

B. These weather conditions can help show when a tornado is developing.

C. Chasers are on the move.

D. Although the NWS appreciates help from storm spotters, it discourages storm chasing.

E. VORTEX was a storm-chasing project that took place in the springs of 1994 and 1995.

F. The NWS wanted to improve that record because early, accurate warnings save lives.

5 Read this paragraph from the passage.

Though the VORTEX projects have ended, scientists are still studying the data the storm-chasing teams collected. The NWS expects the information will help them better protect people and property in the future.

What can you infer about scientific research from these sentences?

A. It is hard to collect data.

B. It takes time to analyze data.

C. Most data never have practical, or useful, purposes.

D. Data are interesting and useful only to scientists.

6 Identify the main idea of the passage and the key details that support the main idea. Then, write a summary of the passage to restate the main idea and details in your own words.

Write your response on the lines below.

LESSON 6

Persuasive Texts

1 GETTING THE IDEA

Persuasive texts try to persuade, or convince, readers to agree with a certain view or take a specific action. Political speeches on television and opinion blog posts online are persuasive texts. Advertisements in newspapers and magazines are also persuasive texts. They try to convince you to buy certain products. Many newspapers and magazines also have an editorial section. In this section, editors write persuasive texts to give their opinions about topics. Readers write letters to the editor to give their opinions about editorials, news stories, and current events.

Text Structure

Many persuasive texts follow a specific structure.

- The **introduction** states the **claim**, or the main point the author wants to make.
- The **supporting paragraphs** give reasons why readers should believe the claim and include evidence to back up the reasons.
- The **conclusion** restates the author's position, summarizes the key points, and leaves readers with a final thought about the topic.

Point of View

Persuasive writing is different from most informational writing. Generally, informational texts are neutral. This means they present the facts about a topic without giving opinions about it. Often, informational texts present both sides of an issue.

Persuasive texts are not neutral. In a persuasive text, an author gives his or her **point of view**, or feelings about a topic. At the beginning of the text, the author makes a claim. The claim states his or her position in support of or against a topic. It is the main idea of the text. The author's claim is usually an opinion. **Opinions** are statements that are based on feelings or beliefs. They cannot be proven true.

Reasons and Evidence

A writer of a persuasive text wants readers to agree with his or her opinions. An author defends a claim by giving reasons to back it up. **Reasons** are supporting ideas that tell readers why they should believe the author's opinions.

Authors also supply evidence to support the reasons. **Evidence** includes facts, examples, quotes, and other data. In contrast to opinions, **facts** are statements that can be proven true or used to prove that something else is true. For a persuasive text to be convincing, it has to include enough evidence for the reader to believe or agree with the author's claim.

Read the sentences below. Circle the opinion. Underline the fact.

> Children need a specific bedtime every night. The National Sleep Foundation recommends that school-age children get ten to eleven hours of sleep each night.

The opinion is a belief. The writer believes that children need a specific bedtime. But that idea cannot be proven true. Other people may hold a different opinion and think children do not need to go to bed at the same time each night. The fact, however, is a true statement. It can be proven that the foundation suggests ten to eleven hours of sleep per night for school-age children.

This chart shows an author's claim and the reasons and evidence used to support it. When you read a persuasive text, pay attention to how the author uses specific evidence to support each reason.

Claim: Children need a strict bedtime to ensure they get enough sleep.		
Reason: Children need more than eight hours of sleep each night to function at their best.	**Reason:** Children need to get enough sleep to stay healthy and alert.	**Reason:** Not getting enough sleep can affect a student's performance in school.
Evidence: The National Sleep Foundation recommends that school-age children get ten to eleven hours of sleep each night.	**Evidence:** Many studies have found connections between too little sleep and a greater risk of health problems.	**Evidence:** Researchers have found that students who get less sleep have more difficulty remembering information.

Methods of Persuasion

Writers have different ways to try to get you to agree with their opinions. Here are some strategies authors may use in persuasive writing.

An author may . . .	An author wants readers to . . .	Example
use strong words that appeal to readers' emotions.	have feelings about the author's views. If readers feel strongly, they may be more likely to change their views or take action.	Why risk your children's health to let them stay up later at night? When children don't get enough sleep, their overall health is affected.
suggest that "everyone is doing it."	feel a need to belong and agree with an idea to "fit in" with others.	Almost all parents give their children a specific bedtime.
use an expert's name to promote something.	believe what an expert says. Readers may be more likely to agree with a view if a trusted expert supports it.	Dr. Pam, a well-known expert on sleep patterns, encourages parents to stick to a set bedtime each night.

Language Spotlight • Persuasive Language

Persuasive writers choose their words carefully. They use precise words to explain exactly what they think and use persuasive language to affect how a reader thinks and feels. An author's word choice affects how convincing the writing is.

Read the paragraph. Underline the persuasive words the author uses. How does the author's choice of words make the information convincing?

> Help student athletes prevent unnecessary injuries! Athletes who do not get the required sleep are less able to focus and risk getting hurt. In one 2012 survey, student athletes who had eight hours of sleep each night reported fewer injuries than those who slept less.

Read the passage.

May 8, 2013
Dear Editor,

What ever happened to Americans' right to personal choice? In places across the country, people are being told what they can and cannot eat, drink, or buy. Recently, some colleges and towns have even banned the sale of personal-sized disposable[1] plastic water bottles. Someone needs to put an end to this insanity. No one should be allowed to ban the sale of plastic water bottles.

First of all, everyone knows that water is a basic need for all human beings. A large amount of the human body is made up of water. People need to drink water to stay hydrated. Doctors and nutritionists recommend that people drink eight glasses of water a day. The easiest way for people to meet this requirement is to carry bottles of water with them. That way they can make sure to have enough water.

This is especially important for people who work or exercise outside. They may not have access to a water fountain or tap. When people sweat, they lose water. They need to replace this water by drinking so they don't get dehydrated. When a person gets dehydrated, he or she may feel dizzy and weak, and may even pass out. So, many workers and athletes rely on disposable water bottles. They are lightweight and easy to carry, and can be thrown away after use.

In addition, there are other situations in which people may not have access to tap water. My family, for instance, goes hiking and camping. We often explore areas that are far from towns and a water supply. We need to carry water bottles with us so we can stay hydrated. Just think of what could happen if we got dehydrated in the middle of nowhere.

Safety experts at government health agencies also recommend that people keep a supply of bottled water in case of emergencies. In some big storms, like a blizzard or hurricane, the water supply may be affected. People may not be able to drink tap water and may need a backup supply of bottled water to drink.

[1] **disposable**: can be thrown away, usually after one use

Unfortunately for some people, this lack of clean tap water is an everyday concern. Many people around the world do not have access to clean tap water. Drinking unclean water can lead to illness and even death. Disposable plastic water bottles can ensure that all people have access to clean drinking water.

I understand that people are concerned by the amount of plastic waste water bottles create. But that's why most towns encourage people to recycle their water bottles. Plastic water bottles can be recycled into new bottles and even be made into other goods, like clothing! Recycling is the better solution to the waste problem.

Banning water bottles is not a suitable option. Without water bottles, people will be more likely to get dehydrated and be exposed to unhealthy drinking water. Why force people to suffer from illness or disease, or even to die, from a lack of clean water? Water bottles should be kept on store shelves so people can get the water they need.

Gianna Levitt

Answer the following questions.

1 What is the author's claim?

A. People should recycle more.

B. Plastic water bottles should not be banned.

C. People should drink eight glasses of water a day.

D. Athletes need to drink more water than other people do.

Hint Think about the main point the author wants people to agree with.

2 Read this sentence from the letter and the directions that follow.

Recently, some colleges and towns have even banned the sale of personal-sized disposable plastic water bottles.

Tell whether this sentence states an opinion or a fact. Explain how you know.

Hint Recall the differences between opinions and facts. Facts can be proven.

3 Write the evidence from the box in the correct locations on the chart to support the opinions from the article.

> Doctors and nutritionists recommend that people drink eight glasses of water a day.
>
> Water bottles are lightweight and can be thrown away after use.
>
> Many people around the world do not have access to clean tap water.

Opinion	Evidence
Personal-sized disposable water bottles are convenient.	
Disposable plastic water bottles help people stay hydrated.	
Disposable plastic water bottles can ensure that all people have access to clean drinking water.	

Hint Read each opinion carefully. Decide which piece of evidence best supports that opinion.

4 The following question has two parts. First, answer Part A. Then, answer Part B.

Part A

What persuasive strategy does the author use in the last paragraph of the letter?

A. words that suggest everyone is using disposable water bottles

B. an expert's opinion to show disposable water bottles are necessary

C. strong words and phrases that appeal to the readers' emotions

D. examples and facts to get readers to buy disposable water bottles

Part B

Which sentence from the letter's last paragraph **best** supports your answer to Part A?

A. Banning water bottles is not a suitable option.

B. Without water bottles, people will be more likely to get dehydrated and be exposed to unhealthy drinking water.

C. Why force people to suffer from illness or disease, or even to die, from a lack of clean water?

D. Water bottles should be kept on store shelves so people can get the water they need.

Hint What type of language does the author use? How does this language affect readers?

Use the Reading Guide to help you understand the passage.

Plastic Water Bottles Are Destroying the Environment

Reading Guide

Look at the introduction to this passage. What is the author's point of view on disposable plastic water bottles?

What kind of evidence does the author provide?

Pay attention to paragraph 4. How does the author address an opposing viewpoint?

The environment is in trouble, and plastic water bottles are to blame! Personal-sized disposable plastic water bottles generate waste that harms the environment. Even recycling isn't an acceptable solution because toxins are still released and too much energy is wasted. We need to find a better solution. Although the sale of water bottles has been banned in some places, more should be done to protect our health and the well-being of the environment. All personal-sized disposable plastic water bottles should be banned.

First, plastic bottles require too many resources and too much energy to make. It takes millions of barrels of oil to make the plastic water bottles that the United States uses each year. And that is just to make the bottles. Think of all the resources that are wasted by large trucks carting the bottles from warehouses to stores.

In a single year, Americans consume more than fifty billion personal-sized bottles of water! That's almost one hundred sixty bottles per person! But people don't need to drink their water from small disposable bottles. Instead of using multiple small bottles, people should refill reusable bottles with tap water. Or, if they don't have clean tap water, they should buy large containers of water and use that water to refill reusable bottles. Using reusable bottles will also save people money.

Small, disposable, plastic water bottles create a huge amount of trash. Although some people may argue that the bottles can be recycled, many people throw plastic in the regular trash. Landfills are quickly filling up with mounds of plastic that people carelessly throw away. The plastic does not break down very quickly. Pretty soon, landfills will be full and there will be nowhere to put the garbage.

Reading Guide

How does the author use persuasive language?

What does the author suggest as alternates to bottled water?

Does the author provide a strong conclusion to the passage? Explain your answer.

Even with recycling, there is a negative impact on the environment. When plastic is recycled, gasses are released into the air. These gasses can harm the air that we breathe. The recycling process also uses a huge amount of energy. If we keep using our natural resources as we are, they will no longer be available to us.

Many people are afraid to drink tap water because they think it's unclean. But there are risks to drinking bottled water, too. Some plastics contain chemicals that can leak into the water. No one knows for sure whether plastic water bottles are completely safe. So, why take a chance on drinking bottled water when there's perfectly good water in your tap?

Of course, some communities do not have access to clean water. But trucking in mass amounts of small water bottles will not help these communities. If anything, that will only create trash problems for these places. Instead, other solutions should be considered. Wells, water tanks, and relocation are all options that have been used to help people gain access to safe, clean water.

The best thing we can do for our health and for the environment is to use reusable glass or aluminum bottles filled with filtered tap water. Some colleges and towns have helped citizens take this step by banning water bottles smaller than one liter. For example, at the University of Vermont, students must carry their own reusable bottles and refill them at water stations. The college hopes this will help reduce waste on the campus.

Other colleges, towns, and even state governments should take a lesson from this plan. They, too, should enforce bans on the use of small water bottles. Landfills are piling up with plastic, and the process of recycling plastic is polluting our air with chemicals. Why isn't anything being done to address these harmful situations? I, for one, refuse to watch the environment be destroyed one plastic bottle at a time. We all need to take action and push to ban plastic bottles around the world. Our health and the future of the planet depend on it!

Answer the following questions.

1. Write the sentences from the box in the correct locations on the chart to show how the author introduces and supports the claim.

In a single year, Americans consume more than fifty billion personal-sized bottles of water!
Small, disposable, plastic water bottles create a huge amount of trash.
All personal-sized disposable plastic water bottles should be banned.

Claim	
Reason	
Evidence	

2. Which statement from the text includes the **most** precise language to support the author's claim?

A. First, plastic bottles require too many resources and too much energy to make.

B. When plastic is recycled, gasses are released into the air.

C. No one knows for sure whether plastic water bottles are completely safe.

D. We all need to take action and push to ban plastic water bottles around the world.

3 The following question has two parts. First, answer Part A. Then, answer Part B.

Part A

Which statement **best** summarizes what the author wants the reader to do?

A. recycle water bottles more often

B. support a ban on water bottles

C. buy larger water bottles

D. clean up landfills and other areas with trash

Part B

Which sentence from the passage **best** supports your answer for Part A?

A. Instead of using multiple small bottles, people should refill reusable bottles with tap water.

B. Landfills are quickly filling up with mounds of plastic that people carelessly throw away.

C. The recycling process also uses a huge amount of energy.

D. We all need to take action and push to ban plastic bottles around the world.

4 The following question has two parts. First, answer Part A. Then, answer Part B.

Part A

In which **two** statements from the passage does the author address an opposing view?

A. But people don't need to drink their water from small disposable bottles.

B. Although some people may argue that the bottles can be recycled, many people throw plastic in the regular trash.

C. Even with recycling, there is a negative impact on the environment.

D. Some colleges and towns have helped citizens take this step by banning water bottles smaller than one liter.

Part B

Which **two** statements give reasons and evidence that the author provides to disprove the opposing views?

A. Some people fail to recycle plastic bottles—instead, they place them in the regular trash.

B. Some plastic bottles contain chemicals that can get into water—this means that it isn't always safe to drink bottled water.

C. University of Vermont students must carry their own reusable bottles and refill them at water stations.

D. It takes energy to recycle plastic bottles, and we cannot afford to waste energy these days.

5 Which of the following reasons does the author give to support the opinion that people should use reusable water bottles instead of disposable plastic water bottles? Choose **all** that apply.

A. People can save money by using reusable water bottles.

B. Some communities do not have access to clean water.

C. People can refill a reusable bottle with filtered tap water.

D. People are afraid to drink tap water because it is not clean.

E. Reusable water bottles are easy to carry.

6 Evaluate how well the author of "Plastic Water Bottles Are Destroying the Environment" supports his or her claim with reasons and evidence. Does the author include enough convincing reasons and evidence to persuade the reader to agree with his or her point of view? Use details from the passage to support your response.

Write your response on the lines below.

LESSON 7

Historical Texts

1 GETTING THE IDEA

Historical text is writing about people and events from the past. When you read historical texts, you look for facts and evidence in both records from the past and writings from the present. From this **evidence**, or proof, you begin to understand what life was like at a certain time. Here are a few types of historical text.

- In a **speech,** a person talks about a topic. The speaker presents an idea to inform or persuade the audience. Evidence is given to support that idea.
- A **government document** provides facts from or about the government. Examples include laws, treaties, and regulations.
- A **nonfiction book** contains facts and ideas about a subject, which the author has gathered through research.
- A **biography** tells about the life of another person. An **autobiography** is a story that a person tells about his or her own life.
- A **newspaper article** provides factual information about a topic or event.

Firsthand and Secondhand Accounts

Some historical texts are written from the author's point of view as he or she experienced an event. This type of historical text is called a **firsthand account.** Firsthand accounts are based on the observations of one person. Therefore, the reader learns only what that person sees, hears, and thinks. Examples of firsthand accounts include diaries, letters, and autobiographies. They often use pronouns such as *I*, *me*, and *we*.

Read the sentences from a letter written by Abigail Adams to her husband, John Adams. At the time, John Adams was attending the Continental Congress, which drafted the Declaration of Independence. How can you tell that this is a firsthand account?

> March 31 1776
>
> . . . in the new Code of Laws which I suppose it will be necessary for you to make I desire you would Remember the Ladies, & be more generous & favourable to them than your ancestors. Do not put such unlimited power into the hands of the Husbands. . . . If particular care & attention is not paid to the Ladies we are determined to foment a Rebellion, and will not hold ourselves bound by any Laws in which we have no voice, or Representation . . .

Most historical texts, however, are written by someone who did not directly experience the events. This type of historical text is a **secondhand account**. The author researches events and writes about them. Secondhand accounts are not as personal. They can be less accurate because they are written after the events happen and because the author was not present. However, they may have a more balanced view of the events than a firsthand account. Examples include biographies, encyclopedia articles, and textbooks. A secondhand account uses pronouns like *he*, *she*, and *they*.

Text Structure

Authors use **text structure** to organize the information they present. The structure helps readers understand how ideas in the text are related. Here are common types of text structures used in historical texts.

- A **sequence** (or **chronological**) **structure** presents events in the order in which they happen. In historical texts, the sequence may use dates or time-order words. Biographies and autobiographies often use sequence structure.
- A **compare-and-contrast structure** explains how two or more topics are alike and different. Signal words, such as *alike, both, unlike,* and *however*, are used in this structure.
- A **problem-and-solution structure** tells about a problem and explains how it was solved. A political speech might use this structure.
- A **cause-and-effect structure** explains what happened (effect) and why it happened (cause). Signal words, such as *because, as a result, due to,* and *if . . . then*, relate the events and help clarify which event came first.

Graphic Features

Historical texts often include graphic features. A **graphic feature** presents information in a visual way. Here are some of the graphic features that might be found in historical texts.

- A **map** shows the location of things or places.

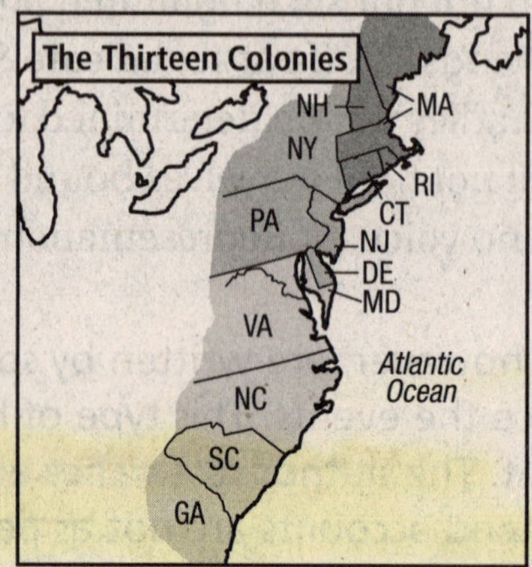

- A **timeline** shows the dates and order of events over time.

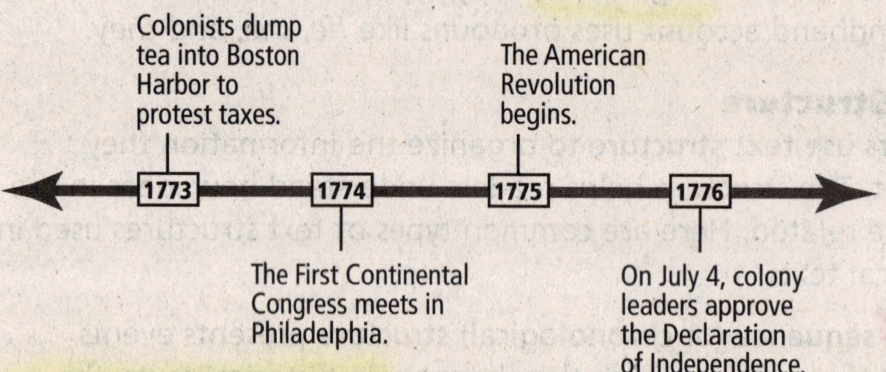

- Graphs, charts, and tables organize information. A **graph** uses bars or lines to show how ideas relate. A **table** or a **chart** lists information in rows and columns, as shown below.

The Thirteen Colonies		
New England Colonies	**Middle Colonies**	**Southern Colonies**
Connecticut Rhode Island Massachusetts New Hampshire	Delaware Pennsylvania New Jersey New York	Maryland Virginia North Carolina South Carolina Georgia

- A **photograph** shows people, events, or objects as they really appeared at the time.

The Wright Brothers military flyer, 1909

- A **flowchart** shows steps in a process or how ideas connect.

Car Assembly Line

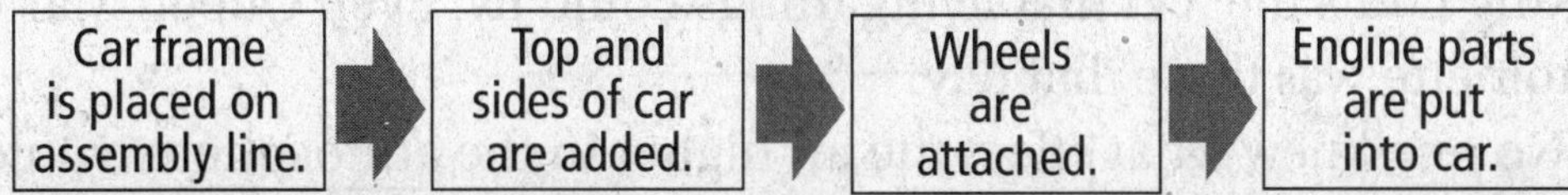

Language Spotlight • Domain-Specific Vocabulary

Historical texts often include **domain-specific vocabulary**, or words that are specific to the subject. The words may be unfamiliar because they are not used in everyday language. Sometimes, words you do recognize have a different meaning when used with a particular subject. Context clues, a glossary, or a dictionary can help you learn what the words mean.

Read the paragraph. Underline two domain-specific words that name landforms.

> An isthmus is a narrow strip of land that connects two large landmasses and separates two bodies of water. The Isthmus of Panama, for example, links the continents of North and South America and separates the Pacific and Atlantic Oceans. Often, a canal is built across an isthmus to connect the two bodies of water. The Panama Canal was built across the Isthmus of Panama to connect the Pacific and Atlantic Oceans.

Read the passage.

The Day I Saw a Sheep Fly!

I once saw a sheep fly! If that wasn't incredible enough, the sheep flew with a duck and a rooster. All three animals rose 1,500 feet into the air above King Louis the XVI's palace at Versailles in France. They were in a cage attached to something that looked like a globe. It was called a balloon.

The date was September 19, 1783, and I was one of thousands of people on hand to witness a hot-air balloon demonstration. Two Frenchmen, Etienne and Joseph Montgolfier, were about to prove to King Louis the XVI that living things could fly. Even Queen Marie Antoinette was there that day.

No one knew what effect the air higher in the atmosphere would have on a person. The king suggested that the brothers launch prisoners up in the balloon. Instead, the Montgolfier brothers decided to use a sheep, duck, and rooster to test what the air would do to the riders. They thought the animals would serve as a better experiment.

People around me seemed doubtful that this experiment was going to prove useful. Everyone wondered how the huge structure was going to get off the ground and into the air. It didn't take long for me to find out.

First, the brothers hung a basket below the balloon. Then, I spied them lifting a cage containing the sheep, duck, and rooster into the basket. That was no easy task. Next, they lit a fire on the ground where the balloon sat. They used straw, manure, and some other materials to get the fire blazing. The heated air flowed into the balloon. Finally, right before my eyes, something amazing happened! The balloon began to rise. I could hardly believe what I was seeing.

For eight minutes, that sheep, duck, and rooster floated in the enormous balloon above us. People on the ground pointed in disbelief. Many clapped. I cheered loudly. Then, the balloon started to make its descent back to Earth, so I ran to the landing place as fast as my feet would carry me.

I got there just as the balloon came down. I could see the animals perfectly. In fact, I saw them so clearly that I noticed during the landing that the excited sheep kicked the rooster, hurting its wing. If it had not been for that clumsy sheep, everything would have been perfect. As it was, the experiment proved successful. I will never forget that momentous day!

Large crowds gathered to watch early balloon flights.

Answer the following questions.

1 This question has two parts. First, answer Part A. Then, answer Part B.

Part A

Read this paragraph from the passage and answer the questions that follow.

> **First, the brothers hung a basket below the balloon. Then, I spied them lifting a cage containing the sheep, duck, and rooster into the basket. That was no easy task. Next, they lit a fire on the ground where the balloon sat. They used straw, manure, and some other materials to get the fire blazing. The heated air flowed into the balloon. Finally, right before my eyes, something amazing happened! The balloon began to rise. I could hardly believe what I was seeing.**

What is the structure of the paragraph?

A. problem and solution

B. comparison

C. cause and effect

D. sequence

Part B

Which group of words from the paragraph **best** supports your answer to Part A?

A. first, then, next, finally

B. spied, lifting, flowed, rise

C. basket, balloon, cage, ground

D. easy, blazing, amazing, hardly

Hint Consider the types of words that can signal a text's structure. Which of those signal words appear in this paragraph? Which text structure do those words show?

2. What caused the balloon to rise? Use details from the passage to explain your answer.

Write your answer on the lines below.

Hint Look for events and ideas that connect the effect of the balloon rising to the causes, or people's actions, that made it rise.

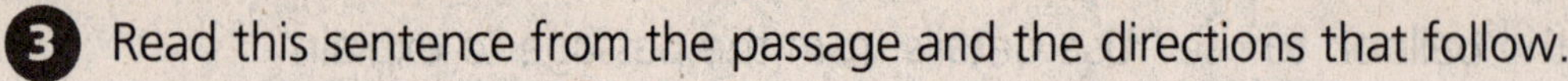

3 Read this sentence from the passage and the directions that follow.

No one knew what effect the air higher in the atmosphere would have on a person.

Which words from the sentence **best** help the reader understand the meaning of the word atmosphere?

A. what effect

B. no one knew

C. air higher

D. on a person

Hint Which words describe where or what the *atmosphere* is?

4 How does the illustration help you better understand the author's written account of the events? Explain **two** details from the picture that help you understand the text.

Write your answer on the lines provided.

____

____

____

____

____

____

____

____

Hint Notice the main objects shown in the drawing. Then, compare them to what you read in the passage.

Use the Reading Guide to help you understand the passage.

The Science of Hot-Air Balloons

Reading Guide

Is this passage a firsthand or secondhand account? Look for details and pronouns that signal the type of account.

What is the text structure of paragraphs 2 and 3? What clues help you decide?

How do signal words make it easier to follow the ideas in the paragraphs?

Near the end of *The Wizard of Oz,* the wizard promises to take Dorothy back to Kansas in his hot-air balloon. Other movies, such as *Up,* have also relied on hot-air balloons for added excitement. Hot-air balloons are used in real life, too. During the Civil War, both the North and South manned spy balloons to gather information about the other side. Today, hot-air balloons are used for pleasure, advertisements, and sports. They also play an important role in scientific research. Weather scientists use them to gather information about daily weather as well as tornadoes and other storms. A special type of balloon that uses the sun's heat to power it might someday explore Mars. This new balloon is a solar Montgolfier balloon, named for the two brothers who built the first hot-air balloon.

The Montgolfier Brothers

Joseph and Etienne Montgolfier were born in France during the mid-1700s. They came from a family of sixteen children. Their father owned a factory that manufactured paper. When the two brothers were older, they worked in the business. However, they were not happy being papermakers. Both brothers enjoyed experimenting. After watching smoke rise as paper burned, the brothers filled some paper bags with smoke to see what would happen. The smoke-filled paper bags floated upward. From this experiment, they learned that smoke is lighter than air.

After that, Joseph built a balloon from silk. At its opening, he placed some paper. Then, he burned the paper, which forced smoke into the balloon. The balloon rose. When the smoke cooled, the balloon returned to the ground. This was the first hot-air balloon.

Reading Guide

How does the example of the coin and the cork help you understand the concept of density?

What information does the diagram show?

How does the diagram work with the text to explain how a hot-air balloon rises?

Why Hot-Air Balloons Rise

The Montgolfier brothers did not really understand the reason why their balloon rose and fell. It had to do with density. Something that is denser than its surroundings will sink. A coin in a bucket of water, for example, sinks because the coin is denser than water. A cork, on the other hand, floats in water. Why? It is less dense than water.

When the air inside a balloon is heated, it becomes less dense than the cooler air outside the balloon. The less-dense warm air rises and lifts the balloon. When the air inside the balloon cools, it becomes denser. The air sinks and the balloon lands.

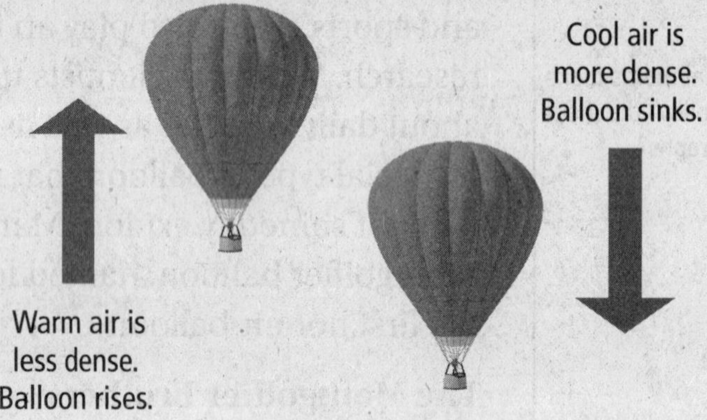

Balloon Design

The Montgolfier brothers' first large-scale hot-air balloon demonstration lasted eight minutes. They had not figured out how to keep hot air inside the balloon. The trip could only last as long as the initial blast of hot air stayed inside the balloon. The trick was to keep hot air flowing into the balloon. Today's balloon designs have solved that problem.

Reading Guide

What is the purpose of the diagram? How does it relate to the text in the passage?

What does each part of the hot-air balloon do? How does each part help the whole balloon work?

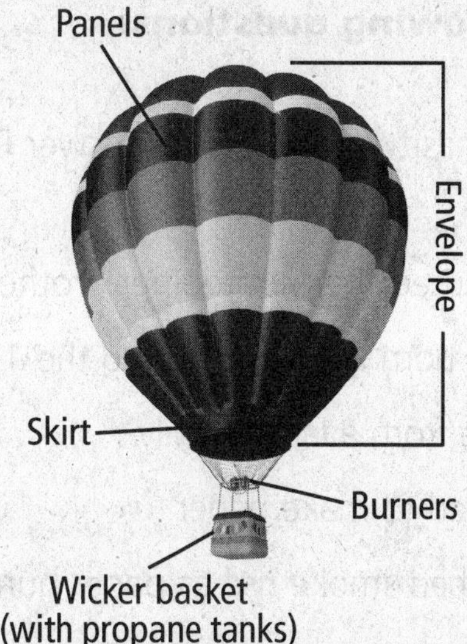

The *envelope* is the actual balloon. It is made from *gores*, or strips of fabric, which are formed from many smaller *panels*. At the bottom of the envelope, the *skirt* holds all the gores together. Balloons are usually made from nylon, which is strong, light, and heat-resistant. Parachutes are made from the same material. The skirt is coated with an extra fire-retardant substance to protect it even more from the nearby flames.

Propane tanks in the basket hold fuel for the burners. Propane is a liquid fuel often used in outdoor grills. The burners shoot out hot flames and can keep heating air as long as there is fuel in the tanks. Today's balloons have controls that allow the balloon operator, or pilot, to let more or less fuel enter the burners, so the balloon can rise or fall. The wicker basket holds the tanks, as well as any passengers or equipment. Baskets are made from wicker, or bendable twigs, because it is sturdy but also flexible. When the balloon lands, the basket bends a little to soften the landing.

To the Future

When the Montgolfier brothers first demonstrated their hot-air balloon, people were amazed. Since that time, people have continued to improve hot-air balloons and have found a variety of uses for them. Today's balloons are lighter and stronger. They fly higher and longer. One day, balloons may fly to outer space. The Montgolfier brothers would be amazed to see how much their experiment paved the way to the future.

Answer the following questions.

1. This question has two parts. First, answer Part A. Then, answer Part B.

Part A

What event caused the Montgolfier brothers to experiment with hot-air balloons?

A. They were born in France during the 1700s.

B. They came from a large family.

C. They learned to make paper.

D. They watched smoke rise as paper burned.

Part B

Which sentence from the passage **best** supports your answer for Part A?

A. Their father owned a factory that manufactured paper.

B. From this experiment, they learned that smoke is lighter than air.

C. Something that is denser than its surroundings will sink.

D. However, they were not happy making paper.

2 Read this paragraph from the passage and the directions that follow.

After that, Joseph built a balloon from silk. At its opening, he placed some paper. Then, he burned the paper, which forced smoke into the balloon. The balloon rose. When the smoke cooled, the balloon returned to the ground. This was the first hot-air balloon.

What kind of structure does the author use to organize the paragraph? Explain how you know. (Which words and phrases help you figure out what the structure is?)

____

____

____

____

____

____

____

____

3 Read the sentence from the passage and the directions that follow.

When the air inside the balloon cools, it becomes denser.

Which word is the **best** synonym for denser?

A. heavier

B. larger

C. stiffer

D. stronger

4 These four parts of a hot-air balloon are out of order. Use the diagram in the passage to number them from top (1) to bottom (4).

__________ wicker basket

__________ panels

__________ skirt

__________ burners

5 The following question has two parts. First, answer Part A. Then, answer Part B.

Part A

What happens to a hot-air balloon when there is no hot air left in the envelope?

A. It rises.

B. It explodes.

C. It sinks.

D. It collapses.

Part B

Which sentence from the passage supports your answer for Part A?

A. The trick was to keep hot air flowing into the balloon.

B. Propane tanks in the basket hold fuel for the burners.

C. Balloons are usually made from nylon, which is strong, light, and heat-resistant.

D. When the air inside the balloon cools, it becomes denser.

6 You have read two passages about hot-air balloons: "The Day I Saw a Sheep Fly!" and "The Science of Hot-Air Balloons." Identify which passage is a firsthand account and which is a secondhand account.

Then, compare and contrast the passages to tell how the authors' points of view, focuses, and information are alike and different. Use examples from the passages to support your answer.

Write your response on the lines below.

LESSON 8

Scientific and Technical Texts

1 GETTING THE IDEA

Scientific and **technical texts** are kinds of nonfiction texts. Scientific texts explain a science topic, such as how rocks form. They include lab reports, magazines articles, and textbooks. Technical texts provide detailed information about a specific subject. They often explain how something works or how to do something. Brochures, recipes, manuals, and how-to guides are types of technical texts.

Main Idea and Details

All scientific and technical texts have a **main idea** that tells what the text is mostly about. They also have **details** that support the main idea, such as statistics, examples, and definitions. Sometimes in a scientific text, the main idea tells about an experiment. In this case, the details are the steps followed to prove the main idea.

What is the main idea of this experiment? What are the details?

> I conducted an experiment to prove that plants take in water. To begin, I got three white carnations, each with a long stem, and three glasses of water. First, I added twenty drops of food color, a different color for each glass, to the water. Next, I asked my mom to cut the end of the flower stems. It's important that the stems are freshly cut and haven't closed up. Then, I placed a flower in each glass. Now all I had to do was wait. I observed the flowers every hour until bedtime but didn't notice a change. By the time I woke up the next morning, the flowers had changed color. My experiment proved that plants take in water.

The most important part of a scientific report like this one is to make sure that the steps are described in order and that none of the steps are skipped.

Text Structure

Text structure is how a text is organized. Like most nonfiction, scientific and technical texts include a lot of information. To make the information easier to understand and remember, authors organize their facts and details using different text structures. Here are some common scientific and technical text structures.

Procedural articles, recipes, and directions use **steps in a process,** or **sequence structure,** to explain how to do something or tell how something was done. Numbers, bullets, or time-order words, such as *first, next,* and *last*, show the order.

In a **whole-to-part structure**, the author states a topic sentence or general idea and then uses facts and details to describe aspects or smaller "parts" of that idea.

> Each part of a plant has a specific job to do. Roots support a plant in the soil and take in water and minerals. The stem gives the plant structure. The leaves produce food for the plant through photosynthesis.

A **problem-and-solution structure** identifies a problem and then tells how it was or could be solved.

> Autumn leaves clog storm drains and cause street flooding during heavy rains. Residents can help solve this problem by disposing of yard waste properly and by clearing the debris from storm drains located in front of their homes.

When authors use **cause-and-effect structure**, they explain what happens (effect) and why it happened (cause).

> Liquid water changes into water vapor when it is heated. This can happen in the form of evaporation when water is heated by the sun or in the form of steam when water is heated to high temperatures.

A **spatial structure** describes where things are. It uses location words such as *top, bottom, front, back, north,* and *west*.

Graphic Features

A **graphic feature** presents information in a visual way. Some graphics clarify the meaning of the text. Others show a lot of information in a small amount of space.

A **diagram** is a drawing with labels. A **model** is a picture or object that represents something that is difficult to see in real life.

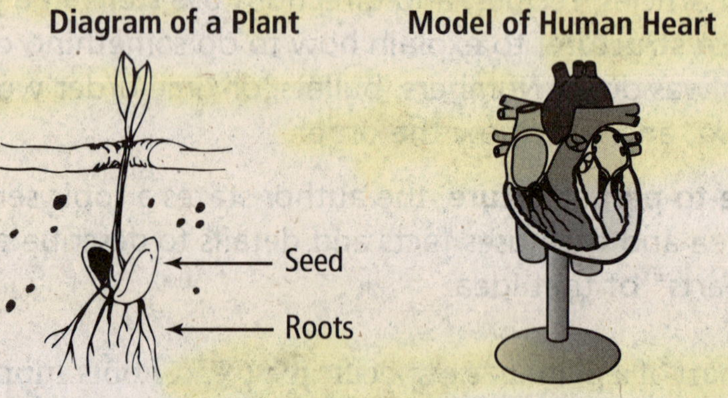

A **table** or **chart** shows data in rows and columns. A **graph** uses bars or lines to compare data or show how ideas relate. Notice that the chart on the left shows the same information as the graph on the right. They both tell how many of each kind of bird was seen in the schoolyard in September.

Birds Seen in the Schoolyard, September

Kind of Bird	Number of Birds
Crows	12
Blue jays	8
Chickadees	20
Bluebirds	2
Cardinals	8

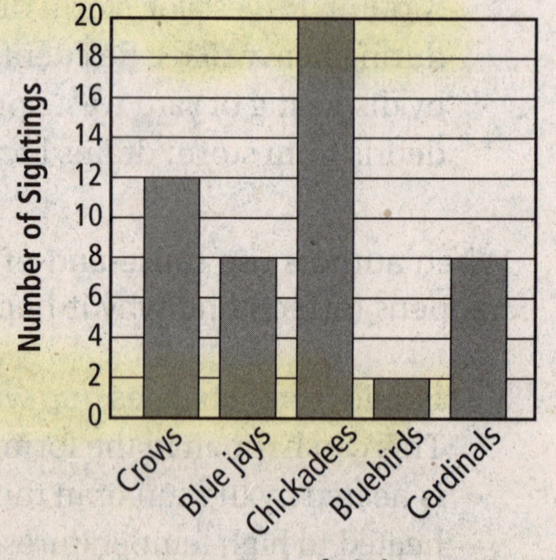

A **flowchart** uses arrows or connecting lines to show steps in a process or to show how things relate to one another.

Ladybug Life Cycle

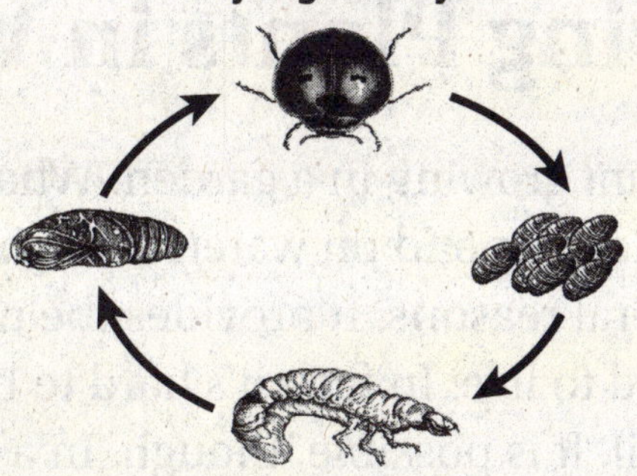

Symbols

A **symbol** is a shape or letter that stands for an idea. In science, for example, a + sign can mean "plus" or "positive," and a – sign can mean "minus" or "negative." You might see temperatures shown as °F for degrees Fahrenheit or °C for degrees Celsius. Knowing what the symbols mean can make it easier to understand what you read.

Language Spotlight • Domain-Specific Vocabulary

Scientific and technical texts often contain **domain-specific vocabulary**. These words have precise meanings for the domain, or area of study. For example, the word *fault* has a specific meaning in Earth science. It means "a break in Earth's crust." Sometimes, a word has a meaning that is different from its scientific or technical meaning. In stories or other texts, *fault* might mean that someone is to blame.

Read the paragraph. Underline two domain-specific words.

Bacteria are single-celled organisms. Some bacteria are harmful to humans and can cause infection and disease. Others, however, are helpful to humans. For example, some aid in human digestion.

2 COACHED EXAMPLE

Read the passage.

Growing Plants in Water

Think about a plant growing in a garden. What does it need to live? Plants in a garden depend on water, sunlight, air, and soil. Soil is important for several reasons. It provides the nutrients, or key minerals, plants need to live. In fact, it's hard to believe that plants can grow without soil. It is possible, though. In a process called hydroponics, plants grow in water instead of soil.

The word *hydroponics* comes from the Greek *hydro*, meaning "water," and *ponics,* meaning "working." As the name suggests, hydroponics means working with water to grow plants. In hydroponics, plants absorb nutrients from water. Something other than soil, such as a frame, holds the plants in place.

Plants growing in a hydroponic frame

Hydroponics History

Hydroponics is not a new, high-tech method for growing plants. It has been used for thousands of years. The ancient civilization of Mesopotamia used hydroponics to grow beautiful gardens called the Hanging Gardens of Babylon. During the tenth century, the Aztecs settled at Lake Tenochtitlan in Mexico. When they were unable to grow crops on the marshy shore, they built large floating rafts of woven reeds. Crops grew on top of the rafts, and the roots grew through the reeds and into the water.

How Hydroponics Works

Water is essential to plant life. In fact, plants are made up of about 90 percent water. Plants use water for photosynthesis, for normal cell functions, and for moving nutrients through the plant. Hydroponic plants grow well in water that contains the same nutrients they would normally get from soil. Because tap water has been purified for human use, hydroponic gardeners must add these nutrients back into the water.

Gardeners must also watch out for the pH level of the water, or how much acid or alkaline is in the water. If the water has too much acid, nutrients dissolve too quickly. If the water is too alkaline, nutrients will not dissolve. Most gardeners use a pH testing kit to make sure they have the correct level for their plants. A good pH level for most plants is between five and six.

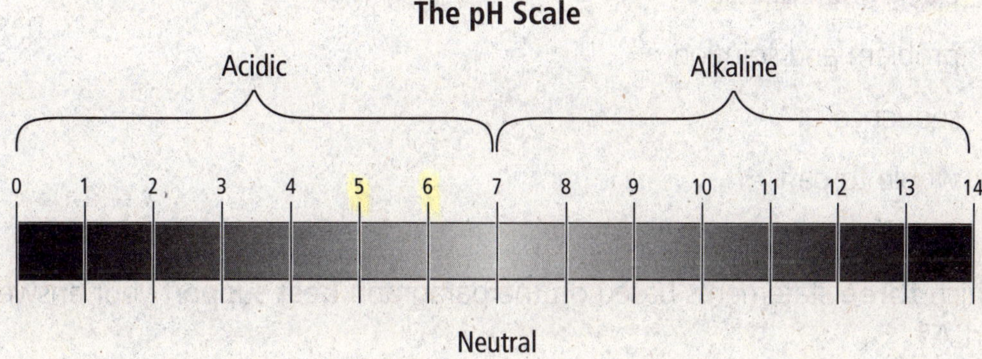

Why Hydroponics?

Hydroponics has many advantages over soil farming. It can save money and effort when land is not available or in places where the soil is poor. Gardens can be planted in classrooms, on city rooftops, and in greenhouses. Because potting soil is expensive and heavy, hydroponics offers an easier and less expensive alternative.

Even though water is the basis of hydroponics, it can actually save water in the long run. The water is reused, and very little is lost or wasted. In addition, hydroponic plants grow faster. When a plant grows in soil, the roots must grow and spread out to seek the water and nutrients the plant needs. With hydroponics, the roots have direct contact with the water and the nutrients. The plant uses less energy growing roots and more energy growing the plant.

Answer the following questions.

1 This question has two parts. First, answer Part A. Then, answer Part B.

Part A

Read this paragraph from the passage and the question that follows.

> **Even though water is the basis of hydroponics, it can actually save water in the long run. The water is reused, and very little is lost or wasted. In addition, hydroponic plants grow faster. When a plant grows in soil, the roots must grow and spread out to seek the water and nutrients the plant needs. With hydroponics, the roots have direct contact with the water and the nutrients. The plant uses less energy growing roots and more energy growing the plant.**

Which text structure is used to organize the information in the paragraph?

A. cause and effect

B. problem and solution

C. sequence

D. whole to part

Part B

Which **three** statements based on the paragraph **best** support your answer to Part A?

A. Hydroponics uses water instead of soil.

B. Because hydroponic farmers use water over and over again, they waste very little.

C. Hydroponic plants grow faster than plants grown in soil.

D. A plant grown in soil needs to spread its roots to find enough water and nutrients.

E. Hydroponic farmers put nutrients into the water they use to grow plants.

F. A plant grown in nutrient-rich water doesn't need to spread its roots to suck up enough water and nutrients.

Hint Look for words and phrases that provide clues showing how the text is organized. The first sentence also provides a clue.

2 Read this paragraph from the passage and the directions that follow.

Think about a plant growing in a garden. What does it need to live? Plants in a garden depend on water, sunlight, air, and soil. Soil is important for several reasons. It provides the nutrients, or key minerals, plants need to live. In fact, it's hard to believe that plants can grow without soil. It is possible, though. In a process called hydroponics, plants grow in water instead of soil.

Underline the sentence that **best** helps the reader identify or explain the main idea of the text.

Hint Look for a sentence that tells what the passage mostly is about.

3 Write **three** of the domain-specific words from the box next to their correct definition in the chart.

dissolve	hydroponics	nutrients	pH	photosynthesis

Domain-Specific Word	Definition
nutrients	the minerals needed by a living thing
pH	the level of acid or alkaline in a substance
hydroponics	the process of using water to grow things

Hint All five words in the box appear in the article. Each is related to the article's scientific topic. Remember to use only three of these domain-specific words. Look back at the passage if you need some context clues.

4 Read this paragraph from the passage and the directions that follow.

> **If the water has too much acid, nutrients dissolve too quickly. If the water is too alkaline, nutrients will not dissolve. Most gardeners use a pH testing kit to make sure they have the correct level for their plants. A good pH level for most plants is between five and six.**

Look at the diagram of the pH scale on the last page of the passage. What can you infer about the pH level most plants need?

A. Most plants need a highly acidic pH.

B. Most plants need a highly alkaline pH.

C. Most plants need either a neutral pH or a very slightly acidic one.

D. Most plants need either a neutral pH or a moderately alkaline one.

Hint Think about what happens if the water has too much acid or too much alkaline. Then, look at the diagram to see where the numbers five and six appear on the pH scale.

Use the Reading Guide to help you understand the passage.

Hydroponic Herb Experiment

Reading Guide

How does the introduction help you understand what type of scientific text this is?

What text structure does the author use to explain the procedure Emma followed? Look for signal words that identify the structure.

Pay attention to the headings. Think about how they help you understand the text.

A student named Emma wanted to try using hydroponics to grow herbs in water. She started with a hypothesis: If plants get nutrients from the soil, then plants need nutrients added to the water in order to grow. They will not grow well in tap water alone.

Materials

Emma gathered these materials.

- four clear, two-liter soda bottles
- scissors
- hydroponic solution
- two small basil plants, as identical as possible, with roots intact

Procedure

This is the procedure Emma followed.

First, Emma washed the soda bottles. She asked her father to cut three inches off the top of two soda bottles and the bottom three inches off the other two soda bottles. Emma then had her father cut a one-inch hole in the base of each of the cut soda-bottle bottoms.

Next, Emma filled one bottle with tap water and the second bottle with water containing two teaspoons of hydroponic solution.

Then, Emma took a basil plant and carefully passed the roots through the hole in one of the bases. She repeated this for the second basil plant and the remaining base.

Finally, Emma placed one base on top of the bottle filled with tap water and one on top of the bottle with hydroponic solution.

Emma watched her plants for twelve days. She recorded observations about plant height and root length every three days.

Reading Guide

Why does the author include this table? What information does it provide?

At what point in the experiment does Emma begin to notice a difference between the plants? What do these differences show?

Data

Emma recorded her observations in the following chart.

Day	Basil in Tap Water	Basil in Hydroponic Solution
Day 1	**Plant**: 3 inches tall, green leaves **Roots**: 2 inches long, thin and wispy	**Plant**: 3 inches tall, green leaves **Roots**: 2 inches long, thin and wispy
Day 3	**Plant**: 4 inches tall, green leaves **Roots**: 3 inches long, thin and wispy	**Plant**: 4 inches tall, green leaves **Roots**: 3 inches long, thin and wispy
Day 6	**Plant**: 4.5 inches tall, green leaves **Roots**: 4 inches long, getting thicker	**Plant**: 5 inches tall, green leaves **Roots**: 3.5 inches long, thin and wispy
Day 9	**Plant**: 5 inches tall, leaves are not as bright in color **Roots**: 5 inches long	**Plant**: 7 inches tall, green leaves, several new leaves growing **Roots**: 4 inches long
Day 12	**Plant**: 5.5 inches tall, some leaves are turning yellow, but a few new leaves are starting to grow **Roots**: 5.5 inches long	**Plant**: 8 inches tall, new leaves are getting larger, and plant is bushier **Roots**: 4 inches long

Conclusion

Emma wrote a conclusion for her experiment.

I grew two basil plants in water, one in tap water and the other in water with nutrients added. The plant in tap water did not grow as tall or produce as many new leaves as the plant with the hydroponic solution. In addition, the leaves of the plant in tap water began to turn yellow. I also observed that the roots of the plant in tap water grew longer. This may be a result of the roots looking for the nutrients the plant needed.

How does the conclusion help you understand Emma's experiment?

The plant in water with the hydroponic solution grew taller, remained green, and produced many more new leaves. Its roots didn't grow as long. I concluded that because the nutrients were easy for the roots to find, the plant used more energy growing taller and growing new leaves than it did growing roots.

Therefore, I conclude that nutrients must be added to water in order for hydroponic plants to grow and remain healthy.

Answer the following questions.

1. Write the heading from the box below next to the description of what information is found under that heading.

Data	Conclusion	Materials	Procedure

Heading	Description
	tells what Emma needed to gather in order to perform her experiment
	describes in time order the steps Emma followed to complete her experiment
	shows a detailed chart in which Emma recorded her observations
	tells what Emma learned from performing her experiment

2 The following steps from the Procedure are out of order. Write a 1, 2, 3, or 4 next to each statement to show the correct order.

☐ Fill one bottle with tap water and the other with water containing hydroponic solution.

☐ Place the bottle bases on top of the bottles filled with solution.

☐ Prepare the soda bottles by washing and cutting them.

☐ Carefully pass the plant roots through the hole in the bottle base.

3 The following question has two parts. First, answer Part A. Then, answer Part B.

Part A

What is the structure of the "Procedure" section of the experiment?

A. cause and effect

B. problem and solution

C. sequence

D. spatial

Part B

Which set of words and phrases from the passage **best** supports your answer to Part A?

A. First; then; Next; Then; repeated this for the second basil plant; Finally; for twelve days

B. Emma washed; She asked; Emma filled; Emma took; Emma placed; Emma watched

C. the soda bottles; her father; two soda bottles; the bottom three inches; a one-inch hole

D. off the top; off the other two soda bottles; in the base; with tap water; through the hole

4 The following question has two parts. First, answer Part A. Then, answer Part B.

Part A

Read these sentences from the passage and the question that follows.

> **I also observed that the roots of the plant in tap water grew longer. This may be a result of the roots looking for the nutrients the plant needed.**

Based on the sentences above, which inference did Emma make?

A. She inferred that the roots of the plant in tap water grew longer.

B. She inferred that the tap-water plant's roots grew longer *because* they were looking for nutrients.

C. She inferred that the roots of the plant in hydroponic solution grew longer.

D. She inferred that the hydroponic-solution plant's roots grew longer *because* the plant was strong and healthy.

Part B

Which observation from Emma's chart **best** supports your answer to Part A?

A. On Day 1, both plants' roots were 2 inches long; both plants' roots were thin and wispy.

B. On Day 2, both plants were 4 inches tall, and both had green leaves and wispy roots.

C. On Day 9, the tap-water plant was 5 inches tall, while the plant in hydroponic solution was 7 inches tall.

D. On Day 12, the tap-water plant's roots were 5.5 inches long, while the roots of the plant in hydroponic solution were 4 inches long.

5 Read these sentences from the passage and answer the question that follows.

> **A student named Emma wanted to try using hydroponics to grow herbs in water. She started with a hypothesis: If plants get nutrients from the soil, then plants need nutrients added to the water in order to grow. They will not grow well in tap water alone.**

Did Emma prove her hypothesis? Explain your answer.

Write your response on the lines below.

6 You read two passages about hydroponics: "Growing Plants in Water" and "Hydroponic Herb Experiment." Choose a graphic feature from one of the passages. Then summarize what it shows. Explain how it relates to the text and helps you understand what you read.

Write your response on the lines provided.

LESSON 9

Analyze Informational Texts

1 GETTING THE IDEA

When you want to know more about a topic, you probably read more than one source. By using multiple sources, you add to your knowledge of a topic. You might read multiple nonfiction texts to:

- locate an answer to a question.
- solve a problem quickly and efficiently.
- learn more about a historical event or scientific concept.
- write or speak about a topic knowledgably.

Analyzing

When you read several nonfiction sources, it is important to make comparisons and connections between the sources. For example, imagine that you are learning about good nutrition. You might read the following texts:

- a section in a science textbook about eating balanced meals
- an essay about students making good snack choices
- a newspaper article comparing the Food Pyramid to My Plate

Each source has nutrition as its main topic, but the text type, text structure, and main idea may be very different. The author's **point of view**, or how the author feels about the topic, may also be different.

Summarizing

The first thing you should do when you read more than one source is to examine each one separately. Identify the main ideas and supporting details. Think about how the ideas and details connect to one another and to the topic. Look for key words and phrases that will help you discuss the topic. Then, **summarize** the text by restating the main ideas and key points in your own words. A good summary helps you remember what you have read and shows that you understand the text.

Making Comparisons

Once you understand each text, you are ready to compare and contrast the texts to deepen your understanding of the topic. When you **compare**, look for ways in which the texts are alike. Notice ways in which they are different to **contrast** them. Consider the text type, its structure, and the author's point of view. Let's take a closer look at some texts about good nutrition as an example.

- A **science textbook** will have a general overview of a science topic. It might use a whole-to-part structure to give you facts and details. The text will be objective because the author keeps a neutral point of view and doesn't share opinions.
- An **essay** might identify the problem of making poor snack choices and then offer solutions. Or, it may use cause and effect to show what happens when poor snack choices are made. The author may choose facts that support his or her opinion.
- A **newspaper article** may compare and contrast the Food Pyramid and My Plate. While the author may express an opinion about which food guide is better, he or she will still present facts and details about each one.

Look for these things when you compare and contrast texts:

- text type and text structure
- author's purpose and point of view
- main idea and supporting details
- graphic features

Read the following paragraphs. Circle elements that are alike. Underline elements that are different. Then, summarize each passage.

from "Healthier Snack Choices"

Kids should stop eating junk food as snacks. While they may taste good, their calories don't add anything to your well-being. Instead, the added sugar can cause tooth decay and weight gain. Healthy food choices involve eating a combination of many different kinds of nutritious foods. Foods with lots of colors are the healthiest. You'll get all the nutrients you need from them.

from "Beware of Sodas"
Sugary sodas can pose many health problems. The additional sugar from these drinks adds calories without the nutrients. It also leads to tooth decay. Another ingredient in soda presents a hidden danger—phosphoric acid. This additive affects the balance of the minerals calcium and phosphorous in the human body, which in turn can affect growth and bone strength. Limit your intake of soda and drink water instead. Water is readily available, calorie-free, and needed by the body. All the important body processes need water in order to function properly.

Making Connections

After you have compared and contrasted different texts, make connections between the texts to **integrate information**. When you integrate information, you combine the important ideas from each source to show your knowledge of a particular topic.

Here is how one student integrated information from both passages in order to share her knowledge about foods to avoid.

Junk food and soda may taste good, but they can pose health risks to kids. The added sugars in these products can cause tooth decay and weight gain. Other ingredients can affect growth and bone strength in negative ways.

Language Spotlight • Shades of Meaning

Synonyms are words that have the same or nearly the same meaning. Certain synonyms, however, also have shades of meaning. Shades of meaning are small, but important, differences in the meanings of similar words. These differences may relate to strength or the feelings that the meanings convey. Think about the words below. How would the meaning of each sentence change if the word *command*, *order*, *demand*, or *advise* were used instead of the word *tell*?

The principal <u>tells</u> the students to line up.
I will <u>tell</u> all my friends to read this book.

Read the passage.

Read Before You Eat

It's snack time, and you're hungry. You reach in the pantry and grab the first thing you see: a small bag of chips. You're about to open the bag. But wait, there's something you need to do before you eat.

Read the Label

All packaged foods have a food label on them. It's usually on the back or side of the product. Find the heading "Nutrition Facts." At first, the label can look confusing, but everyone should know the basics.

Nutrition Facts

Serving Size: 1 oz. (28g/about 21 pieces)
Servings Per Container: About 2

Amount Per Serving

Calories 170 Calories from Fat 110

Serving Size

Begin by looking at the serving size. It's right under the "Nutrition Facts" heading. Serving size is how much there is in one serving of food. Note that the label says that a serving size is one ounce. That amount can be hard to guess, but the label tells you a serving is about twenty-one pieces, or chips. It includes the metric weight of 28 grams, too.

Now comes the tricky part. Look at the servings per container. Although it might seem normal to think of one bag as one serving, that's not always the case. This bag holds about two servings. Does this come as a surprise? If you were to eat one serving of chips, you would eat only half the bag.

Calories

All foods contain calories. A calorie is a unit used to measure energy. Your body burns calories for energy. The nutrition label shows that one serving is 170 calories. But now you know that the bag holds two servings, which means two times the calories. The whole bag contains 340 calories.

Calories from Fat

Move to the right of the calorie listing to the calories from fat. The number 110 means that 110 calories out of the 170 come from fat. That's more than half the calories in the bag. It means the chips are high in fat and aren't something you should eat every day.

The average person needs about 2,000 calories a day. After your body burns the calories it needs, the leftover, unused calories are stored as fat around the body. Experts on nutrition recommend that only about thirty percent, or one third, of the day's calories should come from fat.

Compare and Contrast

Now look at the nutrition facts on a bag of baby carrots and compare them to the chips. One serving size is half a cup of carrots or about six carrots. The total amount of calories in one serving is 25, and there are no calories from fat. Even if you're extra hungry, you can have a second serving of carrots and consume only 50 calories. In fact, you could have three servings of carrots and still eat fewer calories than one serving of chips. In addition, none of the calories come from fat, so your daily allowance of fat can be saved for other foods you eat during the day.

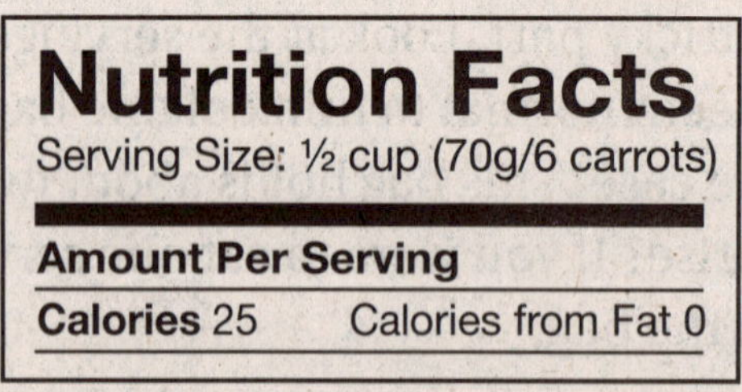

There is much more to learn from a food label, but knowing the basics is a good start. So, the next time you want a snack, go ahead and have one—after you read the label.

Answer the following questions.

1 Which of these points are key details of the passage? Circle **all** that apply.

A. calculating serving size

B. converting ounces to grams

C. determining amount per serving

D. comparing calories and calories from fat

E. eating baby carrots

Hint The headings in an article tell what different sections of the article are about. They also help you focus on the key points the author wants to share.

2 Which sentence **best** states the main idea of the whole passage?

A. At first, the label can look confusing, but everyone should at least know the basics.

B. The average person needs about 2,000 calories a day.

C. Serving size is how much there is in one serving of food.

D. Experts on nutrition recommend that only about thirty percent, or one third, of the day's calories should come from fat.

Hint Remember that the main idea of a passage tells what the text is mostly about.

3 The passage explains the basics of the nutrition facts on the food label. Summarize the main ideas in your own words.

Write your answer on the lines below.

Hint Use the headings to guide your summary. Determine the most important ideas from each section to include in your summary.

4 The following question has two parts. First, answer Part A. Then, answer Part B.

Part A

Read the sentences from the passage.

> **Serving size is how much there is in one serving of food. <u>Note</u> that the label says that a serving size is one ounce.**

Which of the following words would you choose to replace the word <u>Note</u> in the sentence to give it a stronger meaning?

A. Notice

B. Observe

C. Look

D. See

Part B

Which of the following statements **best** supports your answer to Part A?

A. The author hopes that the type size on the label is large enough for most readers to *see* well.

B. The author instructs readers to closely read—to *look* at—food labels.

C. The author knows that most of her readers are scientists who are used to *observing* details.

D. The author wants readers to pay close attention to—*notice*—a detail on the label shown.

Hint To help you find the strongest word, try using each word in the sentence. Then, ask which word feels stronger or sounds more like a command.

Use the Reading Guide to help you understand the passage.

Food Facts

Reading Guide

What is the passage mostly about?

How many calories are in two servings of macaroni and cheese? How do you know?

Everyone has seen the nutrition labels on packaged foods. However, not everyone knows what the different words, numbers, and percentages mean. Learning to read food labels helps people make sense of the information, and make better food choices.

Nutrition Facts

Nutrition facts on food labels usually appear in a certain order. The basic information is listed at the top, right under the heading Nutrition Facts.

Serving Size refers to the amount of food that is equal to one serving. Many packaged foods contain more than one serving. Look right under Serving Size to learn how many servings are in a package. The label shows that this package of macaroni and cheese contains two servings. This is an important fact to consider when deciding how much to eat. It is also important to know that the rest of the label gives information on one serving, not on the total contents of the package.

Nutrition Facts

Serving Size	1 cup (228 g)
Servings Per Container	About 2
Amount Per Serving	
Calories 250	Calories from Fat 110
	% Daily Value
Total Fat 12 g	**18%**
Saturated Fat 3 g	**15%**
Trans Fat 3 g	
Cholesterol 30 mg	**10%**
Sodium 470 mg	**20%**
Total Carbohydrate 31 g	**10%**
Dietary Fiber 0 g	**0%**
Sugars 5 g	
Protein 5 g	
Vitamin A	**4%**
Vitamin C	**2%**
Calcium	**20%**
Iron	**4%**

This food label is from a package of macaroni and cheese.

Reading Guide

How do the headings relate to the food label?

How does reading the headings help you understand how the passage is organized?

How does the macaroni and cheese label help you better understand the information you read in the passage?

Calories and Fat

Calories are fuel for the human body. As the body works, plays, or exercises, it uses calories for energy. The calories a body doesn't use are stored as fat. People need some fat in their bodies. But to be healthy, they should avoid foods that have too many calories from fat. This label shows that 110 of the 250 calories—almost half—come from fat.

Percent Daily Values

The next part of the label lists Percent Daily Values. These percents are based on an average person's diet of 2,000 calories a day. For example, one serving of macaroni and cheese contains eighteen percent of the daily allowance of Total Fat. That leaves eighty-two percent total fat left for other foods for that day.

Percent Daily Values are given for different kinds of nutrients. For the most part, people should avoid foods with too much fat and sodium. Sodium is another word for salt. People should also avoid foods that have too much sugar. Instead, they should try to eat foods that are high in fiber, protein, and vitamins and minerals.

Vitamins and Minerals

Vitamins and minerals are important to a healthy body. Foods that contain ten to twenty percent of the daily value for these nutrients are good choices. Notice that calcium is the only nutrient on the macaroni and cheese label that meets this goal.

Reading Guide

Why is it important for people to read ingredients on a food label?

How does the information on the food label apply to you?

Ingredients

Ingredients include all the things used to make a certain food. It is like a recipe for what is in the food. This list often appears at the end of the food label but can appear in other places. Each ingredient is weighed and then listed in order from most to least. In other words, the foods making up most of the product are listed first.

This list is especially helpful for people with food allergies or special diet concerns. Someone with peanut allergies, for example, would not buy a product with peanut oil as an ingredient. A person who needs to watch out for sugar knows to look for ingredients that name other forms of sugar, such as corn syrup, juice concentrate, sucrose, or honey.

Practice Makes Perfect

It takes practice to read and understand nutrition facts. A good place to start is to compare food labels. Two different brands of macaroni and cheese, for example, can have different daily percent values and different ingredients.

Knowing the serving size, calories, and nutrient values helps consumers make good food choices. It's one more step people can take to have a healthy body.

Answer the following questions.

1. Which is the **best** summary of this passage?

   A. Reading food labels can be confusing because they contain unfamiliar terms, numbers, and percents. Comparing food labels helps people see how foods can be alike and different.

   B. Food labels are on packages to tell you how many calories are in a food and how many calories from fat the food has. This helps people avoid calories that come from fat.

   C. Food labels tell about serving size, amounts of different nutrients, and ingredients. Comparing food labels helps people make better food choices.

   D. Every food label is different, and that is why they can be confusing to read. You can compare food labels to see how the nutrients and ingredients are different.

2. Read the sentences from the passage and the question that follows.

   Knowing the serving size, calories, and nutrient values helps consumers make <u>good</u> food choices. It's one more step people can take to have a healthy body.

   Which of the following words could replace the word <u>good</u> to give the sentence a stronger, more positive meaning?

   A. decent

   B. fine

   C. wise

   D. adequate

Answer the following questions about both passages.

3 Which of these points are facts mentioned in both passages? Circle **all** that apply.

A. Serving size is the amount of food that is equal to one serving.

B. People should avoid foods that are high in fat, sugar, and sodium.

C. Percent Daily Values are given for different nutrients.

D. An average person's diet is about 2,000 calories a day.

E. The list of ingredients includes everything that is in the food.

4 The following question has two parts. First, answer Part A. Then, answer Part B.

Part A

Which claim is **best** supported by evidence from both articles?

A. Most food labels are too confusing and difficult to read.

B. Everyone should read food labels before choosing a snack.

C. Reading food labels can help people make better food choices.

D. Few people know that corn syrup and juice concentrate are forms of sugar.

Part B

Which **two** sentences from the articles **best** support your answer to Part A? (Choose one sentence from each article.)

A. You reach in the pantry and grab the first thing you see: a small bag of chips. (from "Read Before You Eat")

B. Experts on nutrition recommend that only about thirty percent, or one third, of the day's calories should come from fat. (from "Read Before You Eat")

C. For example, one serving of macaroni and cheese contains eighteen percent of the daily allowance of Total Fat. (from "Food Facts")

D. Each ingredient is weighed and then listed in order from most to least. (from "Food Facts")

5 This question has two parts. First, answer Part A. Then, answer Part B.

Part A

Read the paragraph from "Read Before You Eat." Then answer the question that follows.

> **All foods contain calories. A calorie is a unit used to measure energy. Your body burns calories for energy. The nutrition label shows that one serving is 170 calories. But now you know that the bag holds two servings, which means two times the calories. The whole bag contains 340 calories.**

Which **two** sentences from the paragraph give facts that tell what calories are?

A. A calorie is a unit used to measure energy.

B. Your body burns calories for energy.

C. The nutrition label shows that one serving is 170 calories.

D. But now you know that the bag holds two servings, which means two times the calories.

Part B

Which **two** sentences from "Food Facts" tell more about calories?

A. Calories are fuel for the human body.

B. As the body works, plays, or exercises, it uses calories for energy.

C. People need some fat in their bodies.

D. For the most part, people should avoid foods with too much fat and sodium.

E. People should also avoid foods that have too much sugar.

6 You have read two passages about reading food labels: "Read Before You Eat" and "Food Facts." Consider the points each author makes. Integrate the information you read to write three paragraphs demonstrating your knowledge of the importance of reading food labels.

Write your response on the lines below.

Analyze Texts Across Genres

1 GETTING THE IDEA

Authors may present information about a single topic in many different ways. Think about the topic of baseball. One author may write an informational text to give facts about the history of baseball. Another may write a realistic fiction story about a boy whose grandfather teaches him how to play the game.

Readers compare and contrast fiction and informational texts to see how they are similar and different.

Fiction or Nonfiction

Fiction is a made-up story, while **nonfiction** presents facts. Fiction includes fables, myths, and realistic fiction. Some nonfiction texts are newspaper articles, scientific articles, and biographies. Each of these types of texts has unique features that readers can recognize.

Even though fiction and nonfiction are different, they do have some things in common.

Fiction	Both	Nonfiction
• tells a story • includes characters, settings, events, and other details that are completely or partly made up by the author • does not have to be true	• may present information in the form of a story • are told from a certain point of view • can include scientific or historical facts	• gives facts about a topic • may tell a true story • may be broken into sections separated by headings • may include graphic features such as diagrams, charts, and graphs

Some text types include elements of both fiction and nonfiction.

Historical fiction is usually set in a real time or place from the past. It may even include real people and events. What makes it fiction are the made-up characters, events, and details authors add to the historical facts.

Science fiction is often set in the future, in space, or on another planet. Like a scientific text, science fiction may include real-life details about science and technology. But it also tells a story through made-up characters, events, and details.

Literary nonfiction includes biographies and autobiographies. These texts tell true stories about real people. They give facts about people's lives. Writers use storytelling techniques such as vivid details, suspense, and conflict. Dialogue is sometimes used to make the stories more interesting.

Analyze Texts

When you read two related texts, pay close attention to the main ideas and details. Ask questions as you read. This will help you compare and contrast the texts later.

Fiction	Nonfiction
What is the **theme**, or main message, the author wants to share?	What is the **main idea** of the text?
Who are the characters? What is the setting? What are the key events?	What **supporting details** does the author include?

The main message or main idea of a text is not always directly stated. You may have to make inferences to figure it out. Once you know the main idea and details of each text, you can figure out what the texts have in common.

Read each passage below. One is fiction, and one is nonfiction. Pay attention to the settings, events, and people described. Circle any elements that are alike. Underline any elements that are different.

Tea in the Water

"John, come quickly," I called to my brother. "We have to go see what is happening. A group of men with painted faces just snuck past, toward the harbor."

"Finally, their words are turning into action, Richard. Let us go watch this rebellion."

John and I walked quietly down to the water and joined the crowd of spectators. All of us on the shore looked on in amazement. We watched as the disguised men boarded the ships. We hooted and hollered as they lifted each crate and tossed it overboard. Wood cracked and tea splashed into the water. The scent of victory filled the air.

Boston Tea Party

In the years leading up to the revolution, American patriots were unhappy with their rulers. In May 1773, England created a Tea Act that helped the East India Company to sell more tea in America. The patriots did not agree with this law. They pushed merchants, or sellers, to refuse the tea.

In Boston, some people wanted to send tea back to England. When the governor didn't agree with this idea, people took action. On December 16, 1773, Sam Adams and a group of men boarded three tea boats. Many of them were dressed in disguise. They broke the tea chests and threw them overboard. The event became known as the Boston Tea Party. It was just one of many events that would spark a war.

Now let's **compare** and **contrast** the two passages.

"Tea in the Water"	Both	"Boston Tea Party"
• fictional story • narrator is a made-up character • author makes up what it was probably like to watch the Tea Party	• discuss the Boston Tea Party • include a real event from history • use details to describe the historic event	• informational text • gives facts about why the Boston Tea Party happened • includes the name of a real person

Integrate Information

The two passages were on the same topic but presented the information differently. One presented a narrative about fictional characters. The other focused on facts. When you read more than one text on the same topic, you can combine information from the texts to form a better understanding of the topic.

- How can you use both texts to tell about the events of the Boston Tea Party?
- In what other ways might the topic be presented? For example, how might it be different if it were written from Sam Adams's point of view?

Language Spotlight • General Academic Vocabulary

Academic vocabulary consists of words that appear in many school subjects and even in daily language. You can use context clues to help you determine the meaning of academic vocabulary.

The words *examine* and *identify* are both academic vocabulary words. In reading, you may examine two texts and identify how they are alike and different. In art class, you may examine a sculpture and identify the material used to make it.

Now write a sentence using the words *examine* and *identify* in relation to each of the following subjects:

science: ____

social studies: ____

Read the passage.

The Halifax Explosion

Almost one hundred years after the Halifax Explosion, people still wonder how it could have happened. Many people believe that the tragic events of December 6, 1917, could have easily been prevented. No single event caused the devastation. No one person was to blame. But, if any one in a series of missteps and mistakes had been handled differently, the city might have been spared.

In 1917, the Canadian city of Halifax, Nova Scotia, was booming. The city's large harbor helped it to flourish, and ships carrying war supplies frequently docked at its shore. But the harbor was not always properly managed. Ferries, fishing boats, and military ships crowded the harbor. Minor crashes often occurred.

On December 5, a ship named *Mont-Blanc* had arrived near Halifax to join a convoy headed to the war in France. It was packed with a massive amount of explosives. Most ships carrying such cargo would normally fly a warning flag, but the *Mont-Blanc* did not. It would be traveling among enemy boats and did not want them to know what was on board. Although a pilot boarded the ship that night, it was too late for it to depart. So the ship stayed outside the harbor.

Another ship, the *Imo*, was across the harbor. It, too, was supposed to set off on December 5 but did not receive the coal it needed to leave on time. Already behind schedule, the *Imo* sped toward a small area of the harbor called the Narrows the next morning. Like drivers on a road, ship captains must follow certain rules. Traffic should keep to the right and stay below a certain speed. Drivers should clearly communicate where they are turning.

As the *Imo* approached, the *Mont-Blanc* was heading into the Narrows from the opposite direction. The *Mont-Blanc* whistled that it was staying on the right side and would continue on its path. But the *Imo* refused to get out of the way. Facing an impending crash, both ships reacted. The *Mont-Blanc* veered to the left and the *Imo* headed in reverse. Either one of these reactions could have stopped the crash, but the two combined spelled disaster. The ships could not avoid a collision.

At 8:45 a.m., the *Imo* the struck the *Mont-Blanc* and hit parts of the ship carrying the dangerous explosives. Sparks flew, and soon a huge fire raged on board the *Mont-Blanc*. People gathered along the Halifax coast to watch the spectacular blaze. The fire department and its truck, the *Patricia*, arrived on the scene. But their efforts would be fruitless. Twenty minutes after the crash, a tremendous explosion burst through the boat and everything around it. A deafening roar filled the air. Glass shattered and houses crumbled. More fires spread through the city.

The impact of the explosion pushed the water around the *Mont-Blanc* out of the harbor. Then, when the water rushed back in, it created a huge wall of water known as a tsunami. Survivors had barely reacted to the explosion when this great wave of water rushed over them.

Both Halifax and Dartmouth, a city across the harbor, were greatly affected by the explosion and tsunami. Everywhere people looked, they saw devastation. More than 1,500 people were killed, and thousands more were injured. It was a day no one would soon forget. People all over the world learned from the disaster and changed their policies for harbor management. They hoped to prevent such a senseless tragedy from ever occurring again.

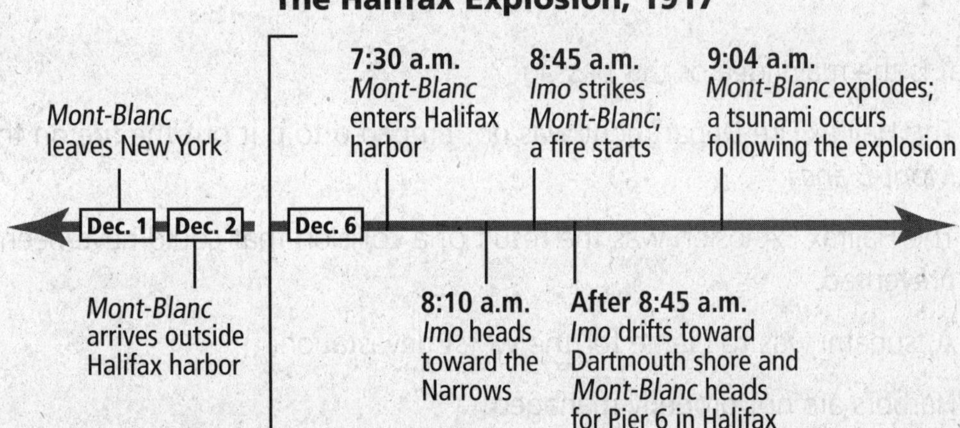

Answer the following questions.

1. This question has two parts. First, answer Part A. Then, answer Part B.

Part A

What type of text is this passage?

A. historical fiction

B. science fiction

C. nonfiction article

D. nonfiction biography

Part B

Which features of the text help you figure out the text type?

A. The text gives facts about a real event from history.

B. The author adds made-up characters and details to the events.

C. The events of the text take place in the future.

D. The author tells about one person's life.

Hint Think about the features of each text type. Which features are present in this passage? Does the author present only facts? Or are there characters and events that are made up?

2. What is the main idea of this passage?

A. The Halifax Fire Department was not prepared to put out the fire on the *Mont-Blanc*.

B. The Halifax Explosion was the result of a collision that could have been prevented.

C. A tsunami was to blame for the worst devastation.

D. Harbors are not properly managed.

Hint Why did the author write this passage? Think about the main point the author is trying to make.

3. The events of December 6, 1917, are out of order. Write numbers 1 through 6 in the boxes to put the events in the correct order.

- [ ] A tremendous explosion occurred.
- [ ] A huge wall of water, called a tsunami, was created.
- [ ] The *Mont-Blanc* and the *Imo* headed toward each other.
- [ ] The *Mont-Blanc* blew its whistle to say it was staying to the right.
- [ ] A fire started on the *Mont-Blanc*.
- [ ] The *Imo* and the *Mont-Blanc* crashed into each other.

Hint Think of how each event led to the next. This will help you place the events in the correct order.

4. What text structure does the author use? Why do you think he or she uses this structure?

Use details from the text to support your answer.

Write your answer on the lines below.

____

____

____

____

____

Hint Think about the main idea of the text. How does the structure help the author convey that main idea? How does the structure help the reader understand the events that occurred?

Use the Reading Guide to help you understand the passage.

Reading Guide

Why does the author include the introduction at the start of this passage?

Look at some of the features the author includes. Which features help you understand what type of text it is?

Why is Olivia surprised by how people in the city are acting this morning?

In a Flash of Light

Three years into World War I, Halifax, Nova Scotia, was a thriving city. Boats carrying supplies for the war moved into and out of the harbor, and factories and mills were bustling from all the business. Yet, on the morning of December 6, 1917, disaster would strike. As city residents looked on, two boats collided in the harbor and set off a chain of events that would lead to unbelievable devastation.

"Johnny, please hurry; we're going to be late for school."

I grabbed my little brother's hand and dragged him toward the door. As the oldest in the family, it was my job to take my little brothers to school, but it was never an easy task. Alden was like a little pocket watch. You could spot him standing at the door and know that it was exactly 8:50 on the dot. Johnny, on the other hand, was a little dickens[1]—or at least that's what our mémé[2] called him. Aside from their identical features, you would never guess that the boys were twins.

We kissed Mama goodbye and then rushed out the door and down the street toward school. All around us, there was a flurry of activity as people pushed past us and ran toward the shore. *Why such a frenzy this morning*? I wondered. Sure, the war had the factories working overtime to handle all the demand, but that was nothing new.

"Look, Olivia!" Johnny pointed. "It's *Patricia*; she's heading to the shore, too!"

Patricia, the fire department's new fire truck, had been the talk of the town for weeks. She was the first motorized truck the city ever had, and everyone in town, not just truck-loving little boys, was amazed by her.

[1] **dickens**: a playful nickname for a troublemaker

[2] **mémé**: grandma

Reading Guide

What do some people think caused the fire? How does Olivia react to the fire?

Look for details the author uses to describe the explosion. How does the explosion affect the characters?

Think about why Olivia has a hard time finding her house. What does this situation show about the explosion?

We raced to follow her and then suddenly saw the reason for all the excitement. Black smoke filled the air around the harbor, and arms of red and orange flames reached toward the sky.

"The Germans are attacking!" someone yelled.

I pulled my brothers in and held them tightly against my chest.

"We should head back home; it's obviously not safe here," I said, trying to guide them back in the opposite direction. But despite my nudging, they both stood frozen, eyes wide in wonder.

"It's not the Germans," I heard a familiar voice say. It was my friend, Anne, from school. "Two boats crashed; I saw it from my kitchen window and came out here for a better look."

"Whatever caused the fire doesn't matter; we really should stay back to keep sa—"

My words were cut short as an eerie silence washed over everything. A burst of bright light flashed across the sky, and then the world turned dark.

I woke up yards away, dizzy and disoriented. Then I heard a soft whimper beside me and turned to see Alden.

"Are you okay, Alden?"

"Yes, Olivia, I'm fine; just a little stunned."

I lifted him up, and we headed to where Johnny was sitting, scratching his head and looking puzzled.

"What just happened?" he asked. "Did something explode?"

"It must have been one of the boats; it was probably carrying supplies for the war. Thank goodness we're all safe, but we should go check on Mama."

We started back toward our house, but I wasn't sure where it was anymore. Huge chunks of metal were scattered everywhere, and piles of rubble marked where familiar homes and stores once stood. I realized then how lucky we were. Many people were hurt, and others walked around in a daze.

Reading Guide

Why do you suppose soldiers herded people uphill, away from the harbor?

Why does the author include the detail that occasionally a person shouted out a name?

How did Olivia and her brothers finally reunite with their mother?

Suddenly, people began shouting. I looked up to see a massive wave of water barreling up from the harbor. I pushed my brothers against an iron gate and told them to hang on. We clung to the gate and waited for the water to pass. Alden and Johnny began to cry. For the longest time, we held onto the gate, afraid to move. Then I saw soldiers herding people uphill, away from the harbor.

"Look," I said, "The soldiers are sending people uphill. Maybe Mama or Papa will go there, too."

We slowly made our way uphill. Occasionally, a person shouted out a name, and two family members were reunited. I kept listening for my name, but no one called "Olivia." Then, I thought I heard my name. I looked around and heard it again. Alden and Johnny heard it, too, and we broke into a run. We ran to Mama, and she squeezed us in a tight embrace.

"I was so worried about you," she said, wiping away a tear from her cheek.

Answer the following questions.

1 Why does the author include an introduction before the events of the story?

A. to tell about the goods made in the city's factories

B. to introduce the character of Olivia's grandmother

C. to show that Halifax is located in the eastern part of Canada

D. to give readers historical background information about the events

2 The following question has two parts. First, answer Part A. Then, answer Part B.

Part A

Read the sentence from the text and the directions that follow.

"Yes, Olivia, I'm fine; just a little stunned."

What does the word stunned mean in this sentence?

A. cheerful

B. alert

C. shocked

D. bored

Part B

Which sentences from the text help you figure out the meaning? Choose **all** that apply.

A. All around us, there was a flurry of activity as people pushed past us and ran toward the shore.

B. I woke up yards away, dizzy and disoriented.

C. I lifted him up, and we headed to where Johnny was sitting, scratching his head and looking puzzled.

D. I looked up to see a massive wave of water barreling up from the harbor.

E. We clung to the gate and waited for the water to pass.

Answer the following questions about both passages in this lesson.

3 Based on information from both passages, what is one conclusion about the events you might make?

A. Olivia and her family never returned to Halifax again.

B. Some people who experienced the explosion and tsunami were confused by what happened.

C. Fire departments stopped using motorized trucks to respond to fires.

D. Residents of Halifax were curious about the fire on the *Mont-Blanc*.

4 Compare and contrast how each author presents information about the events surrounding the Halifax Explosion. How do the features of each text help you identify the type of text? How do they affect your understanding of the topic? Write your answer on the lines below.

5 The following question has two parts. First, answer Part A. Then, answer Part B.

Part A

Read the paragraph from "The Halifax Explosion." Then, answer the question that follows.

> **The fire department and its truck, the *Patricia*, arrived on the scene. But their efforts would be fruitless. Twenty minutes after the crash, a tremendous explosion burst through the boat and everything around it. A deafening roar filled the air. Glass shattered and houses crumbled. More fires spread through the city.**

Which **two** sentences give details about the devastation of the explosion?

A. The fire department and its truck, the *Patricia*, arrived on the scene.

B. But their efforts would be fruitless.

C. Twenty minutes after the crash, a tremendous explosion burst through the boat and everything around it.

D. A deafening roar filled the air.

E. Glass shattered and houses crumbled.

F. More fires spread through the city.

Part B

Which **two** sentences from "In a Flash of Light" add to your understanding of the devastation that the explosion caused?

A. *Why such a frenzy this morning?* I wondered.

B. I pulled my brothers in and held them tightly against my chest.

C. Huge chunks of metal were scattered everywhere, and piles of rubble marked where familiar homes and stores once stood.

D. I realized then how lucky we were.

E. Many people were hurt, and others walked around in a daze.

F. I pushed my brothers against an iron gate and told them to hang on.

6. The two passages you read, "The Halifax Explosion" and "In a Flash of Light," both gave information about the devastating boat crash and explosion that occurred on December 6, 1917. Using information from both texts, describe in your own words what took place on that tragic day. Include details about what people witnessed and how they responded to the events. Be sure to combine information from both passages to help you better understand and describe the event.

Write your response on the lines below.

Read the passage.

America's 200th Birthday Celebration

In 1976, the United States celebrated its two hundredth birthday. This day was so big and important that the party had a special name. It was called the Bicentennial celebration. Planning for the Bicentennial was not much different from planning a regular birthday party. Of course, the guest list was much bigger. Every person living in the United States was invited!

Planning for the Party

In 1967, the U.S. government formed the American Revolution Bicentennial Commission. The group decided that the main celebration would be held in Philadelphia, Pennsylvania. It was also decided that a park would be built in each of the other states, and each state would use its new park for a smaller party.

However, problems soon developed. Some people did not think it was fair for one city to have the biggest party. Because people felt the planning group had failed, another group was formed to create a new plan for America's big day. The new committee agreed that some celebrations would be held for the whole country. It was also decided that each state would plan its own celebrations. Every city and town would decide independently how to celebrate.

Celebrations for Everyone

The committee planned several events for everyone to enjoy. For example, the spacecraft *Viking I* was launched in August 1975. It landed on Mars a few weeks before the big day. The National Air and Space Museum opened in Washington, D.C., on July 1. An old train was restored and turned into a traveling museum. The "Freedom Train" visited cities and towns across the country.

In addition, each state planned ways to honor the things that make it unique. In the past, many people traveled across the United States in covered wagons. The state of Pennsylvania wanted people to remember these trips. Volunteers were asked to travel in covered wagons. Sixty thousand people in many different states began a journey in covered wagons to Pennsylvania. The trip took two years. In states such as Alaska and Ohio, log cabins were repaired and turned into museums. Across the country, other historic buildings, bridges, and cemeteries were restored. Bicentennial parks were created in many states.

Several states made time capsules, filling the containers with items from the present day. Most of the time capsules were small, but one town in Nebraska built a time capsule so big it held a car! The plan is for all the time capsules to be opened in 2076. They will show people what life was like in 1976.

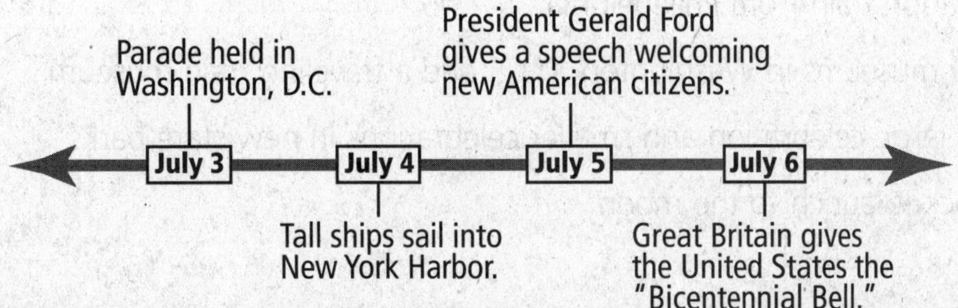

The timeline shows some of the events planned for the Bicentennial celebration.

The Big Day

On July 4, the celebration really began! In Philadelphia, two million people watched a six-hour parade. People from all fifty states marched in the parade. Five hundred thousand people watched a parade in Washington, D.C. In New York City, six million people lined the waterfront as sixteen of the world's tallest ships sailed into the harbor. Ships included Italy's *Amerigo Vespucci*, Chile's *Esmeralda,* and Japan's *Nippon Maru.* There were more than two hundred smaller sailing ships and twenty thousand other ships, too.

There was also a lot of food at these celebrations. Philadelphia made a giant cake. It was fifty feet tall and weighed forty-nine thousand pounds. Many other towns served birthday cakes. Some had picnics and barbecues, too.

At 2:00 p.m. in Philadelphia, bells rang out. At the exact same time, bells in cities and towns across the country tolled. The country was two hundred years old! That night, vivid fireworks filled the night sky. The careful planning had paid off. America's birthday party was a success.

Answer the questions.

1 This question has two parts. First, answer Part A. Then, answer Part B.

Part A

What was the original plan for the celebration?

A. a wagon train from Philadelphia

B. new museums in Washington, D.C., and a traveling train museum

C. one large celebration and smaller celebrations in new state parks

D. a rocket launch to the moon

Part B

Which two sentences from the article **best** support your answer to Part A?

A. The group decided that the main celebration would be held in Philadelphia, Pennsylvania.

B. It was also decided that a park would be built in each of the other states, and each state would use its new park for a smaller party.

C. The new committee agreed that some celebrations would be held for the whole country.

D. It was also decided that each state would plan its own celebrations.

E. Every city and town would decide independently how to celebrate.

2 Which of the following statements about the passage are true? Circle **all** that apply.

A. It is based on one person's observations.

B. It expresses the author's strong opinions.

C. It is written about events that have already happened.

D. It uses pronouns such as *I*, *me*, *we*, and *us*.

E. It contains bias.

F. It contains information found through research.

3 Read the following sentence from the passage.

In addition, each state planned ways to honor the things that make it unique.

Which of the following words is an antonym for honor as it is used in this sentence?

A. illustrate

B. improve

C. insult

D. introduce

4 This question has two parts. First, answer Part A. Then, answer Part B.

Part A

What is **one** main idea of the passage?

A. The U.S. Bicentennial was a celebration meant for the entire country.

B. Small groups are better at planning events like the Bicentennial.

C. The U.S. Bicentennial broke many world records.

D. Many areas planned their own Bicentennial events.

Part B

Which sentence from the passage **best** supports the main idea?

A. It was fifty feet tall and weighed forty-nine thousand pounds.

B. Every city and town would decide independently how to celebrate.

C. In 1967, the U.S. government formed the American Revolution Bicentennial Commission.

D. Every person living in the United States was invited!

5 This question has two parts. First, answer Part A. Then, answer Part B.

Part A

Read this paragraph from the passage.

> **At 2:00 p.m. in Philadelphia, bells rang out. At the exact same time, bells in cities and towns across the country tolled. The country was two hundred years old! That night, vivid fireworks filled the night sky. The careful planning had paid off. America's birthday party was a success.**

Which text structure is used in this paragraph?

A. chronological

B. problem and solution

C. cause and effect

D. compare and contrast

Part B

Which group of words and phrases from the paragraph **best** support your answer to Part A?

A. At 2:00 p.m.; At the exact same time; That night

B. in Philadelphia; in cities and towns across the country

C. bells rang out; bells . . . tolled; vivid fireworks filled the night sky

D. The country; The careful planning; America's birthday party

Read the passage.

The Best Birthday Party Ever

When I was ten years old, the United States celebrated its two hundredth birthday. As the day drew closer, I grew more and more excited! Growing up in New York, the Fourth of July was always a fun occasion. But our family knew that this Bicentennial celebration would be extra special. Even my two-year-old brother knew something exciting was happening. It almost seemed like we were waiting impatiently for our own birthdays to arrive. My sister, brother, and I all shared the same sleepless excitement and sense of butterflies in our stomachs.

There were lots of preparations to make. In June, the kids in our city painted all the fire hydrants. Some got stars and some got stripes, but all now wore red, white, and blue instead of the chipped yellow paint they had been covered in. The firefighters thought it was a good idea, too, and helped paint the hydrants on our street. At the end of the month, my mom bought streamers to hang from our front porch. The tri-colored decoration looked very patriotic, but I thought it was important to display our American flag, too. We hung the flag between the pillars on the porch. Now our house was ready to celebrate.

A few days before the Fourth, a giant flag was hung on a bridge near our house. It was the largest U.S. flag that had ever been made, and it was hung from one of the longest bridges in the country. There was a problem, however. The wind in the harbor pushed the flag against the bridge cables again and again, creating small tears. As a result, the wind was able to whip through the holes and shred the beautiful symbol of our country.

Finally, it was Independence Day. We went down to the waterfront at noon. Mom packed a big picnic—enough for all our cousins, aunts, and uncles. Even Grandpa came, beaming with happiness and pride. He said he was glad that he had lived to see the Bicentennial. He said that this day made him glad he had <u>immigrated</u> to this country sixty years ago. Mom nodded her head. She was happy she had come to the United States, too, and she was proud to be a new citizen.

At about 2:00 p.m. we saw the first ship sail into New York Harbor. It was a tugboat, a tiny craft able to pull ships many times its own weight. It was followed by other tugboats and a fireboat that had a water cannon. That boat shot a blast of water high into the air to announce the arrival of the next ships. They were the tall ships, and they were breathtaking. These ships were made of wood, with sails carried on tall masts. Grandpa said they reminded him of the ships that brought many immigrants to the United States years ago. The ships glided elegantly under the Verrazano Bridge and were met by hundreds of small boats. The tiny boats moved through the harbor excitedly, dancing around each other as they greeted the tall ships that had come from fourteen different countries.

That night we went back to the water's edge to watch the fireworks. We clapped and cheered as rockets hissed and boomed over the inky waters of the harbor. Across the land, we knew people were doing the same thing. Together we celebrated our independence and our country's birthday. The United States was two hundred years old. I was glad that I was at the party!

The tall ship *Amerigo Vespucci* sailed into New York Harbor during the Bicentennial celebration.

Answer the questions.

6 This question has two parts. First, answer Part A. Then, answer Part B.

Part A

Read the sentences from "The Best Birthday Party Ever."

The wind in the harbor pushed the flag against the bridge cables again and again, creating small tears. As a result, the wind was able to whip through the holes and shred the beautiful symbol of our country.

Which of the following statements **best** describes the relationship between the two sentences?

A. The first sentence makes a claim that is supported by the second sentence.

B. The sentences compare two different things.

C. The sentences describe a sequence of events.

D. The first sentence describes the cause of the event in the second sentence.

Part B

Which phrase helped you answer Part A?

A. pushed the flag

B. against the bridge

C. As a result

D. whip through the holes

7 Which sentence from the story does the photograph help readers to understand?

A. It was a tugboat, a tiny craft able to pull ships many times its own weight.

B. That boat shot a blast of water high into the air to announce the arrival of the next ships.

C. Grandpa said they reminded him of the ships that brought many immigrants to the United States years ago.

D. The ships glided elegantly under the Verrazano Bridge and were met by hundreds of small boats.

8 This question has two parts. First, answer Part A. Then, answer Part B.

Part A

Read the sentences from "The Best Birthday Party Ever." Then, answer the question that follows.

> **Even Grandpa came, beaming with happiness and pride. He said he was glad that he had lived to see the Bicentennial. He said that this day made him glad he had immigrated to this country sixty years ago. Mom nodded her head. She was happy she had come to the United States, too, and she was proud to be a new citizen.**

Which **three** phrases from the paragraph provide the **best** help in figuring out what immigrated means?

A. beaming with happiness and pride

B. lived to see the Bicentennial

C. this day made him glad

D. to this country sixty years ago

E. come to the United States, too

F. proud to be a new citizen

Part B

Which is the **best** definition for immigrated, as it is used in this paragraph?

A. hoped for a wonderful new life

B. come to live in a new country

C. left the homeland forever

D. fled from an enemy

9 Write a short summary that restates the main idea and relevant details of "The Best Birthday Party Ever" in your own words.

10 You have read two passages about America's Bicentennial: "America's 200th Birthday Celebration" and "The Best Birthday Party Ever." Compare and contrast the information you learned about the celebrations in each passage. Consider the text types, text structures, and authors' points of view.

Remember to include text evidence from both passages to support your ideas. Write your answer on the lines provided.

STRAND 3

Writing

Writing Foundations

1 GETTING THE IDEA

In school, you may be asked to write different kinds of pieces—stories, reports, opinions. Whatever you write, you need to follow certain steps to get a final piece that is the best it can be. The steps you take make up the **writing process**. These five steps are prewriting, drafting, revising, editing, and publishing.

Prewrite

Prewriting is the first step in the writing process. When you prewrite, you decide on a topic and what you want to say about it. Asking yourself questions about the topic can help you identify important details to include. A graphic organizer like the one below is a good way to keep the details organized.

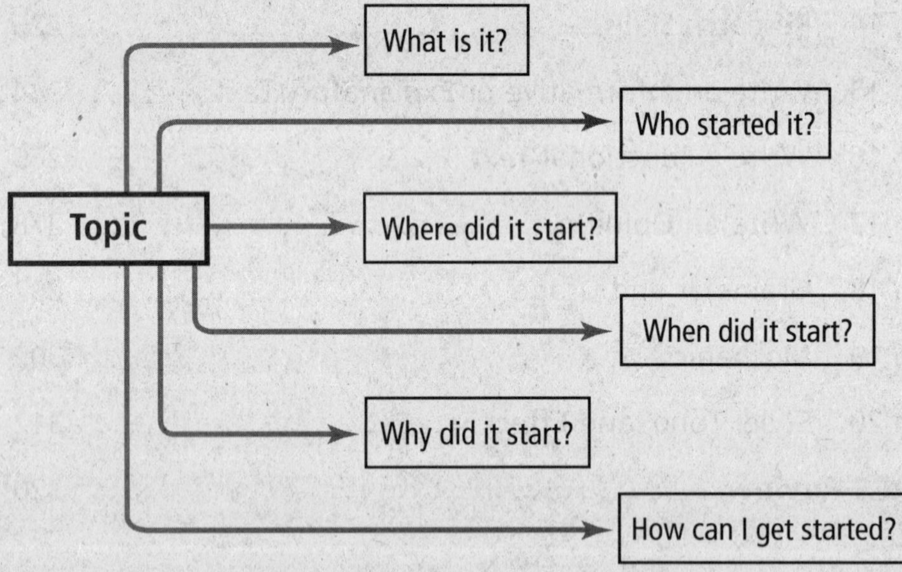

Task, Audience, and Purpose

Prewriting also includes deciding on your task, audience, and purpose. In a test situation, you can find your writing task by reading the question or writing prompt and determining exactly what you are being asked to write. Your **audience** will usually be your teacher. Then, you have to decide on your **purpose,** or what you want to accomplish by writing. Do you want to tell a story about your topic? Do you want to express your **point of view** on a topic? Do you want to provide information about your topic or explain something about it?

Keeping your task, audience, and purpose in mind throughout the writing process is important. Doing so will help you choose an appropriate writing style. For example, a report or an opinion piece should be written in a formal style. It should not contain slang or shortened forms of words.

Draft

Drafting is getting your ideas down on paper. In the first draft of your writing, you will probably have some error. You might be missing some **transitions**, a linking words and phrases such as *another*, *for example*, *also*, and *because*. It's more important to get your ideas down on paper than it is to worry about mistakes at this point.

In some situations, you may not have time to rewrite your draft. So, it's important to follow your writing plan closely and to write neatly. You can't get credit for something your teacher can't read.

Revise

Revising, the third step in the writing process, is the process of improving your writing. This includes adding more facts or details. Add transitions and linking words where needed, and delete unrelated or repeated information. It's also a time to examine word choices to be sure you have used the most effective words for your purpose and audience. If possible, ask a classmate to read your work and give you some feedback on how to improve it.

Edit

Editing, the fourth step in the writing process, refers to correcting mistakes in spelling, grammar, capitalization, and punctuation.

Review Your Work

In a test situation, you will probably need to combine the revising and editing processes. Use the following checklist as a guide.

- ☐ Does my response answer all parts of the writing prompt?
- ☐ Is my main idea or point of view clear?
- ☐ Do I include enough relevant details and information to support my main idea or point of view?
- ☐ Are my ideas presented in a logical order?
- ☐ Do I express my ideas clearly and concisely?
- ☐ Is my writing style appropriate for my task, audience, and purpose?
- ☐ Do I have a clear introduction and conclusion?
- ☐ Is my writing free of spelling, grammar, capitalization, and punctuation errors?

Publish

The final step in the writing process is **publishing**, or making a clean copy of your writing on your paper. It should incorporate all the changes made in the revising and editing processes.

Language Spotlight • Progressive Verbs

Progressive verbs tell about ongoing actions. These verbs use a form of the verb *to be* followed by the main verb that ends with *-ing*. Using progressive verbs in your writing helps you keep the sequence of events in the correct order. Read the following sentences. Each underlined word is a progressive verb. Look at the form of the verb *to be* to tell if the action takes place in the past, present, or future.

present progressive: We are hiking to the cache site.

past progressive: We were searching for hidden treasures.

future progressive: After finding this site, we will be looking for others.

On a separate sheet of paper, write three sentences of your own. Use present, past, and future progressive verbs, and underline them.

2 COACHED EXAMPLE

Read the passage.

Treasure Hunting in the Twenty-First Century

"What are you two up to?" asked Dad, looking at the computer screen.

"We're looking up the guidelines to go geocaching," answered Molly.

Frowning, Dad asked, "What's geocaching?"

"It's like a treasure hunt," said Max, "but it's done with GPS coordinates."

"What does 'GPS' stand for again?" asked Dad.

"Global Positioning System," said Max.

"Here's how geocaching works," said Molly. "You log into the geocaching Web site to see if there are any geocaches in your area. If there is one, you can get its latitude and longitude, and use a GPS device to find it."

"Look," continued Max, "they even give you a clue. It's encrypted, but decrypting it is easy."

"What happens when you find the cache?" asked Dad.

"You open it and sign the logbook that says you found it," said Max.

Molly added, "Most caches have little treasures or trade items in them. You can take one if you replace it with something that's of about the same value."

"That sounds like fun," said Dad. "Are you going to do it?"

"Yes," said Molly, ". . . if you'll drive us to the park."

"I'll drive you," answered Dad, ". . . if I can go on the treasure hunt, too."

Max and Molly readily agreed. After making sure their cell phones were charged, Molly and Max packed water, snacks, gloves, and a flashlight into a backpack.

"What trade items are you going to take?" asked Dad.

Molly volunteered a deck of playing cards that she hadn't yet opened. Max offered a multi-tool that he hadn't used.

“You can’t do that,” cautioned Molly. “Remember, the guidelines said not to put in anything that’s dangerous or sharp. Your multi-tool has a knife in it.”

“Oh, you’re right,” said Max. “What can I contribute?”

Dad suggested one of Max’s new action figures. Max agreed that was a good idea. After all three exchanged their sneakers for hiking boots, they got into the car and drove to the park. Max and Molly turned on their phones as soon as they got out of the car and activated the GPS. Molly read off the geocache coordinates while Max compared them with the coordinates of their current location.

When they honed in on the coordinates, they searched everywhere but couldn’t find a geocache. Then Max remembered the clue he had decrypted. “It said something like ‘If you can’t find the cache right away, keep on rocking.’”

“I’ll bet the geocache is in one of those hollow containers disguised to look like a rock,” Molly said. They started turning over rocks carefully until they found one that felt hollow. It was the geocache! Molly read the note, and Max signed the logbook. The note suggested that they use the disposable camera inside the cache to take a picture of themselves so that the cache’s owner could post it on the geocaching site. Holding the geocache between them, Max and Molly smiled so that Dad could take their picture.

On the ride home, Max and Molly decided that they should make their own geocache to continue the adventure.

Answer the following questions.

1. This question has two parts. First, answer Part A. Then, answer Part B.

Part A

Judging from his actions and dialogue in the story, which words **best** describe Dad's character?

A. suspicious and controlling

B. generous and kind

C. insecure and curious

D. easygoing and fun-loving

Part B

Which sentence from the story **best** supports the answer to Part A?

A. "That sounds like fun," said Dad.

B. "What trade items are you going to take?" asked Dad.

C. Dad suggested one of Max's new action figures.

D. Holding the geocache between them, Max and Molly smiled so that Dad could take their picture.

Hint Recall what Dad said and did in the story. What do these actions show about the kind of person he is?

2. From whose point of view was the story narrated?

A. from Dad's point of view

B. in the third person from an outsider's point of view

C. from Molly's point of view

D. in the first person from Max's point of view

Hint Look at the pronouns used in the story. Did the narrator use first-person pronouns or third-person pronouns to describe the events?

3 The following question has two parts. First, answer Part A. Then, answer Part B.

Part A

Which of the following **best** describes the author's purpose for writing the passage?

A. to inform readers about geocaching

B. to express strong opinions about geocaching

C. to entertain readers with a fantasy story

D. to entertain and inform readers with a realistic story

Part B

Which statement **best** supports the answer to Part A?

A. The author seems to be an expert on the geocaching process.

C. Magical events happen in this story that could not happen in real life.

B. The author seems to think geocaching is too complicated for most people.

D. The events in this story could happen in real life, and the characters are likeable.

Hint What kind of text is this passage? Is it a nonfiction article, a persuasive article, a fantasy story, or a realistic fiction story? Why did the author write this passage?

4 Underline the sentence in the passage that **best** shows the students solving the main problem, which leads to the story's conclusion.

Hint What was the characters' main goal? At what point do you know that the characters achieved their goal and solved the story's problem?

Use the Reading Guide to help you understand the passage.

Geocaching: Treasure Hunting in the Space Age

Reading Guide

Why does the beginning of this passage explain what geocaching is?

How did people learn about geocaching?

How did new Web sites make geocaching more popular?

Going on a treasure hunt may sound like a juvenile activity. When combined with space-age technology, however, it becomes an exciting adventure for people of all ages.

What Is Geocaching?

Geocaching is like high-tech treasure hunting. Instead of a map and a compass, players use GPS (Global Positioning System) technology to hunt for treasure. The word *geocache* comes from the root *geo*, meaning "Earth," and *cache*, meaning "hidden storage place."

How Geocaching Got Started

GPS accuracy got a huge boost on May 2, 2000. That is when twenty-four new satellites were activated. GPS users got much better service around the world. The very next day, a computer engineer named Dave Ulmer decided to test the accuracy of his GPS. He put some objects, including a logbook, into a black bucket and hid it in the woods near his home in Oregon. After noting the coordinates, he posted them on a site for GPS users. Within days, two people had found Ulmer's stash and posted their experiences online.

The rest, as they say, is history. New Web sites for geocaching sprang up. The sites had many new features, such as being able to locate caches by using ZIP codes. This made it easier for more people to play the game. Geocaches increased in number from seventy-five in 2000 to more than two million worldwide today.

Reading Guide

Why does geocaching have rules and tips?

Why is it helpful to the reader to list the rules for finding a geocache?

What things should you keep in mind when selecting trade items for a geocache?

Geocaching Rules

You can start geocaching by finding an online geocaching site. (Be sure to get your parents' or guardians' permission first.) Then, go to the "Hide & Seek a Cache" page, enter your ZIP code, and click "Search." Click on the name of a geocache when the list comes up. Look for a cache that is identified as "regular" or "large" because it is more likely to have trade items to exchange in it. Common trade items include action figures, playing cards, pencil sharpeners, and key chains.

Enter the coordinates of the cache into your GPS, and use them to find the cache. GPS units are accurate to only about twenty feet. At that point, put your GPS away and start searching with your eyes. Once you find the cache, sign the logbook. If the cache contains trade items, take one and put something of equal or greater value in its place. Return the cache to its original place. Be sure to leave the site exactly as you found it. When you get home, log back into the geocaching Web site and record your experiences.

Here are some more things to keep in mind when you find a geocache.

- Do not remove a cache or move it from its original position.
- Do not put food or items with strong odors into a cache because they will attract animals.
- If you don't find the cache, visit the geocaching Web site when you get home and note "Didn't find it" in the log. That way, its owner can check to see if the cache has actually gone missing.

How to Hide a Geocache

When you are ready to hide your own cache, choose a weatherproof container. Clear plastic ones are best. Put some trade items into the container. Be careful not to put anything sharp or dangerous into the container. Include a logbook so that your cache finders can write their names and the dates of their finds. Label the container "Official Geocache," and include contact information.

Reading Guide

How do linking words help connect ideas in this passage?

How does the last paragraph help the reader remember important ideas from the passage?

When your container is ready, think of a good hiding spot. It should not be on private property or government grounds, such as national parks and wildlife preserves. Take your container to the site you select and hide it behind a tree or under some rocks or leaves. Do not bury the container or disturb the environment any more than necessary. Also be sure to note the coordinates of the location so that you can post them on the geocaching site.

Geocaching can be an exciting adventure for people of all ages, but only if all the players follow the same rules. To learn more about the guidelines and selecting GPS devices, log on to a geocaching Web site. You don't have to be a member to read the rules. Happy hunting!

Answer the following questions.

1 The following question has two parts. First, answer Part A. Then, answer Part B.

Part A

What was the author's purpose for writing "Geocaching: Treasure Hunting in the Space Age"?

A. to explain to readers what geocaching is and how it works

B. to tell readers about the tools needed in geocoaching and how to use them

C. persuade readers to try geocaching

D. to entertain readers with an interesting story about geocaching

Part B

Which statement **best** explains the author's main idea for the passage?

A. Geocaching is the best way for parents to teach their children how to use a compass and how to read a map.

B. The term *geocache* comes from the root *geo*, meaning "Earth," and *cache*, meaning "hidden storage place."

C. Geocaching is a fun activity for people of all ages as long as they follow the rules.

D. When you are ready to hide your own cache, choose a weatherproof container.

2 Which sentences tell what happened **immediately after** twenty-four new satellites were activated? Circle **all** that apply.

A. GPS users got a boost in their available service.

B. New Web sites were created that let users find caches by ZIP code.

C. Washington State became the first place where a geocache was put in place.

D. Dave Ulmer decided to test the accuracy of the new GPS technology by hiding a cache and posting its coordinates on a GPS users' site.

3 Here are some additional details the author could have included in the article. Write the letter of each detail next to the heading under which you would include the detail.

A. Look for a place that has some meaning to you or one that provides searchers with a good view.

B. Try to follow the geocaching's tradition "Cache In, Trash Out" by taking a trash bag and collecting trash as you look for your cache.

C. David Ulmer's original site was called "The Great American Stash Hunt."

Heading	Detail
How Geocaching Got Started	C
Geocaching Rules	B
How to Hide a Geocache	A

4 Which of the following statements could be added to the conclusion to make it stronger?

A. GPS devices vary greatly in size and accuracy.

B. To really benefit from the geocaching experience, you need to be familiar with all the rules and guidelines.

C. GPS devices are accurate to only a certain point; then you have to put the device away and rely on your eyesight.

D. You don't need any special equipment or knowledge to go geocaching.

5 In "Treasure Hunting in the Twenty-First Century," you read about a family who went on a geocaching adventure. In "Geocaching: Treasure Hunting in the Space Age," you read about what geocaching is and how to do it. Write a four-paragraph editorial for your school newspaper that explains what geocaching is and tries to persuade the students in your school to form a geocaching club to go on adventures together. Use reasons, facts, and details from both "Treasure Hunting in the Twenty-First Century" and "Geocaching: Treasure Hunting in the Space Age" to support your point of view.

Use the writing process to plan, draft, revise, and edit your writing. Be sure to include a clear introduction, body, and conclusion. You may plan your editorial in the space below. Write your editorial on the following pages.

Plan

main idea:

Things about Geocaching

Supporting detail:

It's even more fun when you do it with friends.

Supporting Detail:

You can tell your sister or brother to geocach with you.

Supporting Detail:

It's basically a scavenger hunt

State your Thesis:

you get help to find them with the GPS

Write your editorial on the lines below.

Facts about Geocaching. There are apps of GPS when you're trying to find a treasure. Maybe when you start it's boring but when you start getting close to one for me it's kind of fun. Geocaching also is described as a series of hide-and-seek games but with objects hidden by someone else. Hiders provide online clues for seekers. Things about caches. Caches are the hidden treasure. After registering online, geocachers look for coordinates of caches. Caches have 2 or 3 parts, a waterproof container. A logbook to list the people who visit the cache, and sometimes a low-cost trinket or geocoin. Fast facts about geocaching. There are more than 3 million active geocaches worldwide. Geocaches are hidden in 191 different countries on all 7 continents. The hobby has changed a little since it's start in Oregon in 2000 when it was called geostashing. They used GPS devices and the internet to re-invent the older hobby of litterboxing. Geocaching started in May 3rd 2000. Geocaching was started by a group of people who were interested in technology and geography. They reinvented the old hobby, letterboxing. Twenty two years ago, Mike Teague became the first person to find the first geocache.

Jeremy Irish launched Geocaching.com, a listing site for geocaches, Groundspeak Inc. Hides and events are reviewed by volunteer regional cache reviewers before publication. The website claims millions of caches and members in over 200 countries.

Write a Response to Literature

1 GETTING THE IDEA

When you write a **response to literature**, you state a position, or give an opinion, about a story, play, or poem you have read. Then, you support your position with evidence from the text. This helps to prove the point you want to make.

Understanding a Prompt

You will often be asked to respond to a **writing prompt** that asks about a text you have read. Read the following example of a writing prompt. Circle the title of the poem you will write about. Then, underline the verb in the prompt.

> Explain how the author Robert Louis Stevenson uses a specific point of view to entertain readers in the poem "My Shadow."

Breaking the prompt down can help you understand exactly what you need to do. The prompt identifies the text you must respond to: "My Shadow." The verb *explain* tells what you need to do. The prompt also identifies the literary element you need to focus on: the point of view featured in the poem.

Forming Your Position

For the prompt above, you have to explain how the author uses a point of view to entertain readers. The first step is to reread the poem, keeping point of view in mind. Then, ask yourself:

- Is the poem written in first-person or third-person point of view?
- What does this point of view allow the poem's speaker to express?
- What about this speaker's voice makes the poem appealing?

Your **position**, or opinion about the poem, can be formed after answering these questions.

Organizing Your Ideas

In the beginning of a response to literature, name the text you're writing about and state your position about it. Stating your position in the beginning helps your readers understand the point you will make in your response. Aim to write a clear, strong introduction to grab the attention of your readers.

Here's one way to state a position about the poem "My Shadow":

> The poem "My Shadow" by Robert Louis Stevenson is written from the first-person point of view of a child. This point of view is entertaining because the child doesn't know what a shadow is and the reader gets to follow along as the child tries to figure that out.

Once you have stated your position, you need to support it. When you support a position, you give reasons why you think the way you do. You provide facts and details from the text, or **text evidence**, to back up your reasons. Be sure to return to the text often while you write to review the reasons you have for your position.

You also have to make sure your opinions are clearly linked to your reasons. The best way to do this is to use **transitions**, or connecting words and phrases, such as *because*, *but*, *consequently*, *for instance*, *in order to*, *in addition*, and *specifically*. These connecting words help your writing flow smoothly from one idea to the next.

The last paragraph of your writing is the **conclusion**. This part restates your position and summarizes the most important ideas.

Using a graphic organizer, like the one on the following page, is a good way to plan and organize your ideas.

Position	"My Shadow" entertains its reader by using the innocent, first-person point of view of a young child.
Reason 1	The child doesn't know what a shadow is; the reader follows along as the child figures that out.
Supporting details	• He thinks his shadow is a person following him around.
	• He is confused by how the shadow grows and shrinks.
Reason 2	The child uses funny words to describe his shadow.
Supporting details	• He calls his shadow a coward.
	• He says his shadow is a sleepy-head.
Conclusion	The point of view of "My Shadow" makes the poem entertaining.

Finishing Up

Reread your draft. Check that your opinion is clear and your reasons are organized in a way that readers can understand. Proofread your work for errors in grammar, capitalization, punctuation, and spelling. As you revise your work, ask yourself the following questions.

- ☐ Does my response answer all parts of the prompt?
- ☐ Is my opinion clearly stated?
- ☐ Do I include enough reasons that support my opinion?
- ☐ Is my response well-organized and focused?
- ☐ Is my writing free of errors?

Language Spotlight • Commas

Using both long and short sentences can make your writing more interesting. If you have mostly short, simple sentences, consider combining some of them to make **compound sentences** using a coordinating conjunction, such as *and*, *but*, or *so*. Remember to use a **comma** before the coordinating conjunction in a compound sentence. How would you combine these two sentences using a coordinating conjunction and a comma?

"My Shadow" rhymes.

The poem is fun to read out loud.

Read the passage.

A Golden Web

In an arbor of yellow roses, a spider began to spin its web. The first thread of spider silk stuck to a perfect yellow bloom. The golden yellow from the rose seeped into the thread. The spider continued to spin, unaware that its web was not made of the usual spider's silk, but spun gold that glistened in the dawn's light.

An old woman was walking through the rose arbor on her way to market when the glittery web caught her eye. "What's this?" she asked herself. She peered into the rose bush for a better look. So intent was she on the gleaming golden web that she didn't even notice the lovely perfume of the roses. But the old woman knew gold when she saw it. She made sure no one was watching her. Then she grabbed the golden web and pressed it in her palm until it became a small golden nugget.

In her zeal to grab the web, the old woman had squashed many of the golden yellow roses. The spider escaped being crushed in its own web and hid inside one of the few remaining blooms. With its web gone, it had no bugs to eat, and it went to sleep hungry.

Meanwhile, the old woman skipped the rest of the way to market with her treasure. She used the gold nugget to buy herself many fine new clothes. The dressmaker who sold the old woman her new clothes asked where she had found the nugget. The old woman did not want anyone to learn the truth. "I found it in the stream," she lied. By that afternoon, the stream was choked with people panning for gold.

The next morning, the old woman went back to the arbor. The spider had just completed a new web of spun gold. The woman trampled several of the rose bushes in her haste to harvest the golden silk. This time the spider barely escaped being crushed in its web, and it still didn't have any bugs to eat. The old woman was so intent on her greedy mission that she did not notice that the dressmaker had followed her into the arbor and seen the golden web.

The dressmaker could not resist bragging about what she had seen, and the next morning the arbor was full of people searching for the golden web. The villagers trampled all the bushes as they shoved each other aside in their frenzy to find gold. But there was no golden web, and when the people finally went home, there were no more golden yellow roses either.

The spider, weak from hunger, spun a new web in the branches of a maple tree. This one did not glitter with spun gold. It was an ordinary web. Soon an ordinary fly got stuck, and the spider ate its meal in peace. The spider lived a long time and was never bothered by the villagers again.

Answer the following questions.

1 This question has two parts. First, answer Part A. Then, answer Part B.

Part A

Which of these words **best** describes the old woman's character?

A. mysterious

B. hardworking

C. clever

D. greedy

Part B

Which sentence from the story **best** supports the answer to Part A?

A. The golden yellow from the rose seeped into the thread.

B. An old woman was walking through the rose arbor on her way to market when the glittery web caught her eye.

C. In her zeal to grab the web, the old woman had squashed many of the golden yellow roses.

D. With its web gone, [the spider] had no bugs to eat, and it went to sleep hungry.

Hint Reread the part of the story in which the woman finds the gold. Why doesn't she tell anyone what she found?

2 Underline a sentence from the story that the author includes to show how the villagers' actions affect the spider.

> **Hint** Reread the parts of the story that describe the spider. How does the spider react as the story goes on? What do the villagers do that causes the spider to act in this way?

3 This question has two parts. First, answer Part A. Then, answer Part B.

Part A

Which main lesson is the storyteller trying to teach readers?

A. Work hard and you will be happy and wealthy.

B. Greed usually leads to destruction and loss.

C. In certain special situations, it is OK to be greedy.

D. Keeping a secret never works out well for the secret keeper.

Part B

Which sentences from the story **best** support your answer to Part A? Check **all** that apply.

A. In an arbor of yellow roses, a spider began to spin its web.

B. The spider continued to spin, unaware that its web was not made of the usual spider's silk, but spun gold that glistened in the dawn's light.

C. With its web gone, it had no bugs to eat and it went to sleep hungry.

D. The woman trampled several of the rose bushes in her haste to harvest the golden silk.

E. The villagers trampled all the bushes as they shoved each other aside in their frenzy to find gold.

F. But there was no golden web, and when the people finally went home, there were no more golden yellow roses either.

> **Hint** Think about the actions of the old woman, the dressmaker, and the villagers in the story. Are they rewarded in the end?

4 A student wrote the following position statement about "A Golden Web."

The author of "A Golden Web" uses magical details to relay a message about the story's characters and about the real world, too.

Which of these details could the student use to support this statement?

A. The author makes one of the characters an old woman with magical powers.

B. The author shows that both the old woman and the villagers want gold.

C. The author includes details about the villagers buying new clothes.

D. The author includes details about roses that can turn things into gold.

Hint The student's claim is about how the author uses magical details. In order to support the statement, the student will have to show readers that there are magical details in the story.

Use the Reading Guide to help you understand the passage.

Rumpelstiltskin

adapted from a story by the Brothers Grimm

Reading Guide

Look at the first sentence of the passage. What information is revealed in this sentence?

What details does the author include to show the king's character in this section?

How does the miller's lie affect his daughter?

Once upon a time, a poor miller wanted to feel more important, so he bragged to the king that his daughter could spin gold from straw.

The king was intrigued. "Bring her to my palace," he commanded.

The young woman was brought to the palace and put in a room covered with heaping piles of straw, a spinning wheel, and a spindle. "You have till dawn to spin the straw into gold," the king said. When he left, the poor woman began to cry.

Suddenly, the door opened, and in stepped a hideous little man. "Why are you crying?" he asked.

The woman told him what the king had commanded. "I have no idea how to spin straw into gold," she said and began to cry again.

"What will you give me if I spin it for you?" he asked.

"My necklace," she replied. The little man took the necklace and began to spin, and by dawn he had spun all the straw into gold.

When the king saw all the gold, he was delighted. He put the woman into a much bigger room full of straw and told her to spin it all into gold before the following morning. The woman didn't know what to do and again began to cry. As before, the little man appeared out of nowhere. "What will you give me if I spin the straw into gold for you?"

"The ring from my finger," answered the woman. The little man took the ring and once again spun all the straw into gold.

Reading Guide

What details does the author include to show the little man's character in this section?

How does the author move the queen toward a solution to her problem in this section?

The king was overjoyed, but his greed was still not satisfied. He put the woman into an even bigger room full of straw. "If you succeed this time, you shall become my wife." Although the woman was just a miller's daughter, the king was convinced he would never find a richer wife even if he were to search the whole world over.

When the woman was alone, the little man appeared and said, "What will you give me if I spin the straw for you once again?"

"I've nothing more to give," answered the woman.

"Then promise me when you are queen to give me your first child," the little man said.

The woman promised, and the little man spun the straw into gold for the third time. When the king found everything as he had hoped, he made the woman his wife.

A year passed, and a beautiful son was born to her. She had forgotten her promise until one day the little man stepped into her room. "Now give me what you promised," he demanded.

The queen offered him all the riches in her kingdom if he would only leave her the child, but the little man said, "No, a living child is dearer to me than all the treasures in the world."

Then the queen began to sob so bitterly that the little man felt sorry for her. "I'll give you three days to try to guess my name. If you guess correctly, you may keep your child."

The queen sent a messenger to scour the land and collect any unfamiliar names he came across. When the ugly little man arrived on the following day, she recited all the names she knew, but at each one the little man gleefully called out, "That's not my name!"

The next day, when the little man once again made his appearance, the queen had a long list of exotic and unusual names. "Is your name, perhaps, Sheepshanks, Cruikshanks, Spindleshanks?"

Reading Guide

How does the author show why Rumpelstiltskin's downfall occurs?

How does the author show the queen solving her problem in this section?

Why does Rumpelstiltskin assume someone told the queen his name?

But he always replied, "No, that's not my name."

On the third day, the messenger returned. "I did not discover any new names, but I came across a grotesque little man dancing around a fire, singing:

"Tomorrow I brew, today I bake.
And then the child away I'll take.
For little deems my royal dame
That Rumpelstiltskin is my name!"

Now the queen was prepared when the little man appeared and asked, "What's my name?"

"Is your name perhaps Rumpelstiltskin?"

At the sound of his name, the little man screamed, "Who told you that?"

In his rage, he hurled himself out the palace window and was never seen or heard from again.

Answer the following questions.

1 The chart below shows three incomplete sentences. Complete each sentence by writing a connecting word or phrase from the box that links the two sentence parts together in a way that makes good sense.

and finally	and that is why	but

First part of the sentence	connecting word or phrase	Last part of the sentence
1. The miller thinks it is fine to lie,		his daughter's situation proves that lying causes trouble.
2. The little man does the miller's daughter's job,		the king sees a roomful of gold—not straw—when he returns to the room the next morning.
3. The little man keeps helping the young woman,		the king makes the miller's daughter his wife.

2 Reread the following sentences about the king from the passage.

He put the woman into an even bigger room full of straw. "If you succeed this time, you shall become my wife." Although the woman was just a miller's daughter, the king was convinced he would never find a richer wife even if he were to search the whole world over.

Explain how the author describes the king's thoughts in this section to show the reader something about the king's character.

Write your response on the lines below.

3 Underline **two** sentences from the story that the author includes to show how the queen tries to stop Rumpelstiltskin from taking her son.

4 Which of the following details from the story could support a claim that Rumpelstiltskin is a mean-hearted character?

A. Rumpelstiltskin feels bad for the queen when she cries.

B. Rumpelstiltskin threatens to take the queen's first child.

C. Rumpelstiltskin spins the straw into gold.

D. The miller lies about his daughter's abilities.

5 A student wrote an essay with the following position and reasons. Fill in a concluding statement to sum up the ideas in this student's essay.

Position	**Rumpelstiltskin deserves to lose in the end.**
Reason 1	**He shows cruelty by demanding payment from the queen.**
Reason 2	**He is not careful enough to keep his name a secret.**
Conclusion	

6 You have read two stories in which a character is threatened or harmed by the greed of other characters but manages to escape in the end. Write an essay describing the spider from "A Golden Web" and the daughter from "Rumpelstiltskin." Be sure to:

- explain how each character is challenged or affected by the greed of other characters.
- compare and contrast the different ways in which each character is able to escape the situation.
- include specific details from each story to support your ideas.
- use connecting words or phrases to clearly link your opinion statements to evidence from the story.
- provide a conclusion.

Plan your response to the writing prompt in the space below.

Write your response on the lines below.

LESSON 13

Write a Narrative

1 GETTING THE IDEA

Narrative writing tells a story. One purpose of narrative writing is to entertain the reader. Some narratives are fictional. Other narratives tell true stories about real people and events. All narratives have characters, a setting, a plot, and a point of view.

Choose a Setting, Characters, Plot, and Point of View

To plan your own narrative, think about these building blocks.

- Your **setting** should be based on what kind of story you want to tell. For example, a science fiction story might be set in space or in the future.
- The **characters** perform the actions in your narrative. Think about the traits (qualities) and motivations (wants) that they will have. How will they act? What will they say?
- To plan the **plot**, or what will happen, decide on a problem the characters have. You will use the events of the story to help the characters find a **solution**.
- The **point of view** of your story will affect what the reader knows while reading. If you use a first-person point of view (with the word *I*), the reader will experience the events as the narrator experiences them. If a third-person narrator tells the story (not using *I*), the reader may know things the characters do not.

Plan Your Story

Suppose you want to write a science fiction story about a family that goes to live on Mars. The characters are an eleven-year-old boy named Jared and his parents. The setting is a spaceship. You can plan your story using a map like the one below.

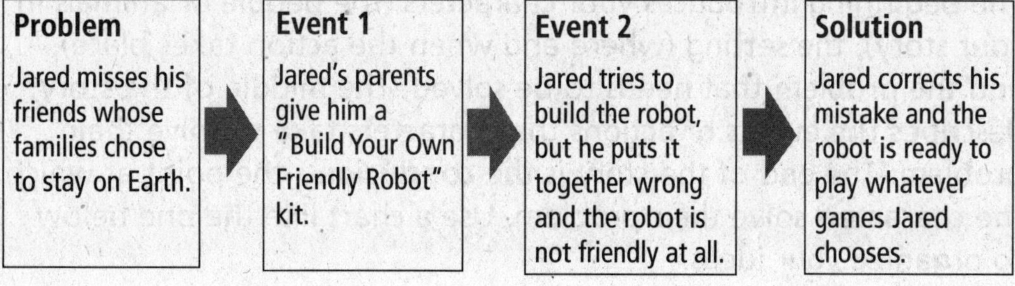

Write Your Narrative Draft: Beginning to End

How you organize your narrative affects how well your reader can understand and enjoy it. The tips below can help you write an organized draft and keep your readers interested from beginning to end. As you write, remember to return to passages you have read for storytelling ideas.

Establish the Situation In the beginning of a narrative, you want to orient your readers, or pull them into the story. The reader needs to know who the story is about and where it is set.

- Some stories start right in the middle of the action. Others grab their readers' attention with an interesting description of the setting or characters.
- Regardless of where you start, be sure to introduce the story's problem early. This will give your readers a reason to keep reading: to find out how the problem will be solved!

Organize the Event Sequence When you write a narrative, you need to be sure that your readers can follow the **sequence of events**. It should be clear what happens first, next, and last. Every good narrative has a beginning, a middle, and an end. These sections make up the plot of a story.

The beginning introduces your characters (the people or animals in your story), the setting (where and when the action takes place), and the problem that needs to be solved. The middle of the story describes the events or actions the characters take to solve their problem. The end of the story is the **conclusion**—the point at which the characters solve their problem. Use a chart like the one below to organize your ideas.

Beginning	Introduce your characters, setting, and problem or goal.
Middle	Develop the plot by describing the actions the characters take to solve the problem.
End	Provide a conclusion that follows from the story events and describes how the problem is solved.

- Use **transition words** and phrases to make the sequence of events clear. Words such as *first*, *then*, *next*, *soon*, and *later* tell when the events are happening and how much time passes between them.
- Make sure each event follows the next in a natural way. The events should lead to an ending that makes sense. They should lead your characters toward a **solution** to the story's problem.

Add Description and Dialogue Description and dialogue bring the characters, setting, and events of your narrative to life. Both are great ways to make readers feel like they're part of the action.

- Add **sensory descriptions**, or details about how things look, feel, taste, smell, and sound. Use concrete words to paint a clear picture of what's going on.
- Think about how characters can show their personalities through **dialogue**, or the words the characters say. You can use dialogue to make your characters more interesting and realistic and to show how they respond to situations in the story.

Write the Conclusion The conclusion, or ending, of the story should show how the characters solved the problem featured in the story. It should make sense, considering the events or experiences that have been narrated in the story.

Revise and Edit

When you revise, try to put yourself in your reader's shoes. Would someone reading your narrative be able to follow it? Would he or she find it interesting? Ask yourself the following questions to figure it out:

- ☐ Do I establish a situation with a setting, characters, and a problem the characters are trying to solve?
- ☐ Is the sequence of events clear?
- ☐ Do I introduce and develop characters in an interesting way?
- ☐ Is there a clear point of view?
- ☐ Do I use exciting dialogue and descriptive details?
- ☐ Does my ending follow from the narrated events? Does it show how the characters solve their problem?

Finally, remember to edit your story to be sure you have fixed any errors in grammar, spelling, and punctuation.

Language Spotlight • Commas and Quotation Marks

When you write dialogue, you use **commas** and **quotation marks** to separate the words someone says from the rest of the sentence that tells about the person speaking. Underline the commas and quotation marks in this sentence.

"The robot is teasing me," Jared complained to his parents.

Where would you add commas and quotation marks in the sentence below?

Check all the connections said Dad.

2 COACHED EXAMPLE

Read the passage.

An Anniversary Adventure

Chandra was stumped. Next week was her grandparents' fiftieth wedding anniversary, and she still had no idea what gift to get them. She didn't want to buy something from a store. She felt that would be too impersonal. *Maybe I could make something*, Chandra thought. But then she couldn't think of a single idea! She decided to ask her parents for help.

"You know you don't need to get them anything," her dad said. "They have everything they could ever wish for, including a wonderful granddaughter." Chandra loved her father, but he was obviously not the best person to ask for this kind of advice.

Fortunately, Chandra's mother had a more helpful suggestion.

"I remember a real-life bedtime story your Grandma used to tell me when I was little. She told me that on the morning of her wedding day, she and my father wrote heartfelt letters to each other. They told each other about their hopes and dreams for their married life together. Then, they sealed the letters inside a time capsule and buried it under a maple tree in the park where they had first met as children."

"What happened to the time capsule?" Chandra asked. "Did they ever dig it up?"

"I don't think so," said her mother. "At least, they never mentioned it to me if they did. My guess is that they forgot all about it."

Chandra knew that those long-lost letters would make a perfect anniversary gift.

"Where is that park?" she asked, thinking that all she had to do was go and dig them up.

"The park *was* where the shopping mall is now," said Chandra's mom. "A lot has changed around here in the past fifty years!"

"When was the mall built?" Chandra asked. She had an idea, but she needed more information.

"About twenty years ago," said her father. "I remember that I was about as old as you are now."

Most people would have given up, but Chandra wasn't most people. Luckily, Dr. Smith, a local scientist, had given Chandra a coupon for a round-trip ride on a time machine that he had invented. Chandra always thought the time machine was fake, but she had recently seen it in Dr. Smith's lab. The time machine was real!

Chandra had been saving the coupon for a special occasion. This was as special as occasions could get. The next day, she cashed in her coupon, set the time machine dial to twenty-two years ago, just to be on the safe side, and pushed the *start* button.

The time machine made a strange knocking noise, but it worked. Soon Chandra landed in the middle of the old park, next to a tall maple tree. But the tree wasn't all she found there. Three bulldozers had already arrived to flatten the park and get the land ready for the mall's construction. They puffed smoke as their engines roared. Chandra knew she didn't have much time.

Answer the following questions.

1 Which sentence describes how the author establishes the situation in this passage?

A. The author introduces the characters and the problem.

B. The author describes where the story takes place.

C. The author tells how the characters solve the problem.

D. The author begins with a history of Chandra's family.

Hint Think about what you learn in the first paragraphs of the passage. What do you know about the passage by this point?

2 Read the last two paragraphs from the story. Then, follow the directions below.

> **Chandra had been saving the coupon for a special occasion. This was as special as occasions could get. The next day, she cashed in her coupon, set the time machine dial to twenty-two years ago, just to be on the safe side, and pushed the *start* button.**
>
> **The time machine made a strange knocking noise, but it worked. Soon Chandra landed in the middle of the old park, next to a tall maple tree. But the tree wasn't all she found there. Three bulldozers had already arrived to flatten the park and get the land ready for the mall's construction. They puffed smoke as their engines roared. Chandra knew she didn't have much time.**

Underline transition words and phrases that tell **when** events happen.

Hint Look for words in the passage that give clues about *when* events are happening, what order they are happening in, and how much time has passed between them.

3 Which of the following sentences does the author include to develop the idea that Chandra is determined to find a good present for her grandparents? Select **all** that apply.

A. Chandra was stumped.

B. She decided to ask her parents for help.

C. Fortunately, Chandra's mother had a more helpful suggestion.

D. Most people would have given up, but Chandra wasn't most people.

E. The next day, she cashed in her coupon, set the time machine dial to twenty-two years ago, just to be on the safe side, and pushed the *start* button.

Hint Which details from the passage show how Chandra works toward the goal of finding a present for her grandparents? What steps does she take to try to find a present?

4 "An Anniversary Adventure" ends with Chandra going back in time to the place where her grandparents buried their letters. Use what you already know about Chandra's character to write an original piece that continues the passage and provides an ending. Your piece should include dialogue with commas and quotation marks, descriptive details, and transition words to make the sequence of events clear to the reader.

Write your ending on the lines below.

Hint Think about the problem in the passage and how your piece can include a satisfying ending that follows naturally from the events so far. Also, remember what you learned about Chandra earlier in the passage. What kind of actions do you think she would take in this situation?

Use the Reading Guide to help you understand the passage.

The Pool Party

Reading Guide

How does the author introduce the characters?

Look at paragraph 3. Underline the words that show the problem in the passage.

Notice how the author uses dialogue to show the characters' traits. How do Henry's parents respond to Henry's problem? What do their responses show about them?

"Henry," Henry's mother called, "You have mail. It's from Sam." She handed Henry a small envelope. Sam's birthday was this month, and Henry was invited to his party.

The two boys had been friends since kindergarten, so Henry had been to a lot of Sam's birthday parties. Henry loved birthday parties, and Sam's were always the best. Every year, Sam's mother made a big chocolate cake with chocolate frosting, and his parents organized amazing party games.

Henry hastily ripped open the invitation to see what this year's theme would be. So far, each theme had been totally unexpected. One year, it was animal cowboys. The following year, it was zombie pirates. But when Henry opened this invitation and saw the word *pool*, his delight turned to panic. Sam was having a pool party, and Henry was *not* a good swimmer.

"I just won't go," Henry told his parents.

"That's silly," said his mother. "You can still have fun even if you don't swim."

"You can wear your floaties," his father added, trying to be helpful.

"Only babies wear floaties!" Henry cried. "Everyone else at the party will be swimming except me. I don't want to go!"

Reading Guide

What sequence of events does the author present in this section? Look for a transition word that shows how the author connects one event to another.

How does the author show how Henry feels about the pool party in this section?

How do Henry's feelings change?

Henry worried about the party all evening, and even when he went to sleep he couldn't seem to forget about it. In one of the many nightmares he had that night, kids were jumping off a diving board into the deep end of a humongous pool. Water splashed all over Henry. When he looked down, he realized he was the only one not wearing a bathing suit. Instead, he was dressed in a dark suit and tie, with bright yellow floaties strapped to his body on top of his fancy clothes.

Everyone stopped playing in the water to stare at him, and then they started to laugh, pointing at his ridiculous outfit. Henry woke in a sweat, with his heart thumping. No way was he going to that party now!

Henry decided to tell Sam at recess that he couldn't come. He'd just have to make up some kind of story about his grandparents visiting from out of town that day. He would say his parents were forcing him to stay home. Yes! That was it! It was a foolproof excuse.

But when recess rolled around, Henry and Sam were surrounded by all of their friends. It was impossible to get Sam alone to break the news. Instead, everyone but Henry kept Sam busy by quizzing him about party plans.

"We're setting up kiddie pools all over the yard for a pretending-to-swim game," Sam explained, "and we bought about a thousand water balloons for a game where you throw the water balloon at a target."

"I can bring my beach ball," Charlie said.

"I'll bring a net," said Nick, "We can play beach volleyball."

"Awesome!" Sam said.

To Henry's great surprise, he found himself listening with more and more interest. He loved beach volleyball, and kiddie pools didn't sound so bad. And so far nobody had said anything about diving off the board into the deep end . . . maybe Henry could do this party after all.

That night, he had an announcement for his parents. "I'll go to the party."

Answer the following questions.

1. The author does a number of things to establish a situation in this passage. Write the phrase from the box in the correct location on the chart to show the purpose that each example serves in the story.

gives information about the characters
states the problem
introduces the characters

Example	Purpose
A. "Henry," Henry's mother called, "You have mail. It's from Sam."	
B. The two boys had been friends since kindergarten, so Henry had been to a lot of Sam's birthday parties.	
C. Sam was having a pool party, and Henry was *not* a good swimmer.	

2 Reread the sentences below. In each one, a transition phrase is underlined.

<u>The following year</u>, it was zombie pirates.

But <u>when recess rolled around</u>, Henry and Sam were surrounded by all of their friends.

<u>That night</u>, he had an announcement for his parents.

How do these three transition phrases help the reader understand the passage?

A. They show Henry's feelings about the party.

B. They make the setting of the story clear.

C. They show time passing between events.

D. They introduce the story's problem.

3 Reread the sentences below.

Everyone stopped playing in the water to stare at him, and then they started to laugh, pointing at his ridiculous outfit. Henry woke in a sweat, with his heart thumping. No way was he going to that party now!

Underline a part of this paragraph in which the author uses sensory details to show how Henry feels about his dream.

4. Why does the author write about Henry's dream? How does that section develop Henry's character and show his response to the news about Sam's pool party?

5 The following question has two parts. First, answer Part A. Then, answer Part B.

Part A

Which of the following events does the author use to lead into Henry changing his mind about the party?

A. Henry has a dream about the party.

B. Henry opens the invitation.

C. Henry talks to his parents at dinner.

D. Henry's friends talk about the party at recess.

Part B

Which sentence from the story **best** supports the answer to Part A?

A. But when Henry opened this invitation and saw the word *pool*, his delight turned to panic.

B. "You can wear your floaties," his father added, trying to be helpful.

C. In one of the many nightmares he had that night, kids were jumping off a diving board into the deep end of a humongous pool.

D. And so far nobody had said anything about diving off the board into the deep end . . . maybe Henry could do this party after all.

6 Write a narrative that tells what happens at the pool party. Make sure that:

- the events you write follow what has already happened in the passage "The Pool Party."
- you build on what you already know about Henry's character.
- you include descriptive details and dialogue.
- you use transition words and phrases to make the event sequence clear.
- you provide an ending.

Plan your narrative in the space below.

Write your narrative on the lines below.

LESSON 14

Research Skills

1 GETTING THE IDEA

Suppose you must write a research report on the exploration of the New World. Would you know what steps to take? Would you know the correct order in which to complete them?

Research writing is informative writing, which shares information about a topic. The word ***research*** means that you must find facts and information about a topic from reliable **sources**, such as books and some Web sites. You do research to learn about the topic. Let's go over the steps you would take to research a topic in order to write about it.

Recall Information

An initial step you can take to focus on a specific topic is to think back on any times you might have already learned about the topic in general. Have you had any experiences at home or on school field trips that can help you focus on something related to the topic? If so, write down these ideas. They might also be useful later when you write your report.

Get Information

Another way to narrow your topic is to look through some sources to get ideas. A source is any material that helps you find information. There are two main places you can do a basic search for information.

- The **library** is filled with books, magazines, encyclopedias, and many other sources. It is a great place to start your research.
- The **Internet** is also very helpful when you use a search engine. Type into the search engine the most specific key words you can think of that are related to the topic.
- Use caution when reviewing Web sites. Some sites on the Internet are more reliable than others. Be sure that you always use a trustworthy source. Sites ending in .gov, .edu, and .org are most likely to be reliable.

Once you begin to look through sources, you will find it easier to narrow your topic. For example, if you are researching the New World, you might want to focus on one explorer in particular or on a famous settlement in the New World. Suppose you decide to write about Christopher Columbus's exploration of the New World. Take a closer look at some sources you could use when doing your research.

Source	Types of Information
Encyclopedias	• Facts that can be trusted • Good starting point for research • May not go into a lot of detail about a topic
Nonfiction books	• Many facts and details • Information that can be trusted
Magazines and newspapers	• Facts and details that can be trusted • May include opinions about different topics
Web sites	• Facts and details that may or may not be correct • .gov, .edu, and .org sites are most reliable

It is important to remember that your sources should always relate to your topic and be trustworthy. When reviewing sources, look through each one or read its table of contents to make sure it has the information you need.

Take Notes on Sources

Gather Information Once you have your sources, the next step is to start taking notes on the information they contain. This involves writing down important facts, details, data, and quotes from each source.

Make sure that you record only important ideas that relate to your topic. Use index cards to write down important facts or details. Remember to record the name of the source and the page where you found the information. Later, you will create a **bibliography** that lists each source you used to write your report.

Sort Information Sort the information from your notes into categories based on related ideas. This will help you organize your notes before you write. See the example on the next page.

Christopher Columbus's Exploration of the New World		
Journey	**Discovery**	**Results**
Ships: *Santa María, Pinta, Niña*	Landed in the Bahamas in October 1492	Claimed new lands for Spain
Set sail in August 1492	Reached Hispaniola in December 1492	Returned a year later with a larger expedition

Once you have finished sorting information, you can use the notes in each category to organize and write your report.

List Sources

Before your report is complete, you must provide a bibliography with an accurate list of sources for every fact, detail, and quote that you found in your research and used in your writing. See below for a review on how to correctly list source titles in your bibliography.

Language Spotlight • Titles of Sources

Follow these guidelines to capitalize titles.

- Capitalize the first and last words in the title and all nouns, pronouns, adjectives, verbs, and adverbs.
- Do NOT capitalize articles, conjunctions, or prepositions.

These guidelines explain how to show titles of sources.

Source	Style	Examples
book, magazine, journal, Web site, newspaper	italics or underlining	*The Sun, The New York Times, www.nasa.gov*
short story, article, poem, chapter	quotation marks	"What Is Pink?" "Over the Rainbow"

On a separate sheet of paper, write your own example for each type of work.

Read this passage from a Web site.

Juan Ponce de León (c. 1460–1521)

Juan Ponce de León was a Spanish explorer. He helped to colonize the island of Puerto Rico. He also discovered Florida. Ponce de León is known for his search for the Fountain of Youth. This is a legend of a fountain that gives health and youth to anyone who drinks from it. There is no proof that he actually looked for this magical place.

Early Years

Ponce de León was born around 1460 in Spain. He sought to make his riches by becoming a soldier and an explorer. As part of this plan, he traveled with Christopher Columbus on his second trip to the New World in 1493.

After Ponce de León arrived in the New World, he showed great skill as a soldier. He fought to stop a fierce attack by natives on a Spanish settlement. The governor of Hispaniola (the Dominican Republic) gave him land as a reward. Ponce de León successfully farmed this land to help support the island. He also married and started a family.

Puerto Rico

During this time, Ponce de León became interested in a nearby island. This island is known as Puerto Rico today. In 1508, he received permission from King Ferdinand of Spain to explore and colonize it. Ponce de León had only just begun to settle the new land when Diego Columbus, the son of Christopher Columbus, challenged him. Diego believed that he had rights as governor of the island. This political struggle continued for a few years. In 1511, Ponce de León was finally forced to leave Puerto Rico. He had to find another land to claim for his own.

Florida

Around this time, natives had told Ponce de León about the "wealthy" island of Bimini (in the Bahamas). There were possibly also rumors of a magical Fountain of Youth on the island, though there is no official record to support this. King Ferdinand allowed Ponce de León to explore the area. But instead of finding Bimini, in 1513 he landed somewhere else. He thought he was on a large island. Ponce de León named it "Florida" for the many flowers that he found there.

After exploring the coast of Florida, he returned to Puerto Rico. Then, he traveled to Spain to tell the king of the beautiful land he discovered. Ferdinand granted him rights to colonize Florida, and he returned there in 1521. But his second trip was not as lucky as his first. His group was attacked by natives upon its arrival. Ponce de León was struck with an arrow, and the ships fled to nearby Cuba. It was there in 1521 that he died of his wounds.

Answer the following questions.

1 A student is writing an informational report about Juan Ponce de León. Read the paragraph from his report and the directions that follow.

> **Ponce de León worked hard with the land he was given in Hispaniola. In the New World, he raised farm animals such as cattle and horses. He also grew vegetables. These food sources helped to support the new settlements in the area.**

The student wants more information about Ponce de León's life as a farmer. Which book would **most likely** give the student more information for his report?

A. *Ponce de León: A New World, a New Life*

B. *European Farming Methods*

C. *The Many Animals of Hispaniola*

D. *Ponce de León's Greatest Discoveries*

Hint First, identify what the student wants to find out. Then, look for connections in the paragraph that suggest the best source. Where does the farming take place?

2 Francis is doing a research report on the discovery of Florida. Read the text from "Juan Ponce de León (c. 1460–1521)." Then, read the directions that follow.

Around this time, natives had told Ponce de León about the "wealthy" island of Bimini (in the Bahamas). There were possibly also rumors of a magical Fountain of Youth on the island, though there is no official record to support this. King Ferdinand allowed Ponce de León to explore the area. But instead of finding Bimini, in 1513 he landed somewhere else. He thought he was on a large island. Ponce de León named it "Florida" for the many flowers that he found there.

After exploring the coast of Florida, he returned to Puerto Rico. Then, he traveled to Spain to tell the king of the beautiful land he discovered. Ferdinand granted him rights to colonize Florida, and he returned there in 1521. But his second trip was not as lucky as his first. His group was attacked by natives upon its arrival. Ponce de León was struck with an arrow, and the ships fled to nearby Cuba. It was there in 1521 that he died of his wounds.

Underline **two** details in the text that tell directly about Ponce de León's discovery of Florida.

Hint Find the text that describes what happened when Ponce de León first stepped on this new land. How did he get there? What did he think and do?

3 Hugo is taking notes on "Juan Ponce de León (c. 1460–1521)." He has made a chart to organize his notes. Write the letters of the notes from the box below in the correct locations to complete his chart.

Notes:
A. tried to explore and colonize Puerto Rico
B. honored with the King's permission to explore and colonize Puerto Rico
C. born 1460; second trip to New World in 1493
D. King Ferdinand gave permission to colonize Florida; natives attacked Ponce de León and his men on his second trip there

Headings	Early Years	Puerto Rico	Florida
Dates		in 1508 left Hispaniola for Puerto Rico; in 1511 had to leave Puerto Rico	in 1513, landed in Florida; in 1521 returned to Florida from Spain; died later that year
Places	born in Spain; sailed to the New World; fought and farmed in Hispaniola		couldn't find Bimini, but found Florida, instead; then returned to Puerto Rico and Spain; then came back to Florida; finally, fled to Cuba
People	sailed with Christopher Columbus; Ponce de León had a wife and children	King Ferdinand gave permission for Puerto Rico trip; Diego Columbus was already there	
Successes	earned land as a reward for soldiering skills; got married and had kids		discovered Florida; was honored with the King's permission to colonize it

Hint Use the bold headings in the left column and at the top of the chart to help you find the correct place for each answer choice.

4 Nicole is writing a report about Ponce de León's life. She wants to organize the information from "Juan Ponce de León (c. 1460–1521)" into three categories before she writes her report. Look at the categories, and then follow the directions below.

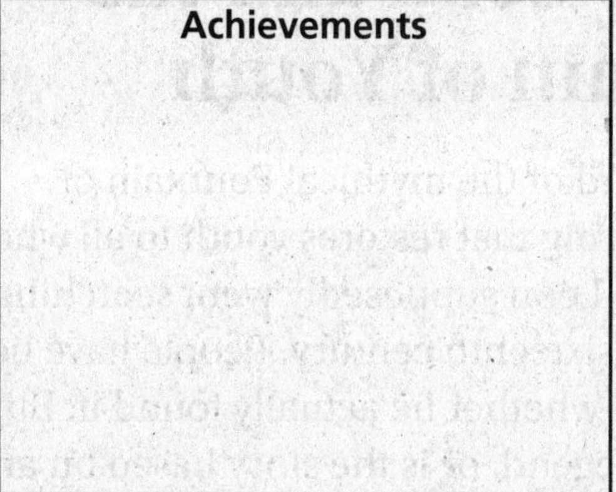

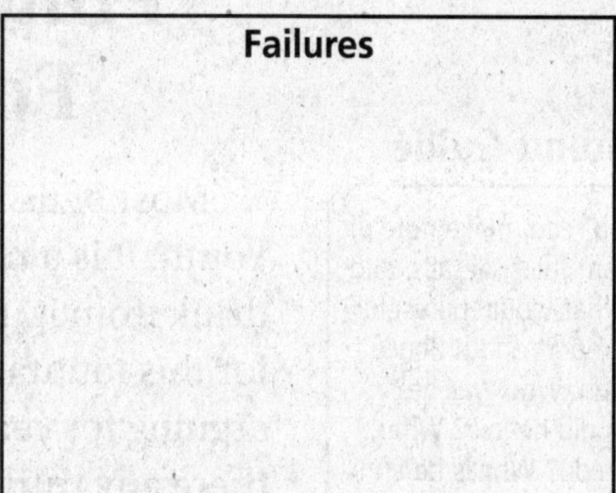

Fountain of Youth

Help Nicole sort the details from the text. Write each detail in the correct box above.

DETAILS

Named a new land "Florida"

Possibly was told of a magical place

Forced to leave Puerto Rico in 1511

Ships fled to Cuba

Helped colonize Puerto Rico

Hint Organize each detail based on the headings provided. Does the detail describe a situation in which Ponce de León succeeded or failed? Or does the information relate to the Fountain of Youth?

Use the Reading Guide to help you understand the passage.

Ponce de León and the Fountain of Youth

Reading Guide

As you read, make note of relevant facts, details, and data that would be useful for a report about Ponce de León. Who was he? When did he live? What did he do? Why is he an important explorer?

Most of us have heard of the mythical Fountain of Youth. It is a natural spring that restores youth to all who drink from it. Ponce de León supposedly went searching for this fountain in the sixteenth century. People have been arguing for years about whether he actually found it. But is there any truth to this legend, or is the story based on an entirely different event?

Ponce de León

Ponce de León lived during the Age of Discovery. This was a time when countries searched for new lands to claim as their own. Ponce de León was eager to become an explorer for Spain. He set out with Christopher Columbus on Columbus's second expedition to the New World. There, he proved himself first as a soldier in fighting the natives and second as a pioneer in settling the island of Hispaniola. Ponce de León then explored Puerto Rico. He began to colonize the island before he was pushed out by Diego Columbus, Christopher Columbus's son. As governor, Diego Columbus claimed rights to the island. A bitter power struggle resulted, and finally Ponce de León was forced to leave.

It was about this time that Ponce de León heard rumors from the natives about the island of Bimini, said to hold riches beyond his imagination. Spain allowed him to look for this island. But instead of finding Bimini, he discovered Florida. Ponce de León explored the coast of Florida for many months. He collected details about the natives and the land. Not once in his records or letters to the king of Spain did he refer to a fountain. Not once did he talk about seeking to be younger. How, then, did his name come to be connected with such a myth?

Reading Guide

What important information does the author provide regarding the Fountain of Youth?

How does the author support this information with historical facts? Think about why a writer might include information about Oviedo in a research report.

The Fountain of Youth

It is certainly possible that the *idea* of the Fountain of Youth existed during that era. The Age of Discovery was a time when people were finding new and exciting places. Anything seemed possible. Christopher Columbus claimed to have found the Garden of Eden. Explorers searched endlessly for El Dorado, the lost city of gold. The Fountain of Youth was just another legend in a list of many. The natives likely spoke of this fountain to Ponce de León. However, there is no evidence that he went in search of it.

Ponce de León focused on exploring and colonizing the land. His letters and other documents show that he was not interested in rumors of magical places. In fact, he spoke only of establishing settlements for Spain and learning more about Florida. There is no reason to think that he had any other purpose for exploring the land. Instead, it is more likely that he was the victim of a cruel joke.

History shows that Ponce de León's name did not become associated with the Fountain of Youth until years after he died. A Spanish court chronicler by the name of Oviedo greatly disliked him. Oviedo supported Diego Columbus. Oviedo was also angry about Ponce de León's actions in Puerto Rico. As a result, he described Ponce de León as someone who was easily fooled and simple-minded. Oviedo made up a story of how Ponce de León was tricked by natives who told him a silly tale about a magical fountain.

The story was likely viewed as a joke when it was first told. However, through the years it slowly became a part of history that was thought to be true. Still, it is not hard to see why so many of us would want to believe such a tall tale. Who wouldn't want to stay young forever?

Reading Guide

What idea is supported by the information about the tourist spot in St. Augustine? How do these details support the author's opinion about the Fountain of Youth?

Even today, people visit a fountain in a tourist spot in St. Augustine, Florida. They drink from the water there, though there is no proof that it can make them younger. There is no proof that Ponce de León even discovered it. But tourists come to drink anyway. Perhaps they hope that Ponce de León had found the fountain after all. Perhaps they come to learn more about the legend. One thing is for certain, though. The famous Spanish explorer at the center of this myth would likely be furious to know he was connected to such a ridiculous idea.

Answer the following questions.

1. Jamal is doing some research for a report about the tourist spot in St. Augustine, Florida. His teacher has asked him to include information from his own personal visit to the park.

   Which **two** pieces of information would be **most important** to include in Jamal's report?

   A. why the fountain at the park was thought to be magical

   B. what street the park was located on

   C. what historical information the park provided

   D. how many people went to visit the park with Jamal

   E. how much it cost to get into the park

2 You are writing a school report about the myth surrounding the Fountain of Youth. Read the paragraphs from the sources you have already reviewed. Then, read the directions that follow.

Juan Ponce de León (c. 1460–1521)

Around this time, natives had told Ponce de León about the "wealthy" island of Bimini (in the Bahamas). There were possibly also rumors of a magical Fountain of Youth on the island, though there is no official record to support this. King Ferdinand allowed Ponce de León to explore the area. But instead of finding Bimini, in 1513 he landed somewhere else. He thought he was on a large island. Ponce de León named it "Florida" for the many flowers that he found there.

Ponce de León and the Fountain of Youth

History shows that Ponce de León's name did not become associated with the Fountain of Youth until years after he died. A Spanish court chronicler by the name of Oviedo greatly disliked him. Oviedo supported Diego Columbus. Oviedo was also angry about Ponce de León's actions in Puerto Rico. As a result, he described Ponce de León as someone who was easily fooled and simple-minded. Oviedo made up a story of how Ponce de León was tricked by natives who told him a silly tale about a magical fountain.

Give **two** details, one from each source, that would support the idea that Ponce de León probably did not search for the Fountain of Youth.

Write your answer on the lines provided.

3 A student is writing a report on how the Age of Discovery affected how people thought and acted in the sixteenth century. She is taking notes on "Ponce de León and the Fountain of Youth." Read the text from the passage and then read the directions below.

> **Ponce de León lived during the Age of Discovery. This was a time when countries searched for new lands to claim as their own. Ponce de León was eager to become an explorer for Spain. He set out with Christopher Columbus on Columbus's second expedition to the New World. There, he proved himself first as a soldier in fighting the natives and second as a pioneer in settling the island of Hispaniola. Ponce de León then explored Puerto Rico. He began to colonize the island before he was pushed out by Diego Columbus, Christopher Columbus's son. As governor, Diego Columbus claimed rights to the island. A bitter power struggle resulted, and finally Ponce de León was forced to leave.**

Use details from the text above to write three important notes that would be helpful for the student's report. Write your answers on the lines provided.

Notes

1. ______________________________

2. ______________________________

3. ______________________________

4 The following question has two parts. First, answer Part A. Then, answer Part B.

Part A

Annika is starting a research report about native people who lived on the Florida coast in the 1500s. Which is the **best** way for Annika to begin working on her report?

A. by organizing her research notes into different categories

C. by writing a detailed outline based on her organized notes

B. by taking notes from library and online information related to the topic

D. by using the library and online search engines to locate information on the topic

Part B

Which source would **most likely** help Annika explore different ideas related to her topic?

A. an educational Web site about modern native cultures

B. a government Web site about laws relating to Native Americans

C. a nonfiction book about the discovery and history of Florida

D. a nonfiction book about discoveries in the sixteenth century

5 A student is creating a list of sources for a report about Ponce de León. Read the source titles and descriptions. Which **two** source titles have incorrect capitalization or punctuation?

A. *Juan Ponce de León: truth and fiction* (book)

B. "A Closer Look at the Legend of the Fountain of Youth" (newspaper article)

C. *Spanish Explorers In History* (Web site)

D. "The Discovery of Florida" (chapter of a book)

E. *History for Everyone* (magazine)

6 You have read two texts about Ponce de León. Both give information about his life and achievements. They also discuss the myth of the Fountain of Youth. The two texts are:

- a Web page titled "Juan Ponce de León (c. 1460–1521)"
- a newspaper article titled "Ponce de León and the Fountain of Youth"

Think about the historical information the texts provide. Write a report that describes the kind of person Ponce de León was, what motivated him to explore new lands, and why people should remember him as a great explorer. Remember to use facts and details from both texts to support your ideas.

Plan your report in the space below. Write your report on the following pages.

Write your report on the lines below.

LESSON 15

Write an Informative or Explanatory Text

1 GETTING THE IDEA

Informative or **explanatory text** tells readers about a topic. It provides them with information or explains something.

In school, you may write informative and explanatory texts for different reasons. For example, you may write a short how-to guide with steps for building a model for science class. Or, you may write a longer informative or explanatory text about a recent event in the news. Your writing should always fit your task, or what you have been asked to do.

State the Topic

To begin writing an informative or explanatory text, state the topic of your essay in a **topic sentence**. A topic sentence explains the main idea of your text. It should be written clearly so it is easy for readers to understand. Readers should immediately be able to tell what your text is about.

Here is an example of well-written topic sentence.

> Many kinds of animals live in the Bay of Fundy.

Develop the Topic

As you continue writing, include facts and details to develop your topic. Your facts and details should be relevant, which means they relate to the topic.

When you use facts and details from sources, you should rewrite the information in your own words. However, sometimes you may want to include a quote from a source. Quotations give the exact words someone else said or wrote. Use quotation marks, and state the name of the source from which you took the quote.

Look at the three facts below. Which one best relates to the sample topic sentence?

- Tourists come from around the world to visit this popular bay.
- The Bay of Fundy is a great place to go swimming or surfing.
- More than a dozen types of whales live in those waters.

Plan Your Informative Text

Once you have written your topic sentence, it's time to start planning the text. Your article, essay, or report should include an introduction, body paragraphs, and a conclusion.

Group related ideas together. Then, place the grouped ideas in an order that makes sense. This will help readers follow the ideas and better understand what you write. A graphic organizer, such as a flowchart, can help you plan.

Use Linking Words

As you organize your ideas, be sure to include **linking words and phrases**. They help readers understand how ideas connect to one another. Some examples of linking words and phrases are *another*, *for example*, *as a result*, *however*, *also*, and *because*.

Use Precise Language

Because your purpose is to inform, readers might not be familiar with your topic. So, be sure to use clear, **precise language**. Using precise language means including nouns, verbs, and adjectives that explain exactly what you mean. This will present your facts in a way that your readers can picture in their minds.

You might also include **domain-specific words** that your readers might not know. If you do, it can be helpful to include definitions in the text. Definitions are another way to provide information and help your readers learn something new.

Provide a Conclusion

Informative or explanatory text should end with a **conclusion**. A conclusion sums up the text. It also leaves readers with a final thought about the topic. For a single paragraph or a short essay, you usually will need to include only a concluding statement. For a longer essay, include a concluding paragraph or section.

> The Bay of Fundy is home to all sorts of wildlife—in the water, in the air, and on land.

Review Your Work

After you have finished, reread your writing. Make sure it is clear and easy to follow. Use this checklist as a guide to make changes.

- ☐ Is my topic sentence clear?
- ☐ Do all the facts and details relate to my topic?
- ☐ Do I use linking words and phrases to connect ideas?
- ☐ Do I include precise language?
- ☐ Does my conclusion sum up the topic?
- ☐ Is my writing free of grammar and spelling errors?

Language Spotlight • Complete Sentences

As you write, pay attention to the structure of your sentences. A **complete sentence** has a subject and a verb. It forms a complete thought. A **sentence fragment** is missing a subject or a verb. It is an incomplete thought. A **run-on sentence** combines one or more sentences without connecting them properly.

Read each group of words below. Write *complete, fragment,* or *run-on* to describe each one.

Stopped by her apartment.

Yesterday, Miguel visited his grandmother.

Miguel helped with chores he went grocery shopping, too.

Read the passage.

How Tides Happen

At dawn, waves from an ocean rush onto a beach. It is high tide,[1] so the water rolls up several feet onto the sand. By noon, waves continue to wash onto the beach. But now it is low tide,[2] so the water comes in only a few inches. These shifts are not caused by changes in the water. It is the position of the sun and the moon that makes the tides change.

Tides shift because of gravity, which is a force that pulls objects toward each other. Earth's gravity pulls objects down to the ground. It keeps people, cars, houses, and anything else on the planet from floating out into space.

The sun's gravity pulls on Earth and keeps it moving in an orbit, or path, around the sun. The moon has a gravitational pull,[3] too. As Earth rotates, the moon's gravity pulls on the planet. This force isn't strong enough to affect the land much, but it is strong enough to affect the seas. That's because water is more flexible[4] than land. As the moon's gravity pulls on Earth, it affects the water on Earth and the tides shift.

When the moon is directly above an area, the water in that area is facing the moon. The moon's gravitational pull causes that water to bulge[5] and this creates high tide. At the same time, the area on the opposite side of Earth also experiences a high tide. Other areas of Earth, which are not directly facing the moon or directly on the opposite side of Earth at that time, experience low tide.

Each day, there are about two high tides. That's because Earth and the moon rotate. As they spin, the tides change. As a result, a high tide happens about every twelve hours and twenty-five minutes. It happens once when the moon is directly above an area and again when it is on the opposite side of the planet.

[1] **high tide**: the time when the sea level rises

[2] **low tide**: the time when the sea level falls

[3] **gravitational pull**: the pull caused by gravity

[4] **flexible**: able to changc

[5] **bulge**: swell

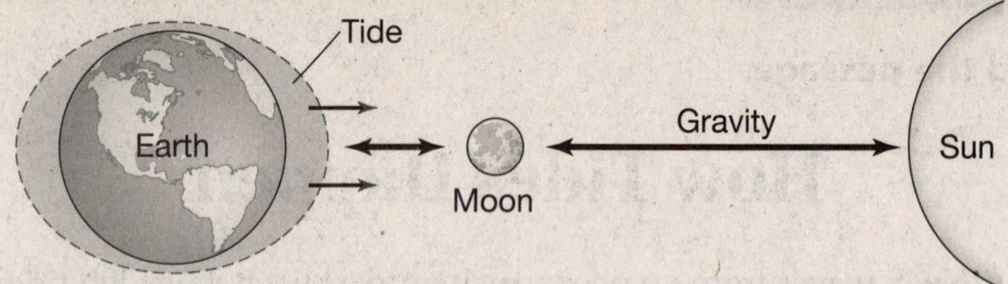

The sun plays an important part, too. It affects how strong or weak the tides are. When the sun and the moon form a direct line with Earth, their gravitational pulls combine. As a result, the tides are stronger. When the sun and the moon form a right angle with Earth, the two forces block each other and the tides are weaker.

Each day, the tide continues to shift from high to low and back again. These changes could not happen without the strong pull of gravity. As Earth moves in relation to the sun and moon, the tides shift here on Earth.

Answer the following questions.

1 This question has two parts. First, answer Part A. Then, answer Part B.

Part A

Which sentence from the passage **best** represents the passage's main topic?

A. At dawn, waves from an ocean rush onto a beach.

B. It is the position of the sun and the moon that makes the tides change.

C. The moon's gravitational pull causes that water to bulge and this creates high tide.

D. As a result, a high tide happens about every twelve hours and twenty-five minutes.

Part B

Which phrase **best** describes the passage's topic?

A. how gravity pulls on Earth

B. how and why tides happen

C. how the moon and sun affect tides

D. why the moon, sun, and Earth have gravity

Hint In Part A you identify a topic sentence. Remember that a topic sentence gives the main idea of the text. For Part B, think about a shorter way to sum up the passage's main topic.

2 You are writing a short informational text about high tides. What details would you include to explain the concept?

____

____

____

____

____

____

____

____

Hint Think about how the author tells about high tides. Include any important facts in your answer.

3 A student is writing a report about how gravity affects high tides. Which of the following facts would be the **most** relevant for him or her to include in the report?

A. When you throw an object into the air, gravity pulls the object back down to the ground.

B. A person's weight relates to the amount of gravity that pulls on his or her body.

C. The moon's gravity has the same amount of pull on Earth's water no matter what phase the moon is in.

D. In space, astronauts are able to float around inside the space station because of microgravity.

Hint Remember that relevant facts directly relate to the topic of a report. The facts and details about gravity should specifically discuss gravity in relation to tides.

4 Read the first two paragraphs of the passage. Then, answer the question that follows.

> **At dawn, waves from an ocean rush onto a beach. It is high tide, so the water rolls up several feet onto the sand. By noon, waves continue to wash onto the beach. But now it is low tide, so the water comes in only a few inches. These shifts are not caused by changes in the water. It is the position of the sun and the moon that makes the tides change.**
>
> **Tides shift because of gravity, which is a force that pulls objects toward each other. Earth's gravity pulls objects down to the ground. It keeps people, cars, houses, and anything else on the planet from floating out into space.**

Which group contains linking words and phrases from the passage?

A. waves, feet, inches, shifts, changes, objects, people, cars, houses

B. dawn, ocean, beach, high tide, water, sand, low tide, gravity, force

C. rush, rolls, continue to wash, comes, makes, shift, pulls, keeps

D. At dawn, so, By noon, But now, caused by, because of, which

Hint Look for places in the passage where the author shows a relationship between two ideas. For example, in this passage, the author used transition words and phrases to give more information about a concept and to show cause and effect.

Use the Reading Guide to help you understand the passage.

Tracking Tides

Reading Guide

Underline the topic sentence in the passage.

Why do scientists keep track of tides?

The author includes details about how tides can affect people. How do these details help you better understand the topic of high and low tides?

High and low tides can have a big impact. So, scientists at research centers keep track of tides and how they change. They use this information to make predictions about tides. Tracking tides and making predictions can help people prepare for changing tides or use the energy they provide.

The Effects of Tides

Tides affect people in many ways. For instance, they affect boats and ships as they sail to shore. If a captain does not know enough about the tides in an area, it can cause a major accident. Fishermen also use information about tides to get bigger catches. That's because some kinds of fish gather during high tides, while others gather during low tides.

Tides can affect people in other ways, too. Workers who construct boardwalks and other things in coastal areas need to know about tides. They need to know when the water will be coming in and going out as they build. During a big storm like a hurricane, it helps to know how the tides will affect cleanup or repair jobs. People who like to surf also try to find out about tides. Knowing when tides are high or low, or weak or strong, can help surfers find the best waves.

Tide Tables

Because tides can have such a big impact, it is important to keep track of them. So, scientists around the world measure the tides. They record information about them on tide tables and use these tables to make predictions. The scientists try to figure out when high and low tides will happen. They also try to figure out how high a tide will be.

Reading Guide

Look for linking words and phrases that connect ideas. How do the linking words and phrases help you understand the relationship between ideas?

What kind of language does the author use?

What final thought does the writer leave for readers?

Different kinds of information can help scientists predict the tides. They consider the past measurements of tides in an area. They also make note of Earth's position in relation to the sun and the moon. They do this because the gravitational pull of the moon creates tides, while the sun and moon together affect the strength of tides. So, knowing where the Earth is in relation to the sun and moon can help predict how the tides will change.

Tidal Energy

Scientists also keep track of tides to find ways to use them. High tides have a lot of power, and people can use this power to create electricity. Known as tidal energy, this type of electricity is made using underwater machines called turbines. The turbines are placed in areas that have very high tides. The flowing water moves the machines, which produce electricity as a result. Tidal power is an alternative form of energy that is renewable; it will never run out like coal or oil will in the future.

People hope to one day produce tidal energy at a place called the Bay of Fundy. A bay is a coastal area that has a small area of water set off from a larger area. The Bay of Fundy is located in the northern part of Maine, and it stretches into Canada. It is a good place to produce tidal energy because the world's highest tides happen there. They often reach as high as fifty feet!

Keeping track of tides helps people in many different ways. It helps fishermen find big catches and surfers find big waves. It helps captains sail their boats safely in to shore. It also helps people produce electricity from the power of tides. So, it's no wonder that scientists around the planet keep an eye on the tides as they come in and go out. Think about that if you are ever on a beach as the tide rolls in.

Answer the following questions.

1. Read these three facts or details that could be added to the passage.

   Circle the sentence that **best** relates to the topic.

Facts and Details
Oil is a nonrenewable resource, which means it will run out one day.
Surfing is a popular sport in many parts of the world, such as Australia.
The Bay of Fundy could produce enough energy to power 100,000 homes.

2. A student is writing an informational text about ocean tides. He wants to connect a sentence about how scientists create tide tables to a sentence about what they can use the information for. Which linking phrase is the **best** to use to connect the two sentences?

   A. of course

   B. for example

   C. in conclusion

   D. on the other hand

3. A student is writing an essay about ocean tides and has included the following text. Which one is a run-on sentence?

   A. The position of Earth in relation to the sun affects the strength of tides.

   B. The power of tides can be used to create electrical energy.

   C. The moon's gravity pulls on the oceans this creates high tides.

   D. Scientists around the world use tide tables to make predictions about tides.

4 Read these four sentences that could be included in the passage. Which one is the **best** example of clear, precise language?

A. Every day, water from the sea comes in and goes out.

B. The tides can do things that make a difference to people.

C. People think about and pay attention to the tides in many places.

D. The gravitational pull of the moon has an effect on Earth's oceans.

5 The following question has two parts. First, answer Part A. Then, answer Part B.

Part A

How does the passage end?

A. with a topic sentence

B. with a supporting fact

C. with a new, related question

D. with a concluding paragraph

Part B

Which phrase **best** explains how the ending helps readers?

A. by summarizing the passage

B. by entertaining readers with a joke

C. by introducing one last interesting detail

D. by adding one more reason to learn about tides

6 Imagine you are a scientist at a research center that tracks tides. Write a report about the kind of work you do. Tell readers about the impact of tides and how tracking them can help people. Use facts from "How Tides Happen" and "Tracking Tides" to support your ideas.

You may plan your report in the space below. Write your report on the following pages.

Plan

Write your report on the lines below.

LESSON 16

Write a Functional Text

1 GETTING THE IDEA

A text that gives you information that helps you **function**, or do things, in your daily life is a **functional text**. Some people call it real-life text. You see it every day in your home, school, and neighborhood. For example:

- Your mom says you can make chocolate milk. The label on the cocoa powder box tells you how much powder to stir into a glass of milk.
- You get a postcard about a toy-store sale. It lists the store's address, the dates when the sale starts and ends, and how much money you can save.
- You see a poster about a play at a high school. The play is based on a book you love! You check to see when the performances are, and how much the tickets cost.
- You go to a swim club for the first time, so you read the safety rules listed on a sign. You learn that running is not allowed in the pool area.

Read the chart below. (A chart is one kind of functional text.) How many of the examples have you seen or used in the last week?

Examples of Functional Texts			
advertisement	directions	letter	rules
appointment reminder	e-mail	list	schedule
blog	flyer	menu	street sign
calendar	food label	note	telephone directory
chart	form	poster	text message
clothing label	instructions	price tag	timeline
diagram	invitation	recipe	Web site

Format and Writing Style

Each kind of functional text has its own format. A **format** is the way information is arranged. For example, a school report card, a recipe, and a party invitation all have different formats.

To make text easier to understand, writers use **text features**. These include **headings** and numbered or **bulleted lists**. (This is a bullet: •.) Writers use headings to help readers understand how the information is organized and what they can expect to learn in sections of the text. Writers also use **bold** or ***italic* type** to help readers notice important words.

Good writers of functional text use a simple, clear writing style. The **writing style** will change depending on the writer's purpose and audience. Sometimes a writer uses **informal language**. When a writer's style is informal, it may sound as though the writer were speaking to the reader. For example, calling a reader "you" in a note to a friend can be informal. It sounds friendly and conversational. Using **contractions**, such as *isn't* and *can't*, is informal, too.

A **formal letter** is one kind of functional text. You might write a formal letter to tell the head of a company how much you love one of their products. Or you might write to complain about a product that does not work. When you write a formal letter, you use **formal language**. You do not use slang or contractions in a formal letter. The envelope in which you mail the letter has its own format, as shown below.

Pablo Ramirez
214 Solano Ave.
Flagstaff, AZ 86001

Prunella Potter, Owner
Toy-Go-Round
2145 Basil Lane
Albany, CA 94706

Who sent this letter? How do you know? Underline the name of the sender. Where is the recipient's address listed? Circle the recipient's address.

Be Concise

When readers read functional texts, they need to quickly understand the main ideas. It is important that functional text writers be concise. **Concise** writing is short and simple. It gets right to the point.

Examples:

- Alarm clock directions: **To stop the buzzer, push the red button.**
- Note: I went to the store. **I'll be back by 4 p.m. - Sam**
- Recipe direction: **Add two tablespoons of cocoa powder.**

It is important for readers of functional texts to get the main idea quickly. As you write a functional text, think to yourself: What facts do your readers need to know? How can you organize the information so that your readers can understand it right away? How can you use text features to draw reader's' attention to important information? Also, think about how much space you have. For example, a party invitation usually needs to fit on a small card:

You're invited to Pablo's tenth birthday party!

When: Saturday, April 9 from 1 to 5 p.m.

Where: Our house at 214 Solano Avenue

Lunch will be served. Parents are welcome!

Please phone or e-mail to tell us if you can come.

Phone number: 510-555-8534

E-mail address: robynramirez@quickmail.com

Does this invitation give party guests all the information they need? What does the invitation ask guests to do? Why doesn't the invitation tell the city, state, and zipcode?

An **e-mail** is another kind of functional text. Most e-mails are informal. Writers use friendly, conversational language to write them. The **subject line** on an e-mail is like a title. It should tell the reader what the e-mail is about. The **body** of the e-mail should be concise, giving only important information about the subject.

Read the following e-mail. What is the writer's reason for writing? Underline the words and phrases that support your answer.

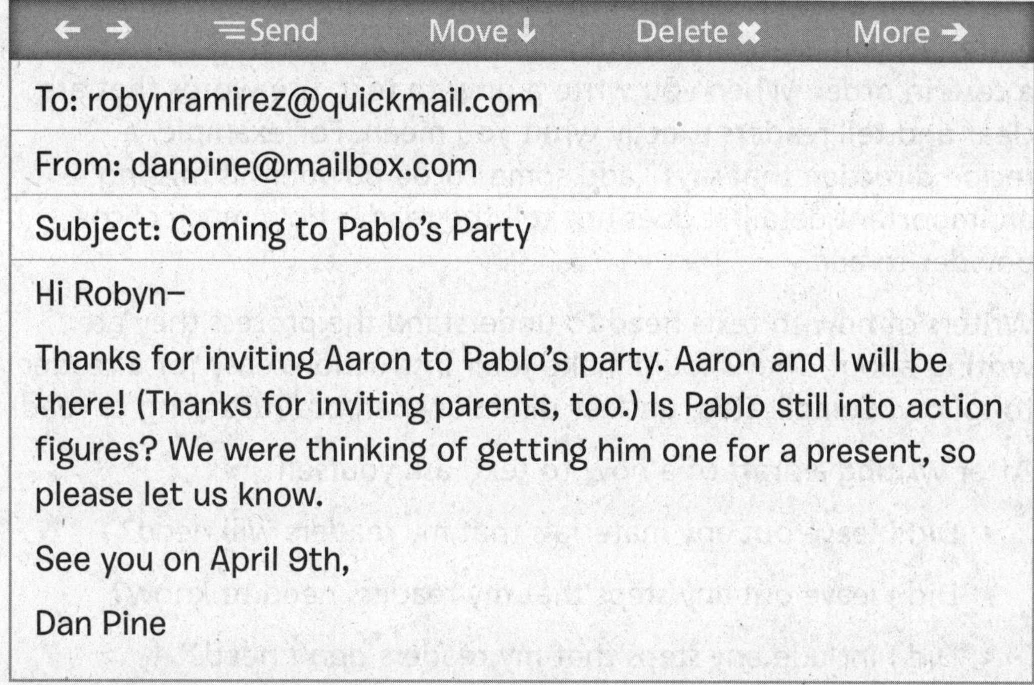

← → ≡Send Move ↓ Delete ✖ More →

To: robynramirez@quickmail.com

From: danpine@mailbox.com

Subject: Coming to Pablo's Party

Hi Robyn–

Thanks for inviting Aaron to Pablo's party. Aaron and I will be there! (Thanks for inviting parents, too.) Is Pablo still into action figures? We were thinking of getting him one for a present, so please let us know.

See you on April 9th,

Dan Pine

Be Precise

Instructions are step-by-step directions that tell you precisely what to do. To be **precise** means to be exact, and to include important details. Instructions may be short, like a clothing tag that reads: *Hand wash. Dry flat.* Or they may be long, like a 10-page **manual** that tells you how to use a computer art program.

A **form** is a **document** you fill in to provide certain facts. For example, you might fill in a form to get a library card. Most forms tell you exactly *what* to *write*, *where* to write, and maybe even what color pen to use.

Please print clearly in blue or black ink to complete each line below.

Last Name First Name

Street Address

City State Zip Code

A **how-to text** is another kind of functional text. It tells how to do something or make something. A **recipe** is a how-to text that gives the reader a set of cooking instructions. It includes: (1) a list of materials you need; and (2) directions that appear step-by-step, in a certain order. When you write a how-to text, use words that are clear and tell readers exactly what you mean. For example, a recipe direction that says "add some cocoa powder" is missing an important detail. It does not tell the reader how much cocoa powder to add.

Writers of how-to texts need to understand the process they are writing about. They should make their instructions easy for a reader to follow. Complicated, unclear directions can be frustrating to read.

After writing a draft of a how-to text, ask yourself:

- Did I leave out any materials that my readers will need?
- Did I leave out any steps that my readers need to know?
- Did I include any steps that my readers *don't* need?
- Did I put the steps in an order that makes sense?

Language Spotlight • Capitalization and Spelling

Functional text is writing you share with at least one other person—and maybe a lot of people. Incorrect capitalization and spelling can make it seem like the writer was careless or did not want to take the time to check his or her work.

Read this e-mail. How many capitalization and spelling errors can you find?

> Dear teammates: Let's celebrite our soccer championship! My parents are throwing a pizza party for our team and our coach. We'll have games and prizes! Its this comming saturday. Hope you can come! We live at 830 race street. The party is at 2:30.
> Love, Jordan

Read the recipe.

How to Make Pancakes That Spell Your Name

Find a partner who has made pancakes before. He or she should be an adult or an older teenager who has permission to cook in your family's kitchen. **IMPORTANT:** Your partner should do—or help you do—all the steps that involve cooking on a stovetop.

You and your partner will need:

- paper and a pencil
- a mirror
- a frying pan
- cooking oil
- pancake batter
- a spatula
- a plastic squeeze bottle with a pointed tip
- a two-cup measuring cup with a spout
- butter
- syrup

Directions:

1. Write your name in all capital letters. Hold your paper up to a mirror. This will show you how each letter looks when it is backwards. For example, if your name is PABLO, you will notice that the A and the O in your name look the same backwards and forwards. Capital letters H, I, M, T, U, V, W, X, and Y are symmetrical, too.

OJBAꟼ

2. Pour a small amount of cooking oil into your pan, and heat it over a low flame. The pan is hot enough when the oil starts to make tiny crackling sounds. Put some batter in your squeeze bottle. Use it to carefully "write" each backwards letter with batter. Make sure your letters have lots of space between them. You should be able to fit about three or four letters in your pan at once.

3. Wait about a minute until tiny bubbles form and pop in your letters. The top of the batter should look drier than it looked at first. Do *NOT* flip the letters over. Next, pour $\frac{1}{4}$ to $\frac{1}{2}$ cup of batter over each backwards letter. Completely cover the letter, forming a small, round pancake. Each pancake should be no bigger than the palm of your hand (not counting the fingers). Wait about two minutes for your pancakes to cook on one side. Flip them and cook them on the other side. Arrange them on a plate so that the letters spell your name.
4. Eat your name with butter and syrup!

Answer the following questions.

1 This question has two parts. First, answer Part A. Then, answer Part B.

Part A

For whom did the writer write this recipe?

A. for adults only

B. for older teenagers aged 16 to 19

C. for kids who aren't old enough to cook by themselves

D. for toddlers who aren't old enough to help their parents cook

Part B

Which sentence from the recipe **best** supports your answer to Part A?

A. Your partner should do—or help you do—all the steps that involve cooking on a stovetop.

B. Capital letters H, I, M, T, U, V, W, X, and Y are symmetrical, too.

C. You should be able to fit about three or four letters in your pan at once.

D. Each pancake should be no bigger than the palm of your hand (not counting the fingers).

Hint This question asks you to do two things. Part A asks you to identify the writer's main audience—the people who will read and use the recipe. Think about the writer's use of the word *you*. Who is "*you*"?

2 Which statement about the recipe's step-by-step directions is **true**?

A. After partners cook their letters on one side, they should flip them over and cook them on the other side.

B. After putting butter and syrup on their pancakes, partners should heat them up in a frying pan.

C. Readers need to fill their squeeze bottle with batter before they hold their paper up to a mirror.

D. Readers need to know how to write their letters backwards before they begin to cook them.

Hint Reread the directions. Which statement makes sense and matches information you read in the directions?

3 The recipe writer sometimes uses all capital letters in the recipe. What is the writer's main reason for doing this?

A. to make readers feel excited about making pancakes

B. to show that those words are parts of headings

C. to call readers' attention to information that is very important

D. to direct readers to read those words very loudly

Hint Think about what you have learned about writers' reasons for using **bold** and *italic* type. Writers may use all capital letters for the same reasons.

4 Write your own recipe or step-by-step instructions for a craft project. Be sure to write about something you already know how to do very well.

Hint In your recipe or how-to text about a craft project, be sure to list materials first. Then list step-by-step instructions. Put them in an order that will make sense for your readers.

Use the Reading Guide to help you understand this letter.

Reading Guide

Who wrote this letter? How do you know? Why did he or she write it?

If you were a student at this school, which job would you pick? Why?

March 5, 2016

Dear Students and Family Members:

As you may know, Warner Avenue School's annual Springy Flingy Fair is coming up on Saturday, April 30th from 1 to 5 p.m. This year we hope to host the springiest flingiest fair *ever*! We also hope to raise *many* dollars for our drama department! To do so, we will need your help. Below you will find a list of committees that need help. Please sign up for at least one job or donate at least one item. E-mail the contact person to let her or him know what job you want and/or what you can donate. Thank you SO much!

Drinks Committee	**Contact:** Robyn Ramirez at robynramirez@quickmail.com
Jobs to Fill—we need: **1.** two strong drivers with big cars to pick up canned drinks and ice from Savings Barn and drive them to school on the morning of the fair **2.** four volunteers to set up the booth and sell drinks at the fair (from noon to 5 p.m.) **3.** two cleanup people to recycle cups, cans, and napkins, wipe down tables, empty ice chests, store leftover drinks, and break down the booth (from 4 to 6 p.m.) **Items we need:** donated recyclable paper cups and napkins; borrowed ice chests	

Reading Guide

Why did the letter writer create a separate chart for each committee?

How does the writer list the different jobs that need to be filled?

Pizza Committee	Contact: Lani Asher at laniasher@maildrop.com

Jobs to Fill—we need:

1. one smart person to help Lani figure out how many extra-large pizzas to buy, and what toppings to choose. (We have a HUGE discount from Place-o-Pizza! And they deliver!)
2. six volunteers to set up the booths and sell pizza slices and salad (from noon to 5 p.m.)
3. four cleanup helpers to recycle pizza boxes, plates, and napkins; compost leftover food; wipe down tables; pack up and distribute uneaten pizza; and break down the booths (from 4 to 6 p.m.)

Items we need donated: recyclable paper plates and napkins; recyclable forks; kid-friendly salads with large serving spoons (Please list the ingredients in your salad and label your bowl and spoon with your name so we can return them to you.)

Desserts Committee	Contact: David Ginsburg at djginsburg@quickmail.com

Jobs to Fill—we need:

1. four volunteers to set up the booth and sell desserts (from noon to 5 p.m.)
2. four cleanup people to recycle plates, bowls, napkins, and utensils; compost leftover food; wipe down tables; wrap and distribute leftover desserts; and break down the booth (from 4 to 6 p.m.)

Items we need: desserts such as cookies, cupcakes, individual slices of cake or pie on paper plates covered with cellophane, and individual servings of gelatin or pudding in paper bowls covered with cellophane; recyclable paper dessert plates, bowls, and napkins; recyclable forks and spoons; storage containers with lids; boxes of cellophane and tin foil

Reading Guide

How many committees are there? What are the other committees for?

Compare a food-related committee chart to a non-food one. How are they alike and different?

Face Painting Committee	**Contact:** Dan Pine at danpine@mailbox.com
Jobs to Fill—we need: **1.** eight talented face painters (hopefully with experience—if you are not experienced, you need to be very talented) to set up the booth and paint kids' faces with cute designs (from 12:30 to 5 p.m.) **2.** two cleanup volunteers to pack up the supplies, wipe down the tables, and break down the booth (from 5 to 6 p.m.) **Items we need donated:** borrowed books on face painting, nontoxic face paint, brushes, recyclable paper cups, clean cloth rags	

Decorating Committee	**Contact:** Veronique Vienne at vvienne@fancymail.com
Jobs to Fill—we need: **1.** six talented folks to help V. V. plan, purchase, and set up the decorations (We will have one planning meeting and one shopping trip before the fair. Decorators will also work from 10 a.m. to 1 p.m. on fair day.) **2.** two cleanup volunteers to take down the decorations (from 5 to 6 p.m.) **Items we need donated:** pushpins, a ball of string, sticky tape, borrowed pairs of scissors	

Racing Committee	**Contact:** our P.E. teacher Gary Green at 555-1718
Jobs to Fill—we need: six helpers to help Gary plan and conduct races, and organize and store equipment (There will be one planning meeting at school. Helpers will also work at the fair from 1 to 5:30 p.m.) **Items we need donated:** two dozen hard-boiled eggs and 24 borrowed metal soup spoons	

Warmly,

Wendy Woodnancy, Principal

Answer the following questions.

1 This question has two parts. First, answer Part A. Then, answer Part B.

Part A

What are the writer's **main** reasons for writing this letter? Choose **two** correct answers.

A. to complain that not enough people have volunteered to work at the fair

B. to help people remember the day, date, and time when the fair is scheduled

C. to introduce parents to teachers such as Robyn Ramirez and Gary Green

D. to boast that this year's event will be the best Springy Flingy Fair ever

E. to make sure that enough people will sign up to do jobs or donate items

Part B

Which two parts of the letter **best** support your answers to Part A?

A. March 5, 2016

B. As you may know, Warner Avenue School's annual Springy Flingy Fair is coming up on Saturday, April 30th from 1 to 5 p.m.

C. Please sign up for at least one job or donate at least one item.

D. two cleanup people to recycle cups, cans, and napkins, wipe down tables, empty ice chests, store leftover drinks, and break down the booth (from 4 to 6 p.m.)

E. (We have a HUGE discount from Place-o-Pizza! And they deliver!)

2 The chart below shows how the letter is organized. Complete the chart by writing the name of each part next to the correct example. Your choices appear above the chart.

names of committees	jobs to fill	contact people	items needed

closing and signature	introductory paragraph	greeting

Letter Part	Example
	Dear Students and Family Members:
	As you may know, Warner Avenue School's annual Springy Flingy Fair is coming up on Saturday, April 30th from 1 to 5 p.m. This year we hope to host the springiest flingiest fair ever!
	Face Painting Committee
	Veronique Vienne at vvienne@fancymail.com
	two strong drivers with big cars to pick up canned drinks and ice from Savings Barn and drive them to school on the morning of the fair
	two dozen hard-boiled eggs and 24 borrowed metal soup spoons
	Warmly, Wendy Woodnancy, Principal

3 This question has two parts. First, answer Part A. Then, answer Part B.

Part A

Where in the letter does the writer use headings?

A. in the greeting

B. in the introductory paragraph

C. in the charts

D. in the closing

Part B

Which text feature does the letter writer use to help readers find headings?

A. **bold text**

B. *italic text*

C. ALL CAPITAL LETTERS

D. underlined text

4 Which sentence below has **one** spelling error and **one** capitalization error?

A. Dear Robyn Ramirez: Are you in charge of the Drinks Committee?

B. I heard that Veronique vienne is in charge of the decarations.

C. I've met Gary green, the physical education teacher at Warner.

D. Wendy Woodnancy, the shool principle, has an interesting last name.

5 The letter writer wants to add the following sentence to the letter.

There are also sign-up sheets for jobs and donations posted in the main office.

Where is the **best** place to add this detail?

A. between the date and the greeting

B. after the greeting and before the introductory paragraph

C. after the sentence that ends with "what you can donate."

D. between the Drinks Committee chart and the Pizza Committee chart

6 Imagine an event you would like to host at home or at school. Write an informal e-mail to family and friends asking for help with the tasks needed to make your event a success. As you write, remember to:

- be concise and precise.
- avoid including unnecessary details.
- make sure your readers can understand the information that you do provide.
- encourage family members and friends to attend even if they are unable to help.
- provide details that will make the event you are planning sound like a lot of fun.

Plan your writing in the space below. Write your response on the following pages.

Plan

Write your response on the lines below.

LESSON 17

Write an Opinion

1 GETTING THE IDEA

Mia says, "I think all schools should provide a tablet for each student to use in school." This is Mia's opinion. An **opinion** tells what someone thinks or believes. It is not a fact. Mia decides to write a letter to the editor of the school newspaper. She will write an opinion piece to persuade students to agree with her opinion.

A well-written **opinion piece** has three main parts. The **introduction**, or beginning, clearly states the opinion. The middle provides reasons for the opinion and facts to support those reasons. The **conclusion**, or end, restates the opinion and the most important points.

Organize Your Information

You can use an outline to organize and plan what information will go into each part of your opinion piece. Which parts of the outline show the beginning, middle, and end?

I. Each student should have a tablet to use in school to boost achievement.
II. There are three main reasons.
  A. Students should have the same opportunities.
    1. Some students might not have a tablet at home.
    2. All students should be able to access the Internet.
  B. Students can learn more.
    1. Students can find current information on the Internet.
    2. Students can find details that may not be in textbooks.
  C. Tablets cost a lot, but so do computers.
    1. Tablets are less expensive than computers.
    2. Tablets are easier to share than computers.
III. If we want all students to have a better and an equal education, providing tablets for them is a great start!

Write Your Opinion Piece

Once you have an outline, use it to guide your writing. The tips that follow explain how to develop each part of your opinion piece to make it as convincing as possible. Remember, your goal is to persuade readers to agree with your opinion.

State Your Opinion The opening sentence of your opinion piece should be a strong position statement. You want your readers to know exactly what you think right from the beginning. For example:

> *Strong Position Statement:* Each student should have a tablet to use in school so that all have the same opportunities to learn.
>
> *Weak Position Statement:* It is probably a good idea for students to have tablets in school.

Provide Reasons The middle part of an opinion piece should include the reasons and facts that support your opinion. When writing your reasons, be sure to do the following:

- Give reasons that support your opinion. Include at least two facts or examples that show why your reasons make sense.
- Explain one or more arguments that differ from your opinion, but then show why readers should agree with your opinion instead.
- Eliminate any reasons that are not related to your opinion. For example, if you want people to agree that all students should have a tablet, do not write about why computers are important.

Use Transitions **Transitions**, or linking words and phrases, connect opinions and reasons. Transitions help readers better understand and follow your ideas. Some transition words and phrases include *because*, *since*, *therefore*, *in addition*, *for instance*, and *in order to*.

Use Appropriate Language As you write, keep your audience in mind. Mia's opinion piece is for other students to read, so she could use informal language. If she were writing to the principal, however, she would use formal language.

- *Informal:* It's time kids got their own tablets for school.
- *Formal:* I would like to suggest that our school provide the entire student body with individual tablets.

Provide a Strong Conclusion Your conclusion should summarize your main points. Be sure to use strong and effective words that fit your audience.

Revise and Edit

Before others read your writing, check that the organization is clear and the reasons are all related to your opinion. Also, check for any spelling and grammar mistakes. Use the following checklist to write your final opinion piece:

- ☐ Do I begin with a clear topic and strong opinion?
- ☐ Do I provide enough reasons and facts to convince readers?
- ☐ Do I have a beginning, middle, and end?
- ☐ Do I use linking words to make ideas easy to follow?
- ☐ Do I use effective words appropriate for my audience?
- ☐ Are my grammar and spelling correct?

Language Spotlight • Relative Pronouns and Adverbs

Relative pronouns introduce clauses that tell more about nouns. Some relative pronouns are *who*, *whom*, *that*, and *which*. **Relative adverbs** also help describe nouns. But these adverbs give specific information about place, time, and reason. The relative adverbs are *when*, *where*, and *why*. Identify the relative pronoun and the relative adverb in these sentences. What nouns do they describe?

Jean bought a new tablet that is easy to use.

Put the package on the shelf where we keep the mail.

Read the passage.

Pets and School Go Together

Many schools allow children to bring pets for show-and-tell. Some classrooms even have their own pets. Why do schools allow this? The answer is simple. Having pets in the classroom is good for students of all ages. Therefore, I think all schools should allow pets.

First of all, students who cannot have a pet at home learn to be comfortable with pets in a classroom. If children are never around animals, they will be afraid of them. By caring for the school pets, they become familiar with animal behavior. They learn how to handle animals safely. This is only one advantage of having pets in school.

Another advantage is learning responsibility. Children share jobs with their classmates. For instance, they can feed the animal and clean its habitat. Also, important life skills such as taking turns, keeping to schedules, and doing assigned tasks are the result of caring for school pets.

In addition, pets in school can provide opportunities for studying other subjects. For example, school pets help students learn math. They can use math to find out how much it costs to feed the pet each week, month, or year. Also, students can make weekly or monthly schedules for animal care.

Learning skills needed to care for pets is not the only advantage of having pets in schools. There are mental advantages as well. Research has shown that caring for animals helps children concentrate. It makes them calm. Having pets in school has also been shown to make classrooms less tense.

Some people may argue that school pets make children ill. However, studies have shown that children who are around pets are better at fighting off infections than those who are not. Research has also shown that children from homes with pets have better attendance at school than those without pets.

I think it is obvious that allowing pets in schools benefits everyone. However, don't just take my word for it. Dr. Harvey Markovitch, a children's doctor, has a similar opinion. He says, "Being around animals is extremely good for children."

Answer the following questions.

1 This question has two parts. First, answer Part A. Then, answer Part B.

Part A

Which sentence **best** states the author's opinion about pets in schools?

A. Some schools sometimes allow pets.

B. Pets cause children to get illnesses.

C. Pets should be permitted in school.

D. Children should have pets at home.

Part B

Which of the following sentences from the passage **best** supports the answer to Part A?

A. Many schools allow children to bring pets for show-and-tell.

B. Therefore, I think all schools should allow pets.

C. Some people may argue that school pets make children ill.

D. He says, "Being around animals is extremely good for children."

Hint This question asks you to do two things. Part A asks you to identify the author's opinion. Think about what the author wants the reader to believe. An introduction and a conclusion should include the author's opinion. For Part B, identify the sentence from the passage that **best** supports the answer you chose in Part A.

2 Circle three examples of linking words or transitions in the passage.

Hint Remember, writers use linking words to connect sentences, paragraphs, and ideas.

3 Read the following reason why some people are against pets in school.

Some people may argue that school pets make children ill.

Which details from the passage argue against this reason? Circle **all** that apply.

A. However, studies have shown that children who are around pets are better at fighting off infections than those who are not.

B. If children are never around animals, they will be afraid of them.

C. Also, important life skills such as taking turns, keeping to schedules, and doing assigned tasks are the result of caring for school pets.

D. Research has shown that caring for animals helps children concentrate.

E. Research has also shown that children from homes with pets have better attendance at school than those without pets.

Hint Be sure to choose only details about the topic in the sentence. The sentence is about whether school pets make children ill. The responses need to give reasons why this may not be true.

4 The writer wants to add one more sentence to the conclusion of the essay.

Which sentence is the **best** one to add to the end of the essay?

A. Thus, the advantages of having pets in school far outweigh the disadvantages.

B. As you can see, allowing school pets has both advantages and disadvantages.

C. Therefore, pets in school allow children to learn how to care for animals.

D. Of course, if we do not allow pets in school, children will no longer be able to study how animals live.

Hint Reread the conclusion. Try each sentence in the choices above as an ending sentence. Which one makes the most sense?

Use the Reading Guide to help you understand the passage.

The Pros and Cons of School Pets

Reading Guide

In which part of the passage can you usually find the author's opinion? How can you tell what the writer's opinion is?

What kind of structure does the author use to organize this passage?

How does the author support each reason given?

Some schools have a policy of "No Pets Allowed." Others invite students to share small pets from home. They also permit students to have their own class pet. Which is the best policy? As you will see, this is not an easy question to answer. I believe there are strong reasons for and against having pets in school.

Opponents of school pets point out that animals in the classroom put students at risk. The Centers for Disease Control states that animals carry germs that can cause vomiting, fever, and stomach pains. In addition, animals can cause injuries. Different kinds of animals may bite, kick, or scratch children who come in contact with them. Also, some students may be allergic to pets.

However, supporters of pets in the classroom point out studies that provide different facts. A university study found that pets make children healthier. They help children build up their immune systems. This allows them to fight off germs that could cause illnesses.

The risk of injuries or sickness is not the only problem with school pets. The animals themselves also can suffer. Often, children may touch the pets too often or too roughly. Sometimes pets are kept in poor conditions where they might have too much or too little light or warmth. School pets can also become lonely or stressed.

Not only can students and the pets have problems, but the teacher can as well. It is often up to the teacher to find someone to care for the pet when school is closed. If no one else takes on the responsibility, the teacher may have to take the pet home every holiday.

Reading Guide

What additional reasons does the author identify?

How do linking words connect paragraphs or sentences?

What is the purpose of the last paragraph? How do you know?

In addition, the cost of keeping a pet is another reason that pets should not be in school. For instance, it can be expensive to provide food and shelter for some pets. What happens if the pet becomes ill? Who pays for a veterinarian to care for it? This is another problem the teacher and school must deal with when pets are allowed in schools.

Supporters say that the key to success with pets in the classroom is choosing the right pet. Not all animals make good pets in school. The pet needs to be quiet. Teachers do not want pets to distract students while they are working. Of course, a good school pet should be easy and inexpensive to care for. It should also be healthy and easy for children to handle. And the pet should be comfortable in a school environment. For example, some may think a rabbit or bird might make a great classroom pet. However, rabbits and birds are bothered by too much noise. Some animals that could make good school pets are fish, guinea pigs, and insects.

Pets also provide learning opportunities for students. Teachers have observed benefits such as children developing responsibility and awareness of others' feelings, as well as a respect for animals. Students can study animals and their needs when pets are allowed in schools. Of course, others point out that pets can cause a distraction when students are learning other subjects. There are other, more safe ways to study animals. Taking field trips to zoos and parks allows children to observe and learn about animals without having to deal with the problems of a school pet.

It seems obvious that allowing pets in schools can have advantages and disadvantages. If your school is deciding whether or not to allow pets, there is lots of research to study. I think reasons for both opinions make sense.

Answer the following questions.

1. Which text evidence supports the opinion that there are advantages to school pets? Circle **all** that apply.

   A. They also permit students to have their own class pet.

   B. A university study found that pets make children healthier.

   C. Teachers have observed benefits such as children developing responsibility . . .

   D. Some animals that could make good school pets are fish, guinea pigs, and insects.

   E. It is often up to the teacher to find someone to care for the pet when school is closed.

   F. They help children build up their immune systems.

2. The following question has two parts. First, answer Part A. Then, answer Part B.

   Part A

   Which of the following statements **best** describes the writer's opinion?

   A. There are good reasons for and against allowing pets in school.

   B. Students and teachers can benefit from school pets.

   C. Animals in school can cause children to get sick.

   D. Studies show that schools with pets help students.

   Part B

   Which of the following sentences from the passage **best** support the answer to Part A? Choose **all** that apply.

   A. I believe there are strong reasons for and against having pets in school.

   B. Different kinds of animals may bite, kick, or scratch children who come in contact with them.

   C. Supporters say that the key to success with pets in the classroom is choosing the right pet.

   D. Pets also provide learning opportunities for students.

   E. There are other, more safe ways to study animals.

   F. I think reasons for both opinions make sense.

3 Reread the following paragraph from the passage.

In addition, the cost of keeping a pet is another reason that pets should not be in school. For instance, it can be expensive to provide food and shelter for some pets. What happens if the pet becomes ill? Who pays for a veterinarian to care for it? This is another problem the teacher and school must deal with when pets are allowed in schools.

Underline **two** transition phrases in the paragraph. Explain how these words connect ideas to make them easier to understand.

4 The writer wants to add the following sentence to the passage.

To decide which is best, you should understand both the pros and cons of having pets in school.

Where in the passage is the **best** place to add this sentence?

A. at the end of paragraph 5

B. at the end of paragraph 7

C. at the end of paragraph 8

D. at the end of paragraph 9

5 Underline and label a relative adverb and a relative pronoun in the passage. Then, circle the word each one describes.

6 "Pets and School Go Together" presented a student's opinion in favor of allowing pets in school. "The Pros and Cons of School Pets" presented information about both sides of the issue. Think about the opinions and reasons in both passages. Then, write an opinion piece **against** allowing pets in school. Be sure to include text evidence from both sources.

You may plan the opinion piece in the space below. Write the opinion piece on the following pages.

Plan

Write the opinion piece on the lines below.

LESSON 18

Grammar and Usage

1 GETTING THE IDEA

Grammar is the system of language you use when you write. Knowing and using grammar rules in your writing lets you express your message clearly.

Sentences

A **complete sentence** contains a **subject** that tells whom or what the sentence is about and a **predicate** that tells what the subject does. A complete sentence tells a complete thought. An **independent clause** has a subject and a verb and can stand on its own as a complete sentence.

There are different kinds of sentences.

- A **simple sentence** has one independent clause. Read the sentence below. Circle the subject, and underline the predicate.

> Neela threw the ball.

- A **compound sentence** has two or more independent clauses. In a compound sentence, a **comma (,)**, and a **coordinating conjunction** join the independent clauses. There are seven coordinating conjunctions: *for*, *and*, *nor*, *but*, *or*, *yet*, *so*. The comma is placed before the coordinating conjunction.

Read the sentence below. Draw boxes around the two independent clauses. What is the coordinating conjunction?

> Neela threw the ball, and her brother caught it.

Every predicate has a verb. A **verb** often shows an action. The subject and verb in a sentence must agree, or match, in number. This means a singular subject must have a singular verb, and a plural subject must have a plural verb.

Josh compares the paintings.

Josh and Alicia compare the paintings.

Common Problems with Sentences

Writers sometimes make mistakes when constructing sentences. A **sentence fragment** is an incomplete sentence. The chart below shows common issues with sentence fragments and how to correct them.

Problem	Solution
Missing a subject: *Fell all night long.*	Add a subject: *The snow fell all night long.*
Missing a verb: *The student in the last row.*	Add a verb: *The student in the last row is asleep.*

A **run-on sentence** connects two complete sentences, but it is missing a coordinating conjunction and/or punctuation. Read this run-on sentence.

The rain created puddles the football field was muddy.

The chart below shows two ways to correct the run-on.

Solution	Example
Make two complete sentences out of the one run-on sentence.	*The rain created puddles. The football field was muddy.*
Add the missing comma and coordinating conjunction.	*The rain created puddles, so the football field was muddy.*

What mistakes were made in the examples below? Rewrite the examples so they are complete sentences.

Never saw the movie.

We wanted to skate on the pond it was not open for skating.

The stains on the carpet.

Verbs

Be sure that you are using correct verb tenses in your writing. The **tense** of a verb shows when an action happens. The chart below shows the simple tenses.

Present Tense	Past Tense	Future Tense
I count.	I counted.	I will count.
She skips.	She skipped.	She will skip.
We worry.	We worried.	We will worry.

The **progressive tense** shows an action in progress. To form the progressive tense, use a form of the verb *be* with the present participle of the main verb. The **present participle** is the verb with the ending *-ing*. The form of *be* that you use changes to show the tense. The chart below shows the progressive tenses.

Present Progressive Tense	Past Progressive Tense	Future Progressive Tense
I *am* counting.	I *was* counting.	I *will be* counting.
She *is* skipping.	She *was* skipping.	She *will be* skipping.
We *are* worrying.	We *were* worrying.	We *will be* worrying.

A **modal auxiliary verb** is a kind of helping verb. It is often used to show conditions such as possibility or need. Some common modal auxiliary verbs are *can*, *could*, *might*, *must*, *should*, *will*, and *would*. Below are two patterns for using modal auxiliary verbs.

- Modal verb + main verb

George *might attend* the concert on Saturday.

- Modal verb + form of *be* + present participle

George *might be attending* the concert on Saturday.

Complete the sentences below with modal auxiliary verbs.

> If I get there before Tara, I ________ help you.
>
> Henry ________ be arriving soon.

Relative Adverbs

An **adverb** is a word or phrase that describes a verb, an adjective, or another adverb. A **relative adverb** introduces a **clause**, or a group of words, that gives information about a **noun**, a person, place, thing, or idea. The relative adverbs *when*, *where*, and *why* are used to show time, place, or reason.

> *To show time*: Tomorrow is the day **when** Grandma will visit the school.
>
> *To show place*: The school **where** Grandma taught has been open for fifty years.
>
> *To show reason*: The school's anniversary is **why** Grandma is visiting the school.

Pronouns

A **pronoun** takes the place of a noun. A pronoun must agree with, or match, its antecedent. An **antecedent** is the noun that the pronoun replaces.

> The boy forgot *his* helmet. The boys forgot *their* helmets.

A **relative pronoun** introduces a clause that gives information about a noun. The relative pronouns are *that*, *which*, *who*, *whom*, and *whose*. The clause comes after the noun it describes.

- *Who* and *whom* refer to people.
- *Which* refers to things. *Which* is often used with information that is not completely necessary to include in a sentence. Use a comma before and after a clause beginning with *which*.
- *That* and *whose* may refer to people or things. *Whose* is used to show possession.

Katherine Paterson is the author **who** wrote the book *Lyddie*.

Erica has a new backpack, **which** she received as a gift.

Prepositional Phrases

A **preposition** is word that comes before a noun or pronoun to show direction, location, or time. A **prepositional phrase** is a group of words that begins with a preposition and ends with a noun or pronoun. To avoid confusion, place the prepositional phrase as close as possible to the noun or pronoun it describes.

Confusing: Mom could see the cat with her glasses on.

Clear: With her glasses on, Mom could see the cat.

Language Spotlight • Adjective Order

An **adjective** is a word that describes a noun or pronoun. When you use more than one adjective to describe the same noun or pronoun, list the adjectives in the correct order. The usual order is shown below.

number/quantity opinion → size/shape → age/temperature → color → origin → material → purpose

Separate the adjectives with commas. An exception is when using a number/quantity adjective.

three big, round, red balls (quantity, size, shape, color)

beautiful, antique, French mirror (opinion, age, origin)

old, brass bell (age, material)

Write sentences for each set of adjectives using correct order.

1. wooden new
2. green ugly cotton
3. American large first

② COACHED EXAMPLE

Answer the following questions.

1 Read the sentence.

The first performer in the talent show ____________.

Choose the words that complete the sentence.

A. who was very nervous

B. thinking about winning first prize

C. and also the last performer

D. danced a jazz routine

Hint A complete sentence has a subject and a predicate. *Performer* is the subject. Which answer choice tells you what the performer did?

2 Read the sentence.

There are several fields ______ the boys can play.

Which word correctly completes the sentence?

A. when

B. where

C. which

D. why

Hint Look carefully at the sentence. Should the missing word refer to a time, place, or reason?

3 Read the information.

Keith is watching TV even though he ______ be helping Marilyn clean out the garage.

Which word correctly completes the sentence to show that helping Marilyn is the right thing for Keith to do?

A. could

B. might

C. should

D. will

Hint Try each word in the blank. Which word makes sense in the sentence and shows that Keith is responsible for helping Marilyn?

4 Which sentence is written correctly?

A. We need to build a strong, rectangular, net frame around our playing field.

B. We need to build a strong, net, rectangular frame around our playing field.

C. We need to build a rectangular, strong, net frame around our playing field.

D. We need to build a rectangular, net, strong frame around our playing field.

Hint Remember the order of adjectives: number/quantity → opinion → size/shape → age/temperature → color → origin → material → purpose.

Answer the following questions.

1 Read the sentence.

Mr. Clark's class was on a field trip so they missed the fire chief's visit.

Where should a comma be added?

A. after <u>class</u>

B. after <u>trip</u>

C. after <u>so</u>

D. after <u>missed</u>

2 Read the sentence.

Maya ran <u>across</u> her yard and <u>below</u> her neighbor's yard chasing <u>after</u> her dog that had crawled <u>under</u> the fence and escaped.

Which underlined word is **not** used correctly?

A. across

B. below

C. after

D. under

Read the paragraphs. There are some errors in grammar and usage.

(1) My aunt and uncle has four cats and a dog. (2) One day I saw them all sleeping on the same couch. (3) Even though the dog doesn't like the cats very much. (4) It was a cold day, so maybe they were cuddled together for warmth.

(5) My aunt usually feeds all four cats on the dining room table so the dog can't reach her food. (6) The dog's food dish is on the floor in the kitchen. (7) Never eat the dog's food—I guess they don't like it.

Answer the following questions.

3 Which word in sentence 1 is used incorrectly, and how should it be changed?

A. The word *My* should be changed to *Our*.

B. The word *aunt* should be capitalized like this: *Aunt*.

C. The word *has* should be changed to *have*.

D. The word *four* should be changed to a numeral *4*.

4 What error can you find in sentences 2 and 3, and how could you fix it?

A. Sentence 2 is incomplete. You could fix it by changing "them all" to "all five of them."

B. Sentence 3 is incomplete. You could fix it by combining Sentences 2 and 3 like this: "The dog doesn't like the cats very much, but one day I saw all five animals sleeping on the same couch."

C. The two sentences should have the same verb tense. You could fix this by changing the word *saw* to *see*, or by changing the word *doesn't* to *didn't*.

D. Both sentences are error-free. Neither needs any changes.

5 Which word in sentence 5 is used incorrectly, and how should it be changed?

A. The word *feeds* should be changed to *feed*.

B. The word *all* should be changed to *those*.

C. The word *so* should be changed to *therefore*.

D. The word *her* should be changed to *their*.

6 What is missing from sentence 7, and how could you fix it?

A. A verb is missing from the first clause. You could add it in like this: "Never taste or eat the dog's food."

B. An adverb is missing from the second clause. You could add it in like this: "I guess they don't really like it."

C. A subject is missing from the first clause. You could add it in like this: "The cats never eat the dog's food —I guess they don't like it."

D. Both clauses need adjectives. You could add them in like this: "Never eat the smelly dog's food—I guess the picky cats don't like it."

Mechanics

1 GETTING THE IDEA

Good writers understand that using correct capitalization, punctuation, and spelling is as important as what they have to say. Using proper mechanics shows readers that you have carefully crafted your writing.

Capitalization

You probably always remember to capitalize the first letter of the first word in a sentence, people's names, and the pronoun *I*. But there are several other important capitalization rules.

Proper Nouns A **proper noun** is a noun that names a specific person, place, or thing. The first letter of a proper noun is capitalized. For example, you do not capitalize the noun *ocean*, but you do capitalize the proper noun *Atlantic Ocean* because it names a specific ocean. Here are other examples of proper nouns.

- Days of the week: *Monday*, *Wednesday*, *Saturday*
- Months of the year: *February*, *June*, *October*
- Holidays: *Memorial Day*, *Fourth of July*, *Thanksgiving*
- Cities, States, Countries: *Allentown*, *Pennsylvania*, *United States of America*

Proper Adjectives A **proper adjective** is an adjective that comes from a proper noun. As with a proper noun, the first letter of a proper adjective is capitalized. For example, *Swiss* is a proper adjective that comes from the proper noun *Switzerland*.

Read the sentences below. Underline the words that should be capitalized.

we do not have school next monday because it is a holiday.

tina says that the white dog café makes the best french fries.

Titles of People When a person's professional or military title is followed by his or her name, capitalize the title.

> *Capitalize*: We are waiting for Coach Brennan to arrive.
>
> *DO NOT capitalize*: We are waiting for the coach to arrive.

Other common personal titles that should be capitalized when used with a person's name are *Mr.*, *Jr.*, *Ms.*, *Mrs.*, and *Miss*.

Titles of Works Follow these guidelines to capitalize titles of books, poems, and more.

- Capitalize the first and last words.
- Capitalize all nouns, pronouns, adjectives, verbs, and adverbs.
- Do NOT capitalize articles, conjunctions, or prepositions.

Besides properly capitalizing a work in your writing, you also need to style it in certain ways. The chart below explains what styles to use for writing the titles of different kinds of sources.

Type of Work	Style	Example
book, play, movie	italics (if text is typed) underlining (if text is hand-written)	*Sideways Stories from Wayside School, Wicked, The Iron Giant*
short story, article, poem, chapter, song	quotation marks (if text is typed or hand-written)	"The Spider and the Fly," "The Boy Who Lived," "Over the Rainbow"

On a separate sheet of paper, write the titles of your favorite book, movie, and song using correct capitalization.

Punctuation with Quotations

A person's quoted words are **direct speech**. The dialogue in a story is an example of direct speech. When writing direct speech, enclose the speaker's words in quotation marks. Usually, the speaker's words are separated from the rest of the sentence by a comma inside the quotation marks.

> "Let's go to the game," Julie said.

If the dialogue tag comes before the speaker's words, the comma comes after the dialogue tag.

> Julie said, "Let's go to the game."

When a speaker asks a question or makes an exclamation, look at the position of the dialogue in the overall sentence. If the dialogue comes first, use the question mark or exclamation point in place of the comma. If the dialogue comes last, use a comma between the tag and the quote. Always keep the end punctuation inside the quotation marks.

> "Are we going to the game?" Julie asked.
> Julie said, "Let's go to the game now!"

If you want to use words from a text in your writing, you need to write them down exactly. Enclose them in quotation marks and use a comma to introduce them.

> The U.S. Declaration of Independence states, "All men are created equal."

Add the missing punctuation below.

> I forgot my ticket Marty said
> Keira cheerfully replied Good thing I have an extra

Spelling

The following spelling patterns and rules will help you correctly spell words.

Words with *ie/ei*

- Write *ie* in most words: *believe, yield*.
- Write *ei* if the letters come after *c*: *perceive, receive*.
- Write *ei* if the vowel sound is NOT a long *e*: *foreign, their*.

Suffixes

The chart below shows rules for spelling words with suffixes.

Spelling Rule	Examples
If the root ends with *e* and the suffix begins with a vowel, drop the *e* before adding the suffix.	cure + *able* → curable smile + *ed* → smiled bake + *er* → baker chase + *ing* → chasing active + *ity* → activity
If the root ends with a consonant + *y* and the suffix begins with a letter other than *i*, change *y* to *i* before adding the suffix.	defy + *ance* → defiance pity + *ed* → pitied berry + *es* → berries mercy + *ful* → merciful happy + *ness* → happiness mystery + *ous* → mysterious
If the root is a noun ending in *-ch*, *-sh*, *-x*, *-s* or *-ss*, add *-es* to the end of the word to form the plural.	branch + *es* → branches ash + *es* → ashes fox + *es* → foxes bus + *es* → buses glass + *es* → glasses

On a separate sheet of paper, correctly spell the new words made from these word parts:

- Add the suffix *-ing* to the root word *amplify*.
- Add the suffix *-ed* to the root word *promise*.
- Add the suffix *-ous* to the root word *luxury*.
- Add the suffix *-ity* to the root word *secure*.

Language Spotlight • Frequently Confused Words

Some words sound alike or nearly alike but have different meanings. Be careful to use the correct word in your writing. The chart below lists several frequently confused words. On a separate sheet of paper, write a sentence for each word.

Word	Definition
coarse *course*	"rough" "a direction" or "a series of classes"
no *know*	used to show a negative response "to understand"
principal *principle*	"the person in charge of a school" or "most important" "a law or fact of nature" or "a belief"
to *too* *two*	"toward" "also" a number
their *there* *they're*	used to show possession used to show location contraction of *they are*

❷ COACHED EXAMPLE

Answer the following questions.

1 Read the sentence.

"Call me as soon as you get there" Mom said as I walked out the door.

Which change corrects the mistake in punctuation?

A. Add a comma after me.

B. Add a comma after there.

C. Add a comma after said.

D. Add a comma after walked.

Hint Remember that in direct speech, a comma is used to separate the speaker's words from the dialogue tag.

2 Read the sentence.

In july, my family is renting a cabin in the northern part of the state.

Which underlined word should begin with a capital letter?

A. july

B. cabin

C. northern

D. state

Hint Proper nouns should be capitalized. Which underlined word names a specific person, place, or thing?

3 Read the sentence.

"Will you be joining us, Kevin? Craig asked.

Which change corrects the mistake in punctuation?

A. Add a quotation mark after the comma.

B. Add a quotation mark after the question mark.

C. Add a quotation mark after Craig.

D. Add a quotation mark after asked.

Hint Quotation marks enclose a speaker's words. They should always come in pairs with one before the speaker's words and one after. Which words does Craig say?

4 Read the sentence.

Bo and Katie do not know which of the two new courses they're friends are taking.

What change needs to be made to correct the error?

A. Change know to no.

B. Change two to to.

C. Change courses to coarses.

D. Change they're to their.

Hint Look carefully at each underlined word and think of its meaning. Does that meaning make sense in the sentence?

3 LESSON PRACTICE

Answer the following questions.

1. Read the sentence.

   With Professor Garcia's <u>guideance</u>, Rudy's <u>laziness</u> <u>decreased</u> and, as a result, Rudy was <u>victorious</u>.

   Which underlined word is misspelled?

   A. guideance

   B. laziness

   C. decreased

   D. victorious

2. Read the sentence.

   Last week at the <u>museum</u>, <u>we</u> saw an outstanding exhibit of <u>chinese</u> <u>porcelain</u>.

   Which underlined word should begin with a capital letter?

   A. museum

   B. we

   C. chinese

   D. porcelain

Read the paragraphs. There are some errors in mechanics.

(1) My grandma lives in Kansas city, in the state of missouri. (2) Since Missouri is in the middle of the United States, Grandma rarely gets a chance to see an Ocean. (3) We live in Los Angeles, California, so it's a treat for her to see the Pacific ocean when she visits us.

(4) Last may Grandma flew to L.A. Airport, which is sometimes called "LAX." (5) When she got off the plane, she heard a voice over a loudspeaker say, "dr. Boynton, please pick up a white courtesy telephone." (6) (Grandma is a doctor, and her last name is Boynton.) (7) The person on the phone was my dad. (8) He told Grandma that he would be an hour late to pick her up. (9) Our next door nieghbor had fallen from a ladder, so Dad had to drive him to Beverly Glen hospital. (10) While she waited for Dad, Grandma reread her favorite book, *Pride And prejudice* by Jane Austen.

Answer the following questions.

3. Which changes correct the **two** mistakes in capitalization in sentence 1?

   A. My grandma lives in Kansas city, in the State of Missouri.

   B. My grandma lives in Kansas City, in the state of Missouri.

   C. My grandma lives in kansas city, in the state of Missouri.

   D. There are no capitalization mistakes in sentence 1.

4. Which changes correct the **two** mistakes in capitalization in sentences 2 and 3?

   A. (2) Since Missouri is in the middle of the United states, Grandma rarely gets a chance to see an Ocean. (3) We live in los Angeles, California, so it's a treat for her to see the Pacific ocean when she visits us.

   B. (2) Since Missouri is in the Middle of the United States, Grandma rarely gets a chance to see an Ocean. (3) We live in Los Angeles, california, so it's a treat for her to see the Pacific ocean when she visits us.

   C. (2) Since Missouri is in the middle of the United States, Grandma rarely gets a chance to see an ocean. (3) We live in Los Angeles, California, so it's a treat for her to see the Pacific Ocean when she visits us.

   D. There are no capitalization mistakes in sentences 2 or 3.

5 Which changes correct the **two** mistakes in capitalization in sentences 4, 5, and 6?

A. (4) Last May Grandma flew to L.A. Airport, which is sometimes called "LAX." (5) When she got off the plane, she heard a voice over a loudspeaker say, "Dr. Boynton, please pick up a white courtesy telephone." (6) (Grandma is a doctor, and her last name is Boynton.)

B. (4) Last may Grandma flew to L.A. airport, which is sometimes called "LAX." (5) When she got off the plane, she heard a voice over a loudspeaker say, "dr. Boynton, please pick up a white courtesy telephone." (6) (Grandma is a Doctor, and her last name is Boynton.)

C. (4) Last May Grandma flew to L.A. Airport, which is sometimes called "lax." (5) When she got off the plane, she heard a voice over a loudspeaker say, "dr. Boynton, please pick up a white courtesy telephone." (6) (Grandma is a doctor, and her last name is Boynton.)

D. There are no capitalization mistakes in sentences 4, 5, or 6.

6 Which changes correct **one** spelling mistake and **three** capitalization mistakes in sentences 7 through 10?

A. (7) The person on the phone was my Dad. (8) He told Grandma that he would be an hour late to pick her up. (9) Our next door neighbor had fallen from a ladder, so dad had to drive him to Beverly glen hospital. (10) While she waited for Dad, Grandma reread her favorite book, *Pride and prejudice* by Jane Austen.

B. (7) The person on the phone was My Dad. (8) He told grandma that he would be an hour late to pick her up. (9) Our next door nieghbor had fallen from a ladder, so Dad had to drive him to Beverly Glen hospital. (10) While she waited for Dad, Grandma reread her favourite book, *Pride And prejudice* by Jane Austen.

C. (7) The person on the phone was my dad. (8) He told grandma that He would be an hour late to pick Her up. (9) Our next door nieghbor had fallen from a ladder, so Dad had to drive him to Beverly Glen hospital. (10) While she waited for Dad, Grandma reread her favorite book, *Pryde And prejudice* by Jane Austen.

D. (7) The person on the phone was my dad. (8) He told Grandma that he would be an hour late to pick her up. (9) Our next door neighbor had fallen from a ladder, so Dad had to drive him to Beverly Glen Hospital. (10) While she waited for Dad, Grandma reread her favorite book, *Pride and Prejudice* by Jane Austen.

LESSON 20

Style, Tone, and Effect

1 GETTING THE IDEA

When you write, the words you choose can have a big impact on your message to the reader. Word choice also adds to your style as a writer. Think carefully about the words and punctuation you use in order to make your writing interesting, informative, and descriptive.

Using Precise Language

When you use precise language, your writing is clearer, more informative, and more effective. Readers are better able to visualize and understand your message. **Precise language** includes specific nouns, vivid verbs, descriptive adjectives and adverbs, and domain-specific vocabulary.

Domain-specific vocabulary includes words that have specific meaning for an area of study, such as science or history. For example, using the social studies word *immigrants* is a better choice than the vague, wordy phrase "people who have moved from another country." It helps the reader pinpoint exactly what the author means.

Read the sentences below. Replace the underlined words with more precise language.

> When the volcano <u>blew up</u>, <u>melted rock</u> <u>came out</u>. People living nearby had to <u>clear the area</u> <u>really fast</u>.

Using Words and Phrases for Effect

Read the sentences below. Whom do you think the writer was happier to see at the party?

> Seeing Jim at the party was a <u>surprise</u>.
>
> Seeing Carla at the party was a <u>shock</u>.

The words *surprise* and *shock* are **synonyms,** or words that have the same or nearly the same meaning. However, while *surprise* and *shock* have similar meanings, they do not have the same effect. The word *shock* suggests a less pleasant reaction than the word *surprise*. This is a difference in the words' **connotations,** or suggested meanings. *Shock* has a more negative connotation than *surprise*.

Read the words below. For each pair, circle the word with a negative connotation.

proud	vain
fearful	shy
confident	pushy
cheat	outwit

Synonyms may also have **shades of meaning,** which relates to the strength of words. For example, *cry* and *weep* have similar meanings, but *weep* is stronger because it suggests a more powerful feeling.

Read the words below. Order the words from 1 to 3, with 1 being the strongest.

ask	challenge	question

Using Formal and Informal Language

When you write a paper for your teacher, you should use formal language. **Formal language** includes proper grammar and full words. It is often written with an objective point of view. Sentences are often longer and more complex.

Informal language is more often used in speaking, but it is also used in narratives or in writing for friends or family members. Informal language may include slang; contractions; improper grammar; and simpler or even incomplete sentences.

> *Formal language*: The child received a new ball since his mom could not find the old one.
>
> *Informal language*: The kid got a new ball since his mom couldn't find the old one.

Circle the words that show informal language below.

> There are tons of really cool stars to look at in the Milky Way Galaxy.

Language Spotlight • Choosing Punctuation for Effect

Punctuation help readers know how to read a text. It can also add meaning to sentences.

Punctuation	Used to show	Example
question mark (?)	uncertainty	At what time are we leaving?
exclamation point (!)	strong emotion	You should not have taken that bag!
ellipsis (. . .)	a thought trailing off	"I just don't know..." he murmured.
dash (—)	an interruption	Joe said, "I think we should—" "It doesn't matter what you think!" shouted Tim.

On a separate sheet of paper, write one sentence that includes an ellipsis and one sentence that includes a dash.

❷ COACHED EXAMPLE

Answer the following questions.

1. Read the sentence.

   James had been taking piano lessons <u>for a long time</u>.

   Choose the **most** specific words to replace the words <u>for a long time</u> in the sentence.

   A. since he was five years old

   B. for several years

   C. as long as anyone could remember

   D. longer than his brother had

> **Hint** Specific language gives the reader a clear understanding of the writer's meaning. Which group of words provides the most exact information?

2. Which sentence **best** uses punctuation to show a thought trailing off?

   A. If only I could remember where I put my keys.

   B. If only I could remember where I put my keys?

   C. If only I could remember where I put my keys—

   D. If only I could remember where I put my keys . . .

> **Hint** Look at the punctuation in each sentence. How is each kind of punctuation normally used? Which sentence best shows that the speaker is distracted?

3 Which sentence has end punctuation that shows excitement?

A. I think that idea will definitely work.

B. I think that idea will definitely work?

C. I think that idea will definitely work . . .

D. I think that idea will definitely work!

Hint Read each option to yourself, changing your tone with each punctuation mark. What kind of end punctuation is used to show strong emotion?

4 Read the paragraph.

(1) Ponce de León lived during the Age of Discovery. (2) This was a time when countries searched for new lands to claim as their own. (3) Ponce de León couldn't wait to go out and explore for Spain. (4) He set out with Christopher Columbus on Columbus's second expedition to the New World.

Which sentence has informal language and should be revised?

A. sentence 1

B. sentence 2

C. sentence 3

D. sentence 4

Hint Remember that formal language uses complete sentences and words. Does one of the sentences use slang words or contractions?

3 LESSON PRACTICE

Answer the following questions.

1. Read the sentence.

   An example of <u>an animal that hunts other animals for food</u> is the cheetah.

   Choose the **most** specific word to replace the words <u>an animal that hunts other animals for food</u> in the sentence.

   A. hunter

   B. carnivore

   C. killer

   D. predator

2. Read the paragraph.

   (1) All animals need food, shelter, and water to stay alive. (2) But some get what they need in really cool ways. (3) For example, clown fish get protection by living among sea anemones. (4) A sea anemone has a dangerous sting, but the clown fish's skin is not bothered by it.

   Which sentence has informal language and should be revised?

   A. sentence 1

   B. sentence 2

   C. sentence 3

   D. sentence 4

Read this e-mail. There are some errors in style, tone, and effect.

(1) Hi, Jill?

(2) I respectfully hope that you, your family members, and all our friends are quite well. (3) Everything here in Flagstaff is really cool. (4) A horrible tragedy befell me, but I am almost over it. (5) I caught my dad's stupid cold. (6) However, Mr. Ramirez has apologized for exposing me to the illness. (7) I miss you SO much. (8) I was hoping to—oops, Mom's calling me, so I'll e-mail you again later, OK?

(9) Sincerely,

Addie

Answer the following questions.

3 Should Addie replace the question mark in the greeting on line 1 with a different punctuation mark? If so, which one should she use, and why?

- **A.** Yes, she should replace it with a dash to show that she was interrupted when her mom called her. (Hi, Jill—)
- **B.** Yes, she should replace it with an exclamation mark to show that she is excited about writing to Jill. (Hi, Jill!)
- **C.** Yes, she should replace it with an ellipsis (three dots) to show that she has paused to think about what to write. (Hi, Jill . . .)
- **D.** No, she should not replace the question mark. The greeting is fine as it is. (Hi, Jill?)

4 Read sentences 2 and 3. Which sentence does not fit the style of a friendly e-mail? Which is the best way to rewrite that sentence?

- **A.** Sentence 2 is too formal. Addie should rewrite it like this: "How are you doing, and how's everybody else back home?"
- **B.** Sentence 3 is too informal. Addie should rewrite it like this: "My family members and I are in good health, and we are enjoying our visit to Flagstaff."
- **C.** Sentence 2 is too informal. Addie should rewrite it like this: "Without being too personal, may I inquire about your health and the health of your respected family members?"
- **D.** Both sentences fit the style of a friendly e-mail. No rewriting is necessary.

5 Read sentences 4, 5, and 6. Then, answer the question that follows.

(4) A horrible tragedy befell me, but I am almost over it. (5) I caught my dad's stupid cold. (6) However, Mr. Ramirez has apologized for exposing me to the illness.

Should Addie rewrite any of these sentences? If so, how should she rewrite them?

A. (4) A horrible tragedy befell me, but thankfully, I have nearly recovered. (5) I caught a dreadful illness from my dear father. (6) However, Mr. Ramirez has apologized for exposing me to the disease, and of course I forgave him, as it is not his fault.

B. (4) Something happened. (5) I got sick. (6) It is a cold.

C. (4) Something not-so-great happened to me, but I am almost over it. (5) I caught my dad's stupid cold. (6) Dad said he was sorry—he's always catching colds from his students.

D. Sentences 4, 5, and 6 are fine the way they are. No rewriting is necessary.

6 Read sentences 7 and 8, and the closing on line 9. Then, answer the question that follows.

(7) I miss you SO much. (8) I was hoping to—oops, Mom's calling me, so I'll e-mail you again later, OK?

(9) Sincerely,

Addie

This is the end of Addie's e-mail to her friend Jill. Which changes would improve the ending?

A. Addie should end sentence 7 with an exclamation mark instead of a period. Sentence 8 is fine as it is. Addie should change the closing on line 9 from *Sincerely* to *Love* or *Your Friend*.

B. Addie should end sentence 7 with a question mark instead of a period. She should change the dash in sentence 8 to a period and capitalize the words *oops*. The word *Sincerely* on line 9 is fine as it is.

C. In sentence 7, Addie should change "SO" to "so." (Words in all capital letters are too informal.) Sentence 8 is fine as it is. Addie should change the closing on line 9 from *Sincerely* to *Your Classmate*.

D. The end of the e-mail is perfect. It needs no changes at all.

STRAND 3 REVIEW

Read this letter. There are some errors in grammar, mechanics, and style.

(1) March 18, 2016

(2) Dear mrs. Grayer:

(3) I am a loyal customer of your bookstore, Readers' paradise. (4) Over the years I have spent hundreds of dollars their. (5) Last week I bought a copy of *The wind in the Willows* for my neice's Birthday present. (6) You'd really like her—she's a very cool twelve-year-old kid!

(7) When I got the book home and flipped through it, I was terrified to discover that someone had scribbled notes in the margins. (8) You ungrateful jerk, you sold me a used book for $25.99— (9) I expect a full refund, and I will be in to collect it next week.

(10) Love,

Mrs. Katrina Kanter

Answer the following questions.

1 Which change corrects a capitalization error lines 1 and 2 (the date and the greeting)?

A. march 18, 2016

B. dear mrs. Grayer,

C. March Eighteenth, Two Thousand and Sixteen

D. Dear Mrs. Grayer,

2 Which changes correct one capitalization error and one spelling error in sentences 3 and 4?

A. (3) I am a loyal customer of your bookstore, Readers' Paradise. (4) Over the years I have spent hundreds of dollars there.

B. (3) I am a loyal customer of your bookstore, Reader's paradise. (4) Over the years I have spent hundreds of $s they're.

C. (3) I am a loyal customer of your bookstore, readers' paradise. (4) Over the years I have spent 100s of dollars their.

D. There are no capitalization errors in the two sentences. In sentence 4, the word *their* should be spelled *they're*.

3. How many errors are there in sentences 5 and 6? What kinds of errors are they?

   A. One error: the word *neice's* should be spelled *nieces'*.

   B. Two errors: the word *wind* in the book title should be capitalized and the word *Birthday* should NOT be capitalized.

   C. Three errors: the word *wind* in the book title should be capitalized, the word *Birthday* should NOT be capitalized, and sentence 6 is too informal.

   D. Four errors: the word *neice's* should be spelled *niece's*, the word *wind* in the book title should be capitalized, the word *Birthday* should NOT be capitalized, and sentence 6 is too informal.

4. Which is the **best** way to rewrite sentences 7 and 8?

   A. (7) When I got the book home and flipped through it, I was horrified to discover that someone had scribbled notes in the margins. (8) You should be ashamed of yourself for selling me a used book for $25.99!!

   B. (7) When I got the book home and flipped through it, I was unhappy to discover that someone had scribbled notes in the margins. (8) You may have been unaware of this, but you sold me a used book for $25.99.

   C. (7) When I got the book home and checked every page, I was devastated to discover that someone had scribbled notes in the margins!! (8) Mrs. Grayer, you are a thief! You sold me a used book for $25.99!!!!!

   D. (7) When I got the book home and flipped through it, I was surprised to discover that someone had scribbled notes in the margins. (8) Mimi, I thought you and I were friends, but I guess we're not. Really? You tricked me into buying a used book for $25.99? I'm really mad at you, Mimi.

5. Identify any error(s) you see in sentence 9 and on line 10 at the end of Mrs. Kanter's formal letter to Mrs. Grayer.

   A. Sentence 9 has no errors. Mrs. Kanter should change her closing from *Love* to *Sincerely* or to another closing that is equally formal.

   B. Sentence 9 is too harsh and formal. The closing on line 10 is fine as it is.

   C. Sentence 9 is too casual and friendly-sounding. Mrs. Kanter should change her closing from *Love* on line 10 to a word or phrase that shows how angry she is.

   D. Sentence 9 and line 10 are fine as they are. No rewriting is necessary.

Read the passages.

The Newbery Medal

Have you ever read a book that had a picture of a medal with the words "Winner of the Newbery Medal" or "Newbery Honor Book" on its cover? Did you wonder what that meant?

The Newbery Medal is awarded every year by the Association for Library Service to Children (ALSC). This group is part of the larger American Library Association (ALA). The medal goes to the author of the best children's book published in the United States during the previous year. Runners-up are recognized as Newbery Honor Books. Many people consider the Newbery to be the most important honor a children's book author can receive.

The History of the Newbery Medal

The Newbery Medal has been awarded every year since 1922. The award is named after John Newbery, a British bookseller who lived during the 1700s. Newbery is considered the world's first publisher of books for children.

The award was the idea of Frederic Melcher, a bookseller and publisher who was a member of the ALA. In 1921, Melcher proposed the idea of an award for children's books at a meeting of children's librarians. The Newbery Medal became the first award given just for a children's book. Since then, other awards have been created. But the Newbery Medal is still the best known and most prized award for children's books.

How Newbery Medal Winners Are Chosen

The Newbery Medal award winner is chosen by a committee made up of ALSC members. Each year, many authors submit books to the awards committee. The committee members read all of them. They discuss what they thought of each book and then compare all of the books. Then they cast a vote. It sometimes takes several rounds of voting, but eventually one book is named the Newbery Medal winner.

Just about any fiction, nonfiction, or poetry book for children published in the United States is eligible for a Newbery Medal. However, several rules help the judges narrow down their choices. For example, only a book written in the previous year—not all of an author's work—may be considered. This gives newer authors an equal chance of winning. The judges consider only the words in a book, not its design or any art it may contain. In addition, a book's popularity is not important. Even a book that not many people have read can still win a Newbery Medal. The judges look at the quality of the writing, not high sales numbers.

The Effect of Winning a Newbery Medal

Being named a Newbery Medal winner or an Honor Book can make an author's career. That author will always be known as a Newbery or Honor Book winner. A picture of the gold Newbery Medal or the silver Honor medal can always be printed on the cover of the winning books. The books will always be known as some of the best books of children's literature.

Newbery books are often among the most read and well-loved books in children's literature. Some famous titles include *A Wrinkle in Time* by Madeline L'Engle (1963), *Maniac Magee* by Jerry Spinelli (1991), and *Holes* by Louis Sachar (1999). The most recent Newbery Medal was awarded to Katherine Applegate for *The One and Only Ivan.* It is told from the point of view of a gorilla, Ivan, who does not mind living at a mall until he meets an elephant who has also been captured and taken from its home.

Newbery Medal winners and Honor Books showcase the best of children's literature. Pick up and read a Newbery book today!

Past Newbery Medal Award Winners

Year	Title	Author
2013	*The One and Only Ivan*	Katherine Applegate
2012	*Dead End in Norvelt*	Jack Gantos
2011	*Moon over Manifest*	Claire Vanderpool
2010	*When You Reach Me*	Rebecca Stead
2009	*The Graveyard Book*	Neil Gaiman
2008	*Good Masters! Sweet Ladies! Voices from a Medieval Village*	Laura Amy Schlitz
2007	*The Higher Power of Lucky*	Susan Patron
2006	*Criss Cross*	Lynne Rae Perkins

This chart lists some recent Newbery Medal winners. How many have you read?

Madeline L'Engle: The Life of a Writer

When people think of well-known children's book authors, Madeline L'Engle is often at the top of the list. L'Engle wrote some of the world's best-loved children's books. She is most well known for her book *A Wrinkle in Time*, which won the Newbery Medal in 1963.

Madeline L'Engle was born in 1918. She grew up in New York City and began writing stories when she was a child. She wrote her first story when she was five years old. When she was in fifth grade, she won a poetry contest. She also kept a journal.

As a child, L'Engle moved with her family several times—first to Switzerland and then to South Carolina. She went to college in Massachusetts. There, she studied English and continued writing. After college, L'Engle published her first two novels while working as an actress in New York City.

After she married, L'Engle and her husband moved to Connecticut and ran a general store. They raised their three children—two daughters and a son—while living there. L'Engle based the book *Meet the Austins* (1960) on this time in her life. The book portrays a real family, but not one that is too perfect or boring. During the next few decades. L'Engle wrote six more books about the Austin family.

It's hard to believe now, but L'Engle's masterpiece, *A Wrinkle in Time*, was turned down by twenty-six publishers before it was finally published in 1962. Since then, it has sold more than eight million copies. The book follows the adventures of Meg Murry and her brother as they travel through time and space to save their father from a planet controlled by darkness. The book's "girl-power" theme was unique because very few books at that time featured a girl as the heroine who led the adventure. L'Engle later wrote *A Wind in the Door, A Swiftly Tilting Planet,* and *Many Waters* to continue telling the story of the Murry family. All the books in the series combine science fiction with elements of love and family relationships.

Throughout her life, L'Engle answered letters that children wrote to her about her books. She also liked to help other writers by participating in writing workshops and speaking about her work. She thought the writing process was very challenging but also very rewarding. Like most authors, she revised and rewrote often when she worked. She said that she always had a plot and characters planned out before writing a book, but in the end they never turned out the way she had planned.

L'Engle often had advice for other writers. For example, she advised young writers to keep a journal of their thoughts and ideas. This journal would be just for the writer and would never be published or shown to anyone else. L'Engle said she often thought about an idea, maybe over the course of writing two other books, before beginning to put it down on paper.

L'Engle continued to write throughout her life. She wrote for adults as well as for children. Her work included poetry, dramas, and nonfiction. She enjoyed writing about topics that make the reader think. She also worked as a librarian at a New York church and enjoyed spending time with her children, grandchildren, and beloved dogs. She continued to win awards for her writing. By the time she died in 2007 at the age of eighty-eight, she had written more than sixty books.

Answer the following question.

6. In "The Newbery Medal" and "Madeline L'Engle: The Life of a Writer," you learned about an important award for children's books and about a writer who won the award. Think about a book that you have enjoyed in the past. Then write an essay to the members of the Newbery Medal judging committee stating why you think the book should win the award. Support your opinion with text evidence from the passages.

Use the space below to plan your essay.

Plan

Write your essay on the lines provided.

STRAND 4

Listening

LESSON 21

Listen to Literature

1 GETTING THE IDEA

When you listen to literature, you listen to a classmate, teacher, librarian, or storyteller read a story or poem aloud. One purpose of reading literature aloud is to entertain the listeners.

It is is important to listen carefully. Often, you will be asked to talk or write about what you hear. Sometimes, your teacher or librarian will tell a story right in front of you. At other times, you may use a computer to play an audio recording or a video presentation of a story.

Purpose

No matter how the literature is presented, your purpose for listening is the same. Your purpose is to:

- identify the **characters, setting, plot**, and **point of view.**
- find **details** about the story elements.
- be ready to **paraphrase**, or retell, portions of a text or the author's sentences or ideas in your own words.

Taking Notes

When you listen, take notes to help you remember what you heard. Taking notes doesn't mean writing down every word you hear. Instead, jot down names, places, and key words and ideas. Draw pictures to help you remember connections between characters and plot events. Your notes should help you get the most from a story.

Illustrations

Some stories that are read or played aloud have illustrations that go with them. The illustrations may include pictures of the story characters and setting or a map that shows where the story takes place. Pay attention to any visuals because they might explain parts of the story or give additional information.

First Listen

The first time you listen to a story, take notes on only the important elements. You should jot down the name of the main character or characters, the setting, and the problem and solution in the plot.

- A story always has a **main character** that the story is mostly about. The main character is usually identified in the first few sentences.
- The **setting**—when and where a story takes place—is also established in the beginning of a story.
- Every story is told from the narrator's **point of view**. You can tell whether the story is told in first person or third person by the pronouns that are used. First person uses first-person pronouns, such as *I, me, we,* and *our*. Third person uses third-person pronouns, including *he, she, they,* and *them*.
- The **plot** tells about a character's problem and how it is solved. Listen for the problem in the beginning. Listen to find out how it is solved at the end.

You might want to draw a story map and fill it in as you listen. Don't try to write down all the details at once. But do jot down questions you might have. During the second listen, listen for the answers to your questions. You can use this chart as a guide.

First Listen		
Story Elements	**Ask Yourself**	**Listen For**
character	Who is this story mostly about?	• the character's name • dialogue or description that gives clues about who the character is
setting	When and where does this story take place?	• place names • dates and time-order words such as *next, last week* • clues that suggest a different time period
point of view	Who is telling the story?	• first-person or third-person pronouns
plot	What happens in the story?	• clues about the character's problem and how it is solved

Second Listen

Your second listen is the time to pay attention to the details. If you started a story map for the first listen, use it to take additional notes.

Second Listen		
Story Elements	**Ask Yourself**	**Listen For**
character	What is the main character like? What does this character want? Who are the other characters?	• descriptions of a character's thoughts and actions • descriptions of other characters' reactions
setting	Is the setting important to the plot? How?	• descriptions of a time and place • clues in the dialogue
point of view	How does the point of view affect how the story is told?	• whether the story tells the thoughts of one or more characters
plot	How does the character try to solve the problem? What happens?	• details about how characters' actions lead to the solution

After Listening

Try to paraphrase the story, or retell it in your own words. Write it down in your notes. That will help you remember the most important parts. Then, think about the theme of the story. What message does the author want the reader to understand?

Language Spotlight • Consult References to Clarify Meaning

Reference materials include print and digital dictionaries, thesauruses, and glossaries. They can help you find or clarify the exact meaning of key words.

Write a definition for the underlined word in each sentence below. Consult references to clarify its exact meaning.

The boys horse around after school.
Riley didn't mind cleaning up.

② COACHED EXAMPLE

Listen to the passage your teacher reads aloud, and look at the picture. Take notes in the space below.

Monique Has a Bad Day

Notes

Answer the following questions.

1 Which sentence describes the point of view of this passage? Circle **all** that apply.

A. It tells the main character's thoughts.

B. It tells only what the characters are doing.

C. It uses first-person pronouns.

D. It uses third-person pronouns.

Hint What does the passage tell you about the characters? What clues can you use to figure this out?

2 How does the picture help you better understand the passage? Circle **all** that apply.

A. It shows the theme of the passage.

B. It shows a character in the story.

C. It shows a key event in the plot.

D. It shows the setting.

Hint What do you see in the picture? Does it show a character? Does it show the setting?

3 Select **three** details from the passage that tell why Monique's day was bad.

A. Monique forgot her lunch.

B. Sloppy joes and coleslaw splattered all over Monique's shirt.

C. Monique picked through the lost and found.

D. Monique and Sasha hardly ever saw each other outside of class.

E. Sasha accused Monique of stealing her sweatshirt.

F. Sasha felt a bit foolish and apologized.

Hint Think about what can happen to make a day bad. Which of these events affected Monique that way?

4 Explain how each event in this passage affects the next one, beginning with Monique's oversleeping. Use details from the passage to explain your answer.

Write your answer on the lines below.

Hint For each event, ask yourself what happened. Then, ask yourself why it happened.

5 Write sentences to paraphrase what happens after Monique wears the purple sweatshirt to class.

Write your answer on the lines below.

Hint When you paraphrase, you retell a passage in your own words. Think about what happens in this part of the passage.

Use the Listening Guide to help you understand the passage your teacher reads aloud. Take notes in the space below.

Listening Guide

What clues does the picture give you about this story?

What are some ways you can check the meaning of an unknown word?

What message does the speaker want you to understand by listening to this story?

The Invisible Warrior

Notes

Answer the following questions.

1. Look at the picture. What does it **best** help you to understand about the passage?

   A. It shows the theme of the passage.

   B. It shows what the invisible warrior looks like.

   C. It shows the culture that the story came from.

   D. It shows how the problem was solved.

2. This question has two parts. First, answer Part A. Then, answer Part B.

   Part A

   Who is the main character?

   A. Strong Wind

   B. Strong Wind's sister

   C. the chief's oldest daughter

   D. the chief's youngest daughter

   Part B

   How can you tell that this person is the main character?

   A. because he or she is the main problem solver

   B. because he or she is the best-looking character

   C. because he or she causes problems in the story

   D. because he or she has the strongest magical powers

3 "The Invisible Warrior" is a traditional legend told by the Algonquin people. Which sentence from the passage gives the **best** clue that it is a traditional legend?

A. Once upon a time, there was a brave warrior who could make himself invisible.

B. Each evening at dusk, Strong Wind's sister walked along the shore of the bay with any girl who wanted to marry her brother.

C. Meanwhile, a great chief lived in the village with his three daughters.

D. The chief's older daughters had both failed Strong Wind's test, but the youngest daughter had not yet tried.

4 This question has two parts. First, answer Part A. Then, answer Part B.

Part A

Read the sentence.

Her sisters teased her and called her a fool, but she paid them no mind.

Based on the clues in the passage, what does mind mean?

A. attention

B. brain

C. reason

D. memory

Part B

Which is the **best** resource to use to check the meaning of mind?

A. an encyclopedia

B. any Web site

C. a dictionary

D. a thesaurus

5 Many cultures use traditional tales to teach important lessons about life. What lessons does "The Invisible Warrior" teach? Use details from the passage to support your response.

Write your answer on the lines below.

LESSON 22

Listen to Presentations

1 GETTING THE IDEA

When you listen to a class lesson or a speaker giving a lecture, you are listening to a presentation. A **presentation** is a talk or speech. Its purpose is to give information or to share an opinion.

Listening to a Presentation

There are different ways to listen to a presentation. Sometimes, the speaker will be in the same room with you. At other times, you might listen to an audio recording or watch a video online.

Purpose

During a presentation, your purpose is to pay close attention. You should listen carefully in order to:

- find out the **main idea** or the speaker's **opinion**.
- identify the **details**, **facts**, and **reasons** the speaker gives to support the main idea or opinion.
- evaluate **evidence** the speaker offers to support the main idea or opinion.

Taking Notes

After you listen to a presentation, you should be able to retell the main points in your own words. Taking notes will help you remember what you hear. Here are some note-taking tips:

- Do not try to write down everything you hear.
- Write down only key words and phrases.
- Keep listening while you take notes.

Graphic Features

Graphic features are images that help you understand a presentation or give new information. Maps, charts, diagrams, and photographs are some graphics that might be included with a presentation.

You might have a chance to listen to a presentation more than one time. If your teacher is reading a passage, for example, he or she might read it twice. You can understand a presentation better if you listen for different things each time.

First Listen

The first time you listen, try to identify the main idea—what the presentation is mostly about. Take notes on that main idea. Often, the main idea is stated at the beginning of the presentation. The speaker usually also restates the main idea at the end, or conclusion, of the presentation. Listen for clues about the main idea in the presentation's title, introduction, and conclusion.

Also, write down any questions you have. During the second listen, you can listen for details and for the answers to your questions.

Nonfiction articles organize information to help readers connect ideas and events. A good presentation has a structure, or a form of organization, too. Listen for clue words that will help you connect ideas in the presentation and identify which structure is used.

Structure	Ask Yourself	Listen For
sequence	Is this about an event? Does it explain a process?	dates; words such as *first, next, last*
cause and effect	What happens? Why does it happen?	words such as *because, since, so*
problem and solution	Is there a problem to solve? Are solutions presented?	words such as *problem, challenge, solution, action*
compare and contrast	Does it explain how things are alike and different?	words such as *alike, same, both, different, however*

Second Listen

Before you listen a second time, look over your notes. Think about what you know about the main idea and structure. Review any questions you have from the first listen. Write down any other questions you now have.

During the second listen, pay attention to the key details. Listen for important points, examples, reasons, and evidence that support the main idea. Take notes on these key details.

Details	Ask Yourself	Listen For
key points	Is this important supporting information about the main idea?	*my first point is, remember that*
examples	Is this a story or a specific thing that helps me better understand an idea?	*for example, ______ is a kind of ______*
reasons	Does this tell me why?	*one reason is, because, this shows that, therefore*
evidence	Does this show proof by giving facts or data?	*one reason is, because, proof of this is*

After the Presentation

After a presentation, summarize it in your own words. Use your notes to help you. Paraphrasing the key parts of a presentation, or retelling them in your own words, will help you understand and remember what you heard.

Language Spotlight • Formal and Informal Language

Formal language is the style used in most presentations. It includes complete sentences, proper grammar, and well-chosen vocabulary. It avoids contractions.

Informal language is how people talk to their friends. It relaxes the rules and can include incomplete sentences, slang, lapses in grammar, and contractions. Informal language is fine for phone calls and conversations among friends. It should be avoided, though, when giving presentations.

How could you rewrite the following sentence so that it is more acceptable for a presentation?

There are tons of really cool stars in the Milky Way Galaxy.

____

2 COACHED EXAMPLE

Listen to the passage your teacher reads aloud. Study the graphic. Take notes in the space below.

The Giant Squid

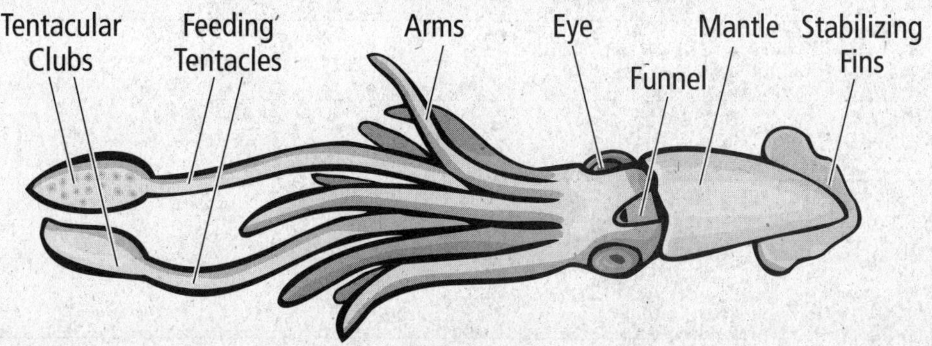

Notes

Answer the following questions.

1. Paraphrase the beginning of the passage that explains what people in the past believed about giant squid.

   Write your answer on the lines below.

   ____

   ____

   ____

   ____

   ____

   ____

   ____

   ____

Hint *Paraphrase* means to retell something in your own words.

2. Before 2004, why was it hard for scientists to learn about giant squid?

   A. Giant squid were too big to study.

   B. No giant squid had been found alive.

   C. Only female giant squid were seen at the surface.

   D. Giant squid are invertebrates.

Hint What reason does the speaker give to explain why scientists had a hard time learning about giant squid?

3 Read this paragraph from the passage and the directions that follow.

> **But there really was something in the ocean. Sometimes a giant carcass, or dead body, would wash up on a beach or be hauled up by a fisherman.**

Underline the phrase that gives evidence that something big really was living in the ocean.

Hint Evidence is facts or data that prove something.

4 What does the diagram show?

A. how giant squid move

B. undersea habitats for giant squid

C. giant squid body parts

D. how big giant squid are

Hint Look carefully at the labels in the diagram to learn what it shows.

Use the Listening Guide to help you understand the passage your teacher reads aloud. Study the graphics and take notes in the space below.

Advantages and Disadvantages of Using Guide Horses

Listening Guide

What is the main idea of this presentation?

What is the structure?

How does the chart help you to understand both the main idea and the structure?

Advantages	Disadvantages
• Good eyesight • Live longer • Do not set off allergies	• Not allowed in some places • Cannot walk well on stairs • Sleep outside • May slip on or scratch floors

Notes

Answer the following questions.

1. Tell the main idea of the passage in your own words.

   Write your answer on the lines below.

2. Why does the passage say that some people *must* work with guide horses instead of dogs?

   A. Horses live longer than dogs.

   B. Dogs cost more to train.

   C. Some people have dog allergies.

   D. Horses work better with people.

3. What evidence does the author give that horses have a long history of being helpful to people?

4 Which choice is the **best** reason to choose guide dogs instead of guide horses?

A. Dogs can work for about eight years.

B. Large dogs and miniature horses are about the same size.

C. Dogs were guide animals first.

D. Dogs can sleep indoors.

5 This question has two parts. First, answer Part A. Then, answer Part B.

Part A

Read this paragraph from the passage. Then answer the question that follows.

> **The idea of using a miniature horse to guide the blind is not as far-fetched as it might sound at first. Horses have been helping people for centuries. Before trains and cars, horses were the main form of transportation. They are also quite loyal and have been known to guide injured owners to safety and protect humans in battle.**

What kind of language does the speaker use in this paragraph?

A. slang

B. formal

C. informal

D. old-fashioned

Part B

Which statement **best** supports the answer to Part A?

A. The speaker is telling about events that happened hundreds of years ago.

B. The speaker wants to teach listeners about an important, interesting topic.

C. The speaker is talking to younger people and wants to use trendy new words.

D. The speaker wants to sound natural—the way people sound in everyday conversation.

6. Retell in your own words the advantages of using guide horses instead of guide dogs to assist the blind. You can use your notes and the chart to help you.

Write your response on the lines below.

Listen to the passage your teacher reads aloud. Take notes in the space below. You will hear the passage twice. Then you will answer questions about the passage.

Notes

1. From whose point of view is the story told?

   A. a first-person narrator whose name is Abuelo

   B. a first-person narrator whose name is Tomas

   C. a third-person narrator from Tomas's point of view

   D. a third-person narrator from Mom and Dad's point of view

2. Read each detail in the box. In the chart below, write the detail under the name of the character it describes. You may write a detail under more than one name.

child	adult	lived in Mexico
helps others communicate	has played soccer	learns a new language

Tomas	**Dad**	**Abuelo**

3 This question has two parts. First, answer Part A. Then, answer Part B.

Read this sentence from the passage.

He said the English words a little differently than Tomas did, but even with Abuelo's accent, Tomas could understand him.

Part A

Choose the **best** meaning of accent as used in the sentence.

A. the different ways that words are pronounced

B. the part that is much different from the rest

C. the mark identifying the sounds to stress in music

D. the symbol showing word parts to say strongly

Part B

Which would be the **best** resource to confirm the definition of accent you chose in Part A?

A. atlas

B. thesaurus

C. dictionary

D. encyclopedia

E. index

4 In each box, write the number 2, 3, 4, or 5 to put the events from the passage in the correct order.

1	Tomas finds out Abuelo is coming to live with him.
	Tomas and Abuelo feel like family.
	Tomas feels like Abuelo is company visiting.
	Tomas and Abuelo start learning each other's language.
	Tomas and Abuelo watch soccer.
6	Tomas tells Dad he is glad Abuelo lives with them.

5 In your own words, summarize how Tomas changes and what he learns by the end of the passage. Include details from your notes to explain how he learns this.

Listen to the presentation your teacher reads aloud. Study the graphics and take notes in the space below. You will hear the passage twice. Then you will answer questions about the passage.

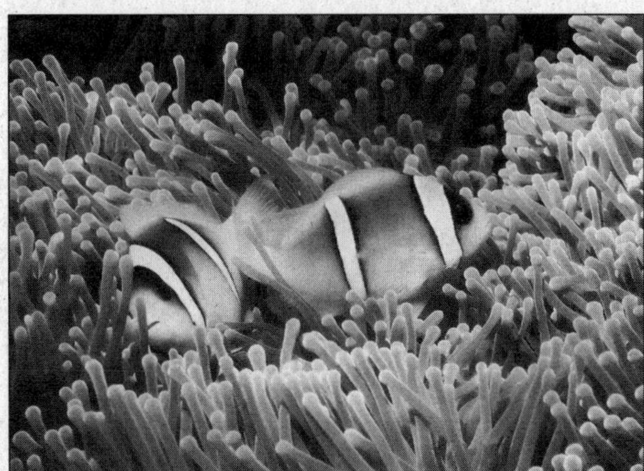

The sea anemone and clown fish on the left have a symbiotic relationship. So do the crab and barnacle on the right.

Notes

6 Which of the following does **not** describe a kind of symbiosis?

A. Both animals are helped.

B. Both animals are harmed.

C. One animal is helped, and the other is harmed.

D. One animal is helped, and the other is not affected.

7 This question has two parts. First, answer Part A. Then, answer Part B.

Part A

Which symbiotic relationship is harmful to one of the animals? Use the photographs and captions to help you remember.

A. one between a barnacle and a crab

B. one between a sea anemone and a clown fish

C. one between an imperial shrimp and a sea cucumber

D. one between a banded sea snake and a harlequin snake eel

Part B

Which sentence from the article **best** supports the answer to Part A?

A. But clown fish have skin that is not bothered by sea anemones.

B. When barnacles are attached to a crab's shell, the crab can't shed its shell.

C. The shrimp hang onto sea cucumbers to help them move through the water in search of food.

D. The harlequin snake eel is helped by looking like the banded sea snake.

8 This question has two parts. First, answer Part A. Then, answer Part B.

Part A

How is mimicry different from the other types of symbiosis described in the presentation?

A. The animals are harmed by each other.

B. The animals have the same enemies.

C. The animals resemble each other.

D. One animal is not affected by the relationship.

Part B

Which evidence from the presentation **best** supports your answer to Part A?

A. So animals are afraid of both creatures and stay away from them.

B. The banded sea snake is a dangerous hunter.

C. But the harlequin snake eel looks just like the banded sea snake.

D. The banded sea snake is neither harmed nor helped.

9 This question has two parts. First, answer Part A. Then, answer Part B.

Part A

Which sentence describes the **best** example of symbiosis?

A. A bird eats tiny bugs off a deer's fur.

B. A squirrel runs up a tree to escape a fox.

C. A mother mouse digs a warm hole for her babies to live in.

D. Two horses share the same stall in a barn.

Part B

Which type of symbiosis does the answer to Part A describe?

A. one in which both creatures benefit

B. one in which one creature benefits, but the other is harmed

C. one in which one creature benefits, and the other is not harmed

D. one in which one creature benefits from mimicking the other

10 Choose two of the animal pairs you learned about in the presentation. Using the notes you took, compare and contrast how the pairs are affected by symbiosis. Include in your answer an explanation of what symbiosis is and why it is important to animals.

Write your answer on the lines provided.

academic vocabulary terms used across many subjects and in everyday language

act a main section of a drama, sometimes made up of *scenes*

adjective a word that describes a noun or a pronoun

adverb a word or phrase that describes a verb, an adjective, or another adverb

affix a word part, such as a prefix or suffix, added to the beginning or end of a word or root to make a new word

alliteration the repetition of consonant sounds

allusion a reference to a person, place, event, or piece of literature

antecedent a word or phrase represented by another word

antonyms words that mean the opposite of each other

article a short nonfiction text that appears online or in newspapers and magazines

audience the readers of nonfiction or fiction, or the people who are listening to someone speaking or reading aloud

author's purpose the reason an author writes a text, usually to inform, entertain, or persuade the reader

bibliography a list of the resources used for a written project

body the main part of a letter or e-mail that comes after the greeting and before the closing

bold type a dark, thick text that readers will notice

bulleted list a list of details or information, using symbols called bullets (•) instead of numbers

caption a phrase or sentence that tells what a photograph or other graphic is about

cast of characters a list of the characters in a drama

cause the reason that something happens

cause-and-effect structure a text organization in which the author explains what happened (effect) and why it happened (cause)

character a person, an animal, or an object that takes part in the action of a story

chronological structure a text organization in which the author presents events in the order in which they happened; also called *sequence structure*

claim a statement that an author makes about an idea, event, or observation

clause a group of words with a subject and a verb

comma the punctuation mark used to separate elements within a sentence; usually represents a brief pause

compare to show how objects, ideas, people, places, events, or passages are similar

compare-and-contrast structure a text organization in which the author points out how two or more things or ideas are alike and different

complete sentence a sentence that forms a complete thought, using a subject and a verb

compound sentence a sentence that contains two or more simple sentences, or main clauses

concise short, simple, and to the point

conclusion the end of a piece of writing in which the author restates his or her position and sums up the text's main points

conflict a problem that the characters solve in a fictional narrative

conjunction a word such as *and*, *but*, or *or* that connects two words, sentences, or phrases

connotations an emotional association with a word; for example, *fragrance* and *stench* are synonyms, but *fragrance* has good connotations and *stench* has bad ones

context clues the words or phrases that help readers understand the meaning of an unfamiliar word

contraction two words combined, using an apostrophe to indicate a missing letter or letters; example: *can't*

contrast to show how objects, ideas, people, places, events, or passages are different

coordinating conjunction a word such as *and*, *or*, *so*, or *but* that joins two independent clauses in a sentence

dash (—) a wide mark of punctuation that shows an interrupted thought

detail information that supports the main idea in a piece of writing

diagram a drawing with labels that shows the different parts of an object or how something works

dialogue the words that characters speak in a drama; in fiction stories, a conversation between characters, with their speech in quotation marks

direct speech the words that someone says, set off by punctuation in writing

directions step-by-step instructions; a set of steps to follow in order to complete a task or project

document printed form that serves as a record or asks for information

domain-specific vocabulary words that have a specific meaning in a particular kind of work or field of study, such as science, history, or technology

drafting creating an early version of a written work; the second step of the writing process

drama a story that is performed on a stage by actors; a play

editing the fourth step of the writing process: correcting mistakes in grammar, spelling, capitalization, and punctuation

effect a result of a cause

ellipsis (. . .) a series of spaced periods showing that text has been omitted

e-mail or email a message sent electronically via the Internet

epic poem a long poem that tells about the adventures of a hero or a historic event

evidence information, or facts, used to support a main idea or claim

exclamation point (!) an end punctuation mark that shows excitement, shock, or surprise

fable a made-up story that teaches a lesson; may have animal characters acting like people

fact information that is true and can be proved

fiction writing about made-up people and events

figurative language words or phrases that mean something different from their dictionary definitions

firsthand account a text in which the author describes an experience or event that he or she is observing or has observed

first-person point of view the perspective in which the narrator is a character in the story and uses the pronoun *I*

flowchart a graphic organizer that uses arrows or connecting lines to show (1) how steps connect or (2) the steps in a process

folktale a story from long ago that has been repeated for many years

form a document that requests certain facts; for example, someone might fill in a form to get a library card

formal language the type of language used in most writing and presentations; includes complete sentences, proper grammar, and well-chosen vocabulary

formal letter a letter written in formal language

format a design for showing information; for example, party invitations and street signs have very different formats

free verse a poem that does not follow fixed rules of rhythm or rhyme

function to work properly

functional text text that helps people do everyday tasks and projects; examples: street signs, invitations, directions, and posters

grammar a system of language used in writing and speaking

graphic feature a photograph, illustration, timeline, diagram, map, graph, or flowchart that adds new information or makes text easier to understand

haiku a very short poem, usually about nature, that has 3 lines and just 17 syllables

heading a word or phrase above a section of text that tells what the section is about

historical fiction a type of writing about made-up people and events that takes place in the past; may involve important people or events from history

historical text nonfiction text that tells about real events or people from the past

how-to text text that explains how to complete a project, such as a recipe or directions for a game

idiom a word or phrase that has a different meaning from the meaning of the individual words

illustration a picture that shows details from text, helping readers better understand and enjoy a story

independent clause a group of words with a subject and verb that represents a complete thought

inference an educated guess that a reader makes about a text, based on evidence the author provides

informal language the type of language that people use in everyday conversation

informational text nonfiction text, such as a biography, essay, speech, or textbook, in which the author presents information, or facts, about the real world

instructions directions; a set of steps that explain how to complete a task or a project

integrate information to make connections between ideas and details from two or more sources in order to better understand a topic

introduction the beginning of a piece of writing that gets the reader's attention and presents the text's main idea

italic type slanted text used to call attention to details or to indicate a book title, for example

label a word or phrase that names something in a photograph, map, or diagram

legend a type of folktale about heroes and their brave actions

limerick a humorous five-line poem that rhymes

line a row of words; the basic building block of a poem

linking words and phrases words and phrases that connect ideas to make writing flow smoothly; also called *transitions*

literal language words or phrases that mean the same as their dictionary meanings

literary nonfiction informational texts, such as biographies and autobiographies, about real people

lyric poem a short poem that is like a song and usually deals with the speaker's thoughts or feelings

main idea the most important idea in a piece of writing

make connections between texts to note how texts are similar and different, often in the same genre

manual a long series of step-by-step instructions

map a drawing that shows the location of physical features, such as cities, roads, or rivers

metaphor a comparison that does not use the words *like* or *as*

meter the "beat," or pattern of rhythm, in a poem

modal auxiliary verb a verb such as *can*, *might*, *should*, *could*, and *must* that shows the possibility or necessity of an action

model a representation of how something looks

multiple-meaning words words that are spelled the same but have more than one meaning

myth a traditional story from a certain place; may give reasons for how something works or how it was created

narrative poem a poem that tells a story

narrative writing the type of writing that tells a story, sometimes fictional and sometimes about real events

narrator the person or character who tells a story

nonfiction writing that tells about the real world—using facts about people, places, events, and things; also called *informational text*

noun a word that names a person, place, thing, or idea

ode a serious poem about a meaningful topic; usually has two or more stanzas and rhyming lines

opinion a belief based on feelings that cannot be proven true

opinion piece a type of writing in which the author states a personal belief and tries to persuade others to agree

paraphrase to retell an author's idea in your own words

personification the type of figurative language in which human qualities are given to nonhuman things

perspective the attitude or feeling of the author toward his or her topic; also called *point of view*

persuasive text nonfiction text in which the author tries to persuade, or convince, the reader to agree with a certain point of view or to take a specific action

plot the series of events in a story that includes the characters' actions, a conflict, and a resolution

plot structure the organization of the events in a story, including the beginning, middle, end, problem, and solution

poetry writing that uses words in lines and stanzas to create a strong feeling, image, or message through meaning, sound, and rhythm

point of view the perspective from which a story or poem is told by a narrator; how an author feels about a topic

precise exact, detailed

precise language words or phrases that tell the writer's ideas in a clear and exact way

predicate the part of a sentence that contains a verb and tells what the subject does

prefix a word part, or affix, added to the beginning of a word or root that changes the word's meaning

preposition a word that comes before a noun or pronoun to show direction, location, or time, such as to, *under*, and *after*

prepositional phrase a phrase that shows time, space, or position; begins with a preposition and ends with a noun or pronoun

present participle a verb form that ends in *-ing* and describes a current action or state of being

presentation a talk or speech that gives information or shares an opinion

prewriting the first step in the writing process, in which writers decide on a topic and determine what to say about it

primary source a source written or recorded at the time of an event by someone who was there

problem a difficult situation, obstacle, or challenge; also called *conflict*

problem-and-solution structure a text organization in which the author states a problem and suggests a way to solve the problem

progressive tense the tense that shows action in progress, using a form of the verb *be* with the main verb

progressive verb a verb form, ending with *-ing* and preceded by a form of the verb *to be*, that is used to express an ongoing action

pronoun a word that takes the place of a noun

proofread to make sure there are no errors in capitalization, punctuation, and spelling

proper adjective an adjective that is capitalized because it describes a specific person, place, or thing, such as *West* in *West Virginia* or *Big* in *Big Dipper*

proper noun a noun that names a specific person, place, or thing, such as *President Kennedy or Scranton, Pennsylvania*

publishing the last step of the writing process; letting others read your work either digitally or in print

punctuation the marks used in sentences that help readers understand the meaning

question mark (?) an end punctuation mark used to show that a question is being asked

quotation text taken—quoted—from a source

quotation marks punctuation used to show the exact words of a speaker

realistic fiction the type of fiction that has characters, events, and a setting that could exist in the real world

reasons in persuasive text, the ideas that support an author's opinions

recipe a how-to text that explains how to cook or prepare something to eat or drink

reference materials resources such as dictionaries, thesauruses, and glossaries that can be used to check word meanings and learn more about research topics

relative adverb an adverb such as *when, where*, and *why* that shows time, place, or reason

relative pronoun a pronoun such as *which, that, who, whom*, and *whose* that is used to add information about a noun

repetition the repeating of a word, phrase, or line

research to gather information from sources such as books and Web sites

response to literature a type of writing in which the author states a position, or gives an opinion, about a story, play, or poem

revising the third step of the writing process: improving writing by changing or making corrections to a draft or piece of writing

rhyme a sound device, often in poetry, in which words end with the same sound

rhythm the pattern of stressed and unstressed syllables in a line of poetry

root the base, or main, part of a word

run-on sentence one or more sentences that have been combined without proper punctuation

scene a smaller section of an act in a drama

science fiction the type of fiction that tells about science and technology; may be set in the future, in space, or in an unusual place

scientific text a nonfiction text, such as a lab report, magazine article, or textbook, that explains a science topic

secondhand account an account of an event written by someone who did not directly experience the event

sensory descriptions details that tell how things look, feel, sound, smell, and taste

sentence fragment an incomplete sentence, lacking either a subject or a verb

sequence of events the order in which events occur

sequence structure a text organization in which the author presents events in the order in which they happen; also called *chronological structure*

setting where and when a story takes place

shades of meaning synonyms that have slight differences in strength or emotion

simile a comparison that uses the words *like* or *as*

simple sentence a sentence that has a subject and a predicate and states a complete thought

solution the answer to a problem

source a book, Web site, or other type of reference material used while doing research

spatial structure a type of organization in which the author describes where things are, using location words such as *top*, *bottom*, *front*, and *back*

stage directions the words in a drama that tell the actors how to speak their lines or how to move; also, information about sound, lighting, props, and costumes

stanza a series of lines that make up a section of a poem

step-by-step one action at a time; arranged in time order

steps in a process a type of text organization in which the writer tells how to do something or how something was done

structure the pattern or organization of a text

subject the part of a sentence that tells what or whom the sentence is about

subject line in an e-mail message, the word or phrase that tells what the message is about

suffix a word part, or affix, added to the end of a word or root that changes the word's meaning

summarize to retell in your own words the most important plot events of a story or the main ideas of a nonfiction text

supporting facts and details facts, examples, or other information that an author includes to explain a main idea

symbol a shape or letter that stands for an idea

synonyms words that have the same or almost the same meaning

technical text an informational text, such as a brochure, recipe, or manual, that provides detailed information about a specific subject or how to do something

tense refers to when the action of a verb takes place, such as past or future tense

text feature an element, such as a heading, bulleted list, or caption, that helps readers find and follow facts and ideas

text structure the way in which text is organized, such as by sequence, cause and effect, compare and contrast, or problem and solution

theme the lesson or message that the author of a story or poem wants to share

third-person point of view the perspective in which the narrator is not a character in the story and describes people and their actions using words such as *he*, *she*, and *they*

timeline a graphic that shows the dates and order of events over a specific time period

topic the subject, or main idea, of a text

topic sentence a sentence that explains the main idea of either a paragraph or an informative text

transition a word or phrase that connects sentences, paragraphs, or ideas to help writing flow

verb a word that shows action or state of being

whole-to-part structure a type of organization in which the author states a topic sentence or general idea and then supports it with facts and details

writing process the steps—prewriting, drafting, revising, editing, and publishing—taken by writers to express themselves in an organized way

writing style might be formal or informal

Short Answer Rubric

Score	
2	The response is correct and answers all parts of the prompt. It uses strong support from the text(s). The student shows understanding of English Language Arts skills.
1	The response only answers some parts of the prompt. It uses weak support from the text. The student shows some understanding of English Language Arts skills.
0	The response is incorrect OR the student has not written a response. The student does not show an understanding of English Language Arts skills.

Analytic Writing Rubric

Score	Focus	Organization	Development and Evidence	Language	Conventions
4	The response answers all parts of the prompt. It makes connections between ideas in the text. The language fits the purpose and audience.	The response presents ideas in an order that makes sense. There is a clear introduction and conclusion. The response uses a variety of transitions.	The response uses strong text support and shows understanding of the text. It includes clear reasons, details, and/or description.	The response uses exact language and strong vocabulary.	There are few mistakes in grammar, punctuation, capitalization, and spelling.
3	The response answers most parts of the prompt. It makes some connections between ideas in the text. The language mostly fits the purpose and audience.	The response often presents ideas in an order that makes sense. There is an introduction and conclusion. The response uses some transitions.	The response uses text support and shows understanding of the text. It includes reasons, details, and/or description.	The response mixes some exact language with more general language.	There are some mistakes in grammar, punctuation, capitalization, and spelling. The mistakes do not affect the meaning of the response.
2	The response answers some parts of the prompt. It does not make many connections between ideas in the text. Some of the language does not fit the purpose or audience.	The response does not present ideas in an order that makes sense. There is a weak introduction and conclusion. Transitions are used incorrectly.	The response uses some text support but shows little understanding of the text. It includes weak reasons, details, and/or description.	The response uses simple and broad language.	There are many mistakes in grammar, punctuation, capitalization, and spelling. The mistakes sometimes make it hard to understand the response.
1	The response only answers the prompt in a general way. It makes weak or incorrect connections between ideas in the text. The language does not fit the purpose or audience at all.	The response has no clear structure. Some ideas do not relate to the response. Few transitions are used.	The response uses little or no text support. It shows a misunderstanding of the text. There are few reasons, details, and/or descriptions.	The response uses confusing or incorrect language.	There are serious mistakes in grammar, punctuation, capitalization, and spelling. The mistakes make it hard to understand the response.
0	The response does not answer the prompt, is incomplete, or cannot be read.				

Informative and Opinion Writing Rubric

Score	Focus	Organization	Development and Evidence	Language	Conventions
4	The response answers all parts of the prompt. It focuses on a clear main idea or opinion statement. The language fits the purpose and audience.	The response presents ideas in an order that makes sense. There is a clear introduction and conclusion. The response uses a variety of transitions.	The response uses strong text support and shows understanding of the source text(s). It includes clear reasons and descriptions.	The response uses exact language and strong vocabulary.	There are few mistakes in grammar, punctuation, capitalization, and spelling.
3	The response answers most parts of the prompt. It usually focuses on a main idea or opinion statement. The language mostly fits the purpose and audience.	The response often presents ideas in an order that makes sense. There is an introduction and conclusion. The response uses some transitions.	The response often uses text support and shows understanding of the text(s). Text support may be general. The response includes some reasons and descriptions.	The response mixes some exact language with more general language.	There are some mistakes in grammar, punctuation, capitalization, and spelling. The mistakes do not affect the meaning of the response.
2	The response answers some parts of the prompt. It sometimes focuses on a main idea or opinion statement. The language does not always fit the purpose and audience.	The response does not present ideas in an order that makes sense. There is a weak introduction and conclusion. Transitions are used incorrectly.	The response uses some text support for the main idea or opinion statement. It does not show a complete understanding of the text(s). Text support may not make sense with the response, or may be incorrect.	The response uses simple and broad language.	There are many mistakes in grammar, punctuation, capitalization, and spelling. The mistakes sometimes make it hard to understand the response.
1	The response only answers the prompt in a general way. It does not have a clear main idea or opinion statement. The language does not fit the purpose or audience at all.	The response has no clear structure. Some ideas do not relate to the response. Few transitions are used.	The response uses little or no text support for the main idea or opinion statement. The text support does not relate to the response.	The response uses confusing or incorrect language.	There are serious mistakes in grammar, punctuation, capitalization, and spelling. The mistakes make it hard to understand the response.
0	The response does not answer the prompt, is incomplete, or cannot be read.				

Narrative Rubric

Score	Focus	Organization	Development and Evidence	Language	Conventions
4	The narrative responds to all parts of the prompt. It has a clear setting, narrator, and/or characters. It fits the purpose and audience.	The narrative has a strong plot. The sequence of events makes sense. There is a clear opening and closing. The response uses a variety of transitions.	The response uses strong narrative techniques. Details, dialogue, and description move the plot along or help the reader imagine the scene.	The narrative uses strong examples of sensory, concrete, and figurative language.	There are few mistakes in grammar, punctuation, capitalization, and spelling.
3	The narrative responds to most parts of the prompt. It has a setting, narrator, and/or characters. It mostly fits the purpose and audience.	The narrative has a plot with an opening and closing. The response uses some transitions.	The response often uses narrative techniques, such as details, dialogue, and description.	The narrative uses some examples of sensory, concrete, and figurative language.	There are some mistakes in grammar, punctuation, capitalization, and spelling. The mistakes do not affect the meaning of the response.
2	The narrative responds to some parts of the prompt. It has a setting, narrator, and/or characters, but sometimes loses focus. It does not always fit the purpose and audience.	The narrative has a confusing plot with a weak opening and closing. The response uses some transitions.	The response may use some narrative techniques, but they do not add anything to the story.	The narrative uses weak example of sensory, concrete, and figurative language.	There are many mistakes in grammar, punctuation, capitalization, and spelling. The mistakes sometimes make it hard to understand the response.
1	The narrative only responds to the prompt in a general way. It is missing a setting, narrator, and/or characters. It does not fit the purpose and audience.	The narrative has no plot. Some ideas do not relate to the response. Few transitions are used.	The response uses few or no narrative techniques. The narrative techniques do not relate to the plot or the prompt.	The narrative uses unclear and confusing language.	There are serious mistakes in grammar, punctuation, capitalization, and spelling. The mistakes make it hard to understand the response.
0	The response does not answer the prompt, is incomplete, or cannot be read.				

AzMERIT Practice Test 1

Directions

This Practice Test is designed to help you prepare for tests that you will take on the computer. It includes new types of questions that have been adapted to work in a paper-and-pencil format. Some questions have direction lines that will tell you how to complete the question and indicate your answer. Always read the directions carefully. You will mark your answers and write your responses directly into the Practice Test book.

This Practice Test includes two main parts:

1. English Language Arts
2. Writing Task

The English Language Arts part of the test contains reading, editing, and listening sections. After completing the reading and editing sections, stop and wait for your teacher to give you instructions on taking the listening section of the Practice Test. Your teacher will give you instructions on when and how to complete the Writing Task.

Read the story, and answer the questions that follow.

The Princess and the Pea

1 Once upon a time, there was a prince who was looking to marry. He had searched the land to find just the right woman. She had to be strong and intelligent, but she also had to be sensitive enough to be a compassionate princess to the kingdom's people.

2 The queen knew how much her son wanted to find just the right woman to be his bride. However, none of the princesses they had met so far had the qualities they were looking for.

3 One stormy night, a young woman appeared at the castle, asking to come in. "Welcome, my dear," said the queen. The queen guided the woman to the fire in the library. "Why are you out alone on such a cold and rainy night?" the queen asked.

4 "I was riding with my family, but we became separated in the storm," the young woman answered.

5 "And who are your family?" the queen asked.

6 The young woman blushed and replied, "Actually, I am Princess Angelica, the daughter of Queen Evangeline and King Desmond. They'll be very upset when they find out I've ended up so far from home."

7 The queen was struck by the young woman's grace and took a liking to the poor, drenched princess. She decided to test the woman's honesty and led the princess to a special guest chamber.

8 "What an unusual bed!" the princess remarked, gazing up at a pile of twenty mattresses.

PRACTICE TEST 1

9 “We want you to be comfortable,” the queen smiled.

10 What the princess didn’t know was that the queen had hidden a small pea under the very bottom mattress. Only the most sensitive soul would know that it was there.

11 The princess climbed the ladder to the top of the bed and went to sleep.

12 In the morning, the queen entered and asked the princess how she slept.

13 “Oh, Your Majesty, I’m sorry to report that I did not sleep well at all,” the princess replied.

14 “Whatever was the matter?” the queen asked.

15 “I don’t know,” the princess replied. “It was as if there was a rock underneath the mattresses!”

16 The queen smiled. “You didn’t sleep well? My dear, that’s wonderful!”

17 “I beg your pardon?” The princess stood staring at the queen, confused.

18 “I didn’t mean that I was glad for your discomfort,” the queen said. “Join us downstairs.”

19 The princess headed downstairs when she was ready. She found the king, the queen, the prince, and some of the servants in the dining room smiling happily at her.

20 “What is going on?” the princess asked, her hands to her face.

21 The prince ran to her and dropped down on his knee. He grabbed the princess’s hand and blurted, “Will you marry me?”

22 The princess blushed and said, “Why me?” Despite her question, she found herself quite attracted to this handsome young man.

23 "You have proved yourself sensitive enough to be princess to my people," the prince said. He gazed into her warm, brown eyes.

24 "Well, I am often told I'm very sensitive," the princess said tentatively, "but I'm not sure people mean it in a good way."

25 "We think it's a *very* good thing," the queen said. "When you couldn't sleep because of the tiniest pea under twenty mattresses, you proved yourself to be a highly sensitive young woman. We know you will feel compassion for the people of our land."

26 The princess looked into the eyes of the adoring prince. He looked as if he had been struck through the heart by Cupid's arrow.

27 "I have been wondering how I might be helpful to others," she said, as the prince reached for her hand. "Now I know!"

1

This question has two parts. First, answer part A. Then, answer part B.

Part A

Which of the following **best** describes the reasons for the queen's actions in the story?

Ⓐ The queen likes being in charge of things. She wants to make sure her son's wife has a similar personality.

Ⓑ The queen wants to keep her son from choosing someone she doesn't like. She knows that she will be spending a lot of time with her son's wife.

Ⓒ The queen wants to find someone who will be a good wife to her son. She loves her son and wants him to be happy.

Ⓓ The queen feels lonely and locked up in such a big castle. She wants someone to keep her company when the king and prince are away.

Part B

Underline the sentence from the story that supports your answer in part A.

1 Once upon a time, there was a prince who was looking to marry. He had searched the land to find just the right woman. She had to be strong and intelligent, but she also had to be sensitive enough to be a compassionate princess to the kingdom's people.

2 The queen knew how much her son wanted to find just the right woman to be his bride. However, none of the princesses they had met so far had the qualities they were looking for.

PRACTICE TEST 1

2

This question has two parts. First, answer part A. Then, answer part B.

Part A

Which of the following **best** describes the theme of "The Princess and the Pea"?

Ⓐ Someone who is sensitive usually has a difficult time sleeping.

Ⓑ A queen is the best person to choose a suitable partner for her son or daughter.

Ⓒ Someone who is sensitive to the smallest thing would be more sensitive to people's needs.

Ⓓ A prince should quickly marry the first princess he meets.

Part B

Choose the sentence from the story that **best** supports your answer to part A.

Ⓐ "She had to be strong and intelligent, but she also had to be sensitive enough to be a compassionate princess to the kingdom's people."

Ⓑ "The queen was struck by the young woman's grace and took a liking to the poor, drenched princess."

Ⓒ "'Well, I am often told I'm very sensitive,' the princess said tentatively, 'but I'm not sure people mean it in a good way.'"

Ⓓ "'I have been wondering how I might be helpful to others,' she said, as the prince reached for her hand."

3

Which of the following **best** describes what happens when the princess enters the dining room after spending the night at the castle?

Ⓐ The princess is greeted with mixed emotions by the king, queen, prince, and their servants. They're not sure what to make of her.

Ⓑ The princess is suspicious of the prince and his family and isn't sure what they are up to. They look at her with equal suspicion.

Ⓒ The prince, queen, king, and their servants greet the princess with joy and excitement. They are sure that she is the person they need.

Ⓓ The prince, his parents, and the servants greet the princess happily, but she just wants to return home.

4

This question has two parts. First, answer part A. Then, answer part B.

Part A

Read this sentence from the story.

> **"Well, I am often told I'm very sensitive," the princess said <u>tentatively</u>, "but I'm not sure people mean it in a good way." (paragraph 24)**

What does the word <u>tentatively</u> mean as used in this sentence?

Ⓐ uncertainly

Ⓑ surprisingly

Ⓒ angrily

Ⓓ joyfully

Part B

Explain which clues help you understand the meaning of the word.

Write your answer in the space provided.

PRACTICE TEST 1

5

Why does the prince **most likely** want a sensitive wife?

Ⓐ She would get along well with him because he is sensitive too.

Ⓑ She would be like the queen, whom the prince adores.

Ⓒ She would rule with understanding and kindness.

Ⓓ She would alert him when things went wrong.

6

Read the sentences from the story.

> **The princess looked into the eyes of the adoring prince. <u>He looked as if he had been struck through the heart by Cupid's arrow.</u> (paragraph 25)**

Which statement **best** reflects the meaning of the underlined sentence?

Ⓐ The prince is wounded and may not live to marry the princess.

Ⓑ The princess has played a trick on the prince, but he does not seem to notice.

Ⓒ The princess has asked her friend, Cupid, to fall in love with the prince.

Ⓓ The prince is gazing at the princess with whom he has fallen in love.

7

This question has two parts. First, answer part A. Then, answer part B.

Part A

Which words **best** describe the princess in the passage? Choose all that apply.

- **A.** ☑ gentle
- **B.** ☑ silly
- **C.** ☐ unhappy
- **D.** ☐ angry
- **E.** ☑ truthful
- **F.** ☐ understanding

Part B

Write **two** details from the story that support your answer to part A.

Write your answer on the lines provided.

Reading

Read the articles, and answer the questions that follow.

Text A

Pioneer Women

1 When we hear about American homesteaders, or people who moved to territories and states to claim land for their own, we usually hear about the men. What many people do not know is that according to historians' estimates, nearly 12 percent of the homesteaders in the western parts of the United States were single women.

2 Why would single women risk the difficulties of traveling across the country to start new lives in new, and sometimes hostile, lands? They did it for the same reasons men did—to have their own land. They had no rent to pay and no fear of losing their jobs. Their work was their own. If they worked hard, they were bound to make their lives better.

3 The Homestead Act of 1862 allowed a woman aged twenty-one or older and head of her own household the right to take ownership of some federal land. Some women took the government up on the offer.

4 How did those pioneer women get to their new lands and build their new homes? After the Homestead Act first passed, cross-country travelers did not have many choices. Many joined wagon trains, which were groupings of horse-pulled wagons that traveled together. Since the railroad system was not yet complete, the safest way to travel was with another group of homesteaders. Women traveling on their own were forced to join up with strangers on long and difficult journeys.

5 When the railroad spread far enough across the country, homesteaders finally had another transportation option. Still,

traveling by train depended on when and where they were traveling. Eventually, the railroad expanded, and more and more people moving west were able to get there by train. Women who were traveling alone most likely thought it was safer to travel on a train full of many fellow travelers and a conductor than as part of a wagon train.

6 What happened to the pioneer women when they arrived in their new destinations? The number of women who were able to stake out their land, build their homes, and start their new lives was small at first. Many women had to find work until they could save up enough to buy the materials necessary to build a house. Some found work as teachers, schooling the children of other settlers. Others hired themselves out to cook, do laundry, or clean for others. Even though it was difficult at the time for women to be hired for "men's jobs," some women also found this kind of work. They got jobs as clerks in stores or as secretaries for newspapers.

7 The federal government did provide some money for homesteaders, but the requirements were strict. The homesteaders had to stay on the land for a certain amount of time and show that they had improved it before they could claim it as their own. Single women faced a particularly hard time because some people did not believe women could take care of land and property on their own.

8 Elinore Rupert Stewart was one of the best-known female homesteaders in the early 1900s. Stewart's husband passed away, and she was raising a young daughter on her own. She left Denver, Colorado, and traveled to seek her fortune. She and her daughter settled in Wyoming, where she worked as a housekeeper for a Scottish homesteader named Clyde Stewart. Eventually, the two married. Stewart is just one of the many women who chose to follow adventure—and seek independence—as they became a part of this country's westward movement.

Text B

The Joys of Homesteading

adapted from a letter
by Elinore Rupert Stewart

January 23, 1913

Dear Mrs. Coney,

1 I am afraid all my friends think I am very forgetful and that you think I am ungrateful as well, but I am going to plead not guilty. Right after Christmas Mr. Stewart came down with *la grippe*[1] and was so miserable that it kept me busy trying to relieve him. Out here where we can get no physician we have to give medicine to ourselves, so that I had to be housekeeper, nurse, doctor, and general overseer. That explains my long silence.

2 And now I want to thank you for your kind thought in prolonging our Christmas. The magazines were much appreciated. They relieved some weary night-watches, and the box did Jerrine more good than the medicine I was having to give her for *la grippe*. She was content to stay in bed and enjoy the contents of her box.

3 When I read of the hard times among the Denver poor, I feel like urging them every one to get out and file on land. I am very enthusiastic about women homesteading. It really requires less strength and labor to raise plenty to satisfy a large family than it does to go out to wash, with the added satisfaction of knowing that their job will not be lost to them if they care to keep it. Even if improving the place does go slowly, it is that much done to stay done. Whatever is raised is the homesteader's own, and there is no house-rent to pay.

[1]**la grippe**: an old-fashioned term for influenza or "the flu"

This year Jerrine cut and dropped enough potatoes to raise a ton of fine potatoes. She wanted to try, so we let her, and you will remember that she is but six years old. We had a man to break the ground and cover the potatoes for her, and the man irrigated them once. That was all that was done until digging time when they were ploughed out and Jerrine picked them up. Any woman strong enough to go out by the day could have done every bit of the work and put in two or three times that much, and it would have been so much more pleasant than to work so hard in the city and then be on starvation rations in the winter.

4 To me, homesteading is the solution of all poverty's problems, but I realize that <u>temperament</u> has much to do with success in any undertaking, and persons afraid of coyotes and work and loneliness had better let ranching alone. At the same time, any woman who can stand her own company, can see the beauty of the sunset, loves growing things, and is willing to put in as much time at careful labor as she does over the washtub will certainly succeed; will have independence, plenty to eat all the time, and a home of her own in the end.

5 Here I am boring you to death with things that cannot interest you! You'd think I wanted you to homestead, wouldn't you? But I am only thinking of the troops of tired, worried women, sometimes even cold and hungry, scared to death of losing their places to work, who could have plenty to eat, who could have good fires by gathering the wood, and comfortable homes of their own, if they but had the courage and determination to get them.

6 I must stop right now before you get so tired you will not answer. With much love to you from Jerrine and myself, I am

Yours affectionately,
Elinore Rupert Stewart

8

Which sentence from Text A **best** supports the author's point that "[w]omen who were traveling alone most likely thought it was safer to travel on a train full of many fellow travelers and a conductor than as part of a wagon train"?

Ⓐ "After the Homestead Act first passed, cross-country travelers did not have many choices."

Ⓑ "Many joined wagon trains, which were groupings of horse-pulled wagons that traveled together."

Ⓒ "Women traveling on their own were forced to join up with strangers on long and difficult journeys."

Ⓓ "Still, traveling by train depended on when and where they were traveling."

9

Which statement **best** describes the importance of the Homestead Act?

Ⓐ The Homestead Act made it legal for people to travel by trains to territories in order to set up homes.

Ⓑ The Homestead Act provided transportation and money for men who were willing to build homes and start farms.

Ⓒ The Homestead Act offered men and qualified single women the opportunity to move to the West and settle the land.

Ⓓ The Homestead Act offered money to women who were willing to take jobs as teachers or secretaries in the West.

10

This question has two parts. First, answer part A. Then, answer part B.

Part A

How is the information in Text A organized?

Ⓐ by cause and effect

Ⓑ in a time sequence

Ⓒ by compare and contrast

Ⓓ by problem and solution

Part B

Which sentence **best** supports your answer in part A?

Ⓐ "When the railroad spread far enough across the country, homesteaders finally had another transportation option."

Ⓑ "The federal government did provide some money for homesteaders, but the requirements were strict."

Ⓒ "What many people don't know is that according to historians' estimates, nearly 12 percent of the homesteaders in the western part of America were single women."

Ⓓ "Stewart is just one of the many women who chose to follow adventure—and seek independence—as they became a part of this country's westward movement."

11

What does Elinore Rupert Stewart, the writer of Text B, think about women and homesteading? Choose **all** that apply.

A. ☐ She thinks homesteading is something women would find difficult.

B. ☐ She thinks that homesteading allows women to worry less.

C. ☐ She thinks Mrs. Coney should move to Wyoming to homestead.

D. ☐ She thinks women would be taking too much of a risk by homesteading.

E. ☐ She thinks women who homestead have a chance to succeed in new lives.

12

Elinore Rupert Stewart believes that homesteading is the solution to many women's problems. Give three examples from Text B that support this belief.

Write your answer on the lines provided.

13

This question has two parts. First, answer part A. Then, answer part B.

Part A

What is the meaning of the word <u>temperament</u> as it is used in this sentence from Text B?

> **To me, homesteading is the solution of all poverty's problems, but I realize that <u>temperament</u> has much to do with success in any undertaking, and persons afraid of coyotes and work and loneliness had better let ranching alone. (paragraph 4)**

Ⓐ bad behavior

Ⓑ sensitivity to poverty

Ⓒ someone's personality

Ⓓ someone's training

Part B

Which of the phrases from Text B describes people who would **not** have the right temperament for homesteading?

Ⓐ "persons afraid of coyotes and work and loneliness"

Ⓑ "any woman who can stand her own company"

Ⓒ "troops of tired, worried women"

Ⓓ "scared to death of losing their places to work"

PRACTICE TEST 1

14

How are Text A and Text B similar? Choose **all** that apply.

A. ☐ They describe events in the 1800s.

B. ☐ They describe advantages of the Homestead Act of 1862.

C. ☐ They describe the personal qualities needed for homesteading.

D. ☐ They describe how homesteading provided opportunities for women.

E. ☐ They describe the negative aspects of homesteading.

F. ☐ They describe how homesteading offered opportunities for men.

G. ☐ They describe events in the 1900s.

15

What would Elinore Rupert Stewart **most likely** say to someone who did not think that women could take care of land and property? Use details from Text B to support your answer.

Write your answer in the space provided.

Read the story, and answer the questions that follow.

The Storm

1 A gray dawn had begun to creep into my bedroom. The room was bitterly cold—so cold that two heavy blankets and a down-filled comforter could not keep out the chill. The wind howled, rattling the windows and causing our old farmhouse to creak and moan.

2 I peered out the window. The snow that had begun to fall yesterday morning was still falling. Snowdrifts stood as high as five feet among the <u>scattered</u> buildings of the farmstead. Shivering, I pulled the covers over my head and tried to snuggle more deeply into my bed. The cold and the snow had told me all I needed to know. Our electric lines were certainly down and our water pipes frozen. No power, no lights, no water, no heat.

3 "Tim! Timmy! Breakfast is ready," my mother called from the bottom of the stairs. "At least the gas stove is working! Hurry now—before your oatmeal gets cold."

4 I struggled out from under the weight of the covers and dressed quickly. I pulled a winter coat from my closet and put it on as I ran down the stairs. The house was dark and gloomy. A blanket had been hung in the doorway that separated the kitchen from the dining room. Pushing it aside and entering the kitchen, I breathed in the wonderful smells of fresh-brewed coffee and frying bacon.

5 "It's warmer in here," I said.

6 "Yes," Dad answered. "We're using the gas burners to cook, and they provide a little heat at the same time. Looks like the kitchen is going to be our home until we get some electricity."

7 "Here, Timmy. Sit down and eat your breakfast," Mom said. She handed me a bowl of steaming oatmeal. "Do you want a couple of slices of bacon, too?" she asked. She set the milk carton and an empty glass on the table.

8 "Yes, please," I said. I took off my coat and ate silently, listening to Dad fiddle with the dial on a battery-powered radio. He was trying to find an update on the weather. The radio buzzed and whined and whistled, but finally Dad tuned in to radio station WLAN in Lancaster. According to the radio, the storm would continue through early afternoon and begin to clear up toward evening. Snowplows were standing by throughout the area. They would begin to clear roads at the first sign that the snow was slowing down.

9 "Well," Dad said, "I predict that we will have power before tomorrow morning. Meanwhile, I think Timmy and I had better bundle up and do our chores. After that, maybe we could play a game or something. What do you think?"

10 I agreed and then put on my coat again. When Dad and I stepped out of the house and into the teeth of the storm, I could hardly see the barn. Snow swirls stung my eyes and skin. The wind, tearing through a grove of pine trees, sent pine needles through the air like tiny darts. We struggled through snowdrifts, sometimes sinking to our waists. I put my head down, pulled my hood as far forward as it would go, and tried to keep Dad in sight.

11 Finally reaching the barn, I was freezing cold and nearly out of breath. The cattle were sheltered in a large covered area at the west side of the barn. I carried bucket after bucket of shelled corn from the grain bin to the animals' feed troughs. Meanwhile, Dad grabbed an ax. He went back into the stinging snow and broke through the ice on their watering tank with the ax. Our work done, we made the painful trip back to the house.

12 Dad and I got out of our wet clothes and hung them up to dry. Then Mom fixed us each a cup of hot chocolate. After we drank the hot chocolate and thawed our limbs in the warm kitchen, Dad pulled all our board games out of the hall closet.

13 We played all that afternoon. And because Dad's lantern gave off plenty of light, we played well into the evening. I was even starting to wish that it would keep on snowing. Just then, though, I heard the roar and crunch of a snowplow clearing the gravel road in front of our house.

14 Moments later, I had the chance to buy the Electric Company in our board game. I decided to go for it. Just as I handed over my play money, our lights flickered and came back on. Then the furnace kicked in.

15 "Timmy," Dad said, laughing. "Why didn't you buy that Electric Company this morning?"

16

Which detail from the paragraph gives a clue that there is no power at Timmy's home? Underline the detail below.

1 A gray dawn had begun to creep into my bedroom. The room was bitterly cold—so cold that two heavy blankets and a down-filled comforter could not keep out the chill. The wind howled, rattling the windows and causing our old farmhouse to creak and moan.

17

This question has two parts. First, answer part A. Then, answer part B.

Part A

How can the narration of this story **best** be described?

Ⓐ first person, told from Timmy's point of view

Ⓑ first person, told from Dad's point of view

Ⓒ third person, telling mostly about Timmy's thoughts

Ⓓ third person, telling about characters' actions but not their thoughts

Part B

Write **two** details from the story that support your answer to part A.

Write your answer in the space provided.

18

What does the word scattered mean as it is used in the sentence?

Snowdrifts stood as high as five feet among the scattered buildings of the farmstead. (paragraph 2)

Ⓐ cold

Ⓑ not very tall

Ⓒ spread out

Ⓓ of different kinds

19

What is meant by the sentence "The cold and the snow had told me all I needed to know" in paragraph 2? Use details from the story to support your answer.

Write your answer in the space provided.

20

Which traits **best** describe Timmy's dad? Choose **two** traits.

A. ▢ dull

B. ▢ strict

C. ▢ worried

D. ▢ easygoing

E. ▢ excited

F. ▢ hardworking

21

Read this entry from a dictionary.

> **fix** (fiks) *v.* 1. to repair or mend 2. to make firm or place permanently 3. to decide or determine 4. to get or prepare food

Which is the meaning of the word <u>fix</u> as it is used in the sentence?

> Then Mom <u>fixed</u> us each a cup of hot chocolate. (paragraph 12)

Ⓐ meaning 1

Ⓑ meaning 2

Ⓒ meaning 3

Ⓓ meaning 4

22

This question has two parts. First, answer part A. Then, answer part B.

Part A

Why does Timmy seem to like the snowstorm better by the end of the story?

Ⓐ He gets to eat oatmeal and bacon for breakfast.

Ⓑ He has fun feeding the animals in the barn in the cold weather.

Ⓒ He has a good time playing games in the kitchen with his family.

Ⓓ He enjoys the adventure of helping his father while getting stung by pine needles.

Part B

Which of the following **best** supports your answer to part A?

Ⓐ "Our electric lines were certainly down and our water pipes frozen. No power, no lights, no water, no heat."

Ⓑ "Snowplows were standing by throughout the area. They would begin to clear roads at the first sign that the snow was slowing down."

Ⓒ "When Dad and I stepped out of the house and into the teeth of the storm, I could hardly see the barn."

Ⓓ "We played all that afternoon. And because Dad's lantern gave off plenty of light, we played well into the evening."

Read the article, and answer the questions that follow.

Finding Your Way with GPS

1 For centuries, travelers needed to navigate, or find their way, by observing the sun, moon, stars, and planets. They did this whether on foot, on an animal, or onboard a ship. The compass was invented around the year 1300 and helped travelers by telling them which direction was north. However, navigation still presented a challenge. It wasn't until the 1960s that navigation started to change from a skill requiring a lot of practice to something most people could do easily and quickly. Today, people can use devices that rely on high-tech satellites in space to determine where they are and how to get to where they need to go, no matter how far away it is.

2 You have to understand satellites to understand today's navigation systems. A satellite is any object that orbits, or revolves around, a planet. In fact, the moon is Earth's first satellite. You can use it to determine which way you're headed. For example, if it is early in the night and you see a full moon on your right, you're facing north. But if it is cloudy, you would be unable to use the moon. That's where the modern, human-made satellites and the Global Positioning System (GPS) come in.

3 In the 1960s, the United States military began creating a system that eventually became the GPS. The military first used navigation satellites that orbited Earth to help submarines find their way. The satellites transmitted radio signals between receivers on the moving submarines and stations on Earth. The receiver on one of the submarines would calculate the time it took the signal to return from the satellite to Earth. This would help determine the submarine's

exact location. These transmissions could sometimes take hours. So they kept improving the system and, by the end of 1978, they had launched the first two Navstar satellites.

4 Since then, this technology has grown into the GPS that is used by most people and companies today. It's important to know that although GPS has *global* in its name, the satellite navigation system is owned by the United States. Satellite navigation is also used throughout Europe. At about the same time the United States was developing satellite navigation, Russia was developing its own system. The European system was initially intended for military use, but then it was expanded to include nonmilitary, or civilian, use. EGNOS, a modern satellite navigation system in Europe, improves the accuracy of GPS. Another European system, called Galileo, will be an all-civilian satellite navigation system.

5 Modern, high-speed GPS needs at least four satellites in orbit and an antenna on Earth. The antenna is a GPS device that sends a signal up to the satellites and receives the signal that returns from the satellites. Each satellite carries an atomic clock. These clocks keep time extremely accurately, so they can record the exact time when the signal is received from Earth. A computer within the GPS device then uses the time lapse between each signal sent back from the satellites to calculate the device's location.

6 Today's GPS can determine a device's location to within ten feet, and sometimes even closer. A GPS device can be installed on just about anything. It can be in cell phones, computers, tablets, cars, planes, or even your dog's collar. These devices can help you determine where you are and how to get to a specific place.

7 GPS devices and programs have gone beyond simply telling you where you are on the planet. The GPS satellites' signals can be connected to telephones or Internet networks, allowing many to access the information. Technology can take the GPS signals and translate them into specific step-by-step directions from the GPS device's current location to another location.

8 Technology can translate GPS directions into words that can be spoken aloud by computers. Some devices can even provide voices based on popular TV characters. Alternatively, the directions can be shown on an animated map that shows you (or your car) as you make your way to your destination with your GPS device. You can either type in the address of your destination or say aloud where you want to go, and your GPS will show you the way.

9 Whether carried in a cell phone, attached to the dashboard of an automobile, or installed in a ship, GPS can be used by nearly anyone with access to the technology. It can also be incorporated into almost any electronic device. GPS keeps all who carry it from getting lost.

23

Based on the article, why was satellite navigation created?

Ⓐ because of problems with cloudy weather

Ⓑ so military vessels could find their way

Ⓒ to help the United States make money

Ⓓ to help astronauts travel in outer space

24

This question has two parts. First, answer part A. Then, answer part B.

Part A

What is the main idea of "Finding Your Way with GPS"?

Ⓐ GPS makes navigation easier.

Ⓑ GPS is better than the European satellite navigation system.

Ⓒ If GPS didn't exist, no one would be able to find their way.

Ⓓ All satellites are simple machines.

Part B

Which detail from the article **best** supports your answer to part A?

Ⓐ "In the 1960s, the United States military began creating a system that eventually became the GPS."

Ⓑ "In fact, the moon is Earth's first satellite."

Ⓒ "These devices can help you determine where you are and how to get to a specific place."

Ⓓ "Modern, high-speed GPS needs at least four satellites in orbit and an antenna on Earth."

25

This question has two parts. First, answer part A. Then, answer part B.

Part A

Which is the **best** description of the overall structure of "Finding Your Way with GPS"?

Ⓐ comparison

Ⓑ cause and effect

Ⓒ problem and solution

Ⓓ chronology

Part B

Underline **three** words or phrases in the paragraph below that support your answer to part A.

3 In the 1960s, the United States military began creating a system that eventually became thc GPS. The military first used navigation satellites that orbited Earth to help submarines find their way. The satellites transmitted radio signals between receivers on the moving submarines and stations on Earth. The receiver on one of the submarines would calculate the time it took the signal to return from the satellite to Earth. This would help determine the submarine's exact location. These transmissions could sometimes take hours. So they kept improving the system and, by the end of 1978, they had launched the first two Navstar satellites.

26

This question has two parts. First, answer part A. Then, answer part B.

Part A

Which claim does the author make about GPS?

Ⓐ GPS can be used by many people on many devices.

Ⓑ Satellite navigation is too high-tech for some.

Ⓒ European satellites are better than other systems.

Ⓓ Using GPS to navigate is the best choice for everyone.

Part B

Which sentence from the passage **best** supports your answer to part A?

Ⓐ "Today's GPS can determine a device's location to within ten feet, and sometimes even closer."

Ⓑ "The GPS satellites' signals can be connected to telephones or Internet networks, allowing many to access the information."

Ⓒ "Whether carried in a cell phone, attached to the dashboard of an automobile, or installed in a ship, GPS can be used by nearly anyone with access to the technology."

Ⓓ "GPS keeps all who carry it from getting lost."

27

What does the word transmissions mean as it is used in these sentences from the article?

> **The receiver on one of the submarines would calculate the time it took the signal to return from the satellite to Earth. This would help determine the submarine's exact location. These transmissions could sometimes take hours. (paragraph 3)**

Ⓐ the launching of a satellite into space

Ⓑ the signals sent to and from Earth

Ⓒ the calculations GPS devices make

Ⓓ the information used by Russian satellites

28

How has modern technology made GPS more accessible to ordinary users? Use details from the article to support your answer.

Write your answer in the space provided.

Read the poem, and answer the questions that follow.

The Pet Rabbit

by Lizzie Lawson and Robert Ellice Mack

I have a little Bunny with a coat as soft as down,
And nearly all of him is white except one bit of brown.
The first thing in the morning when I get out of bed,
I wonder if my Bunny's still safe in his little shed.

And then the next thing that I do I dare say you have guessed;
It's to go at once and see him, when I am washed and dressed.
And every day I see him I like him more and more,
And each day he is bigger than he was the day before.

I feed him in the morning with bran and bits of bread,
And every night I take some straw to make his little bed.
What with carrots in the morning and turnip-tops for tea,
If a bunny can be happy, I'm sure he ought to be.

Then when it's nearly bedtime I go down to his shed,
And say "Good night you Bunny" before I go to bed.
I think there's only one thing that would make me happy quite,
If I could take my Bunny dear with me to bed at night?

29

Which statement **best** summarizes the poem?

Ⓐ The speaker tells why she loves a pet rabbit.

Ⓑ The speaker tells how much she loves a pet rabbit.

Ⓒ The speaker tells how she cares for and loves a pet rabbit.

Ⓓ The speaker tells how quickly a pet rabbit is growing.

30

Which statement **best** explains why "The Pet Rabbit" is a poem and not a story?

Ⓐ It has words that rhyme, even though there is no set pattern for them.

Ⓑ It has a meter, or rhythmic structure, that varies from one part to the next.

Ⓒ It is written in free verse, meaning the lines do not rhyme.

Ⓓ It has a set pattern of rhyming lines and a set meter.

31

This question has two parts. First, answer part A. Then, answer part B.

Part A

Which word is a synonym for the words ought to as they are used in this line from the poem?

If a bunny can be happy, I'm sure he ought to be. (line 12)

Ⓐ cannot

Ⓑ should

Ⓒ might

Ⓓ won't

Part B

Which line of the poem tells why the bunny ought to be happy?

Ⓐ "I wonder if my Bunny's still safe in his little shed."

Ⓑ "And every day I see him I like him more and more,"

Ⓒ "And each day he is bigger than he was the day before."

Ⓓ "I feed him in the morning with bran and bits of bread,"

32

Which characteristics **best** describe the girl and the bunny? Write the characteristics in the boxes below.

Girl	**Bunny**

well fed

loving

soft coat

good caretaker

growing fast

eager

33

What is the meaning of the word <u>down</u> as it is used in this line?

I have a little Bunny with a coat as soft as <u>down</u>, (line 1)

Ⓐ silk

Ⓑ feathers

Ⓒ straw

Ⓓ velvet

34

This question has two parts. First, answer part A. Then, answer part B.

Part A

Which statement **best** describes how the little girl feels about her bunny?

Ⓐ She worries about him a lot and thinks he is not very happy.

Ⓑ She gets tired of having to check on him.

Ⓒ She thinks her bunny is the best pet a child could possibly have.

Ⓓ She wishes she could be with him even more.

Part B

Underline two lines that support your answer to part A.

I feed him in the morning with bran and bits of bread,
And every night I take some straw to make his little bed.
What with carrots in the morning and turnip-tops for tea,
If a bunny can be happy, I'm sure he ought to be.

Then when it's nearly bedtime I go down to his shed,
And say "Good night you Bunny" before I go to bed.
I think there's only one thing that would make me happy quite,
If I could take my Bunny dear with me to bed at night?

35

Read these lines from the poem.

> And then the next thing that I do I dare say you have guessed;
> It's to go at once and see him, when I am washed and dressed.
> (lines 5 and 6)

Why does the little girl tell the reader, "I dare say you have guessed"?

Ⓐ She suspects that the reader is familiar with taking care of bunnies.

Ⓑ She thinks she has made it clear that she wonders about her bunny as soon as she wakes up.

Ⓒ She isn't sure what the reader will think, but she is trying to guess.

Ⓓ She has a schedule for the bunny that she follows, and the reader should know what she does next.

Read the article, and answer the questions that follow.

Marie Curie

1 Marie Curie was born in Poland in 1867. As a child, she amazed people with her great memory. She learned to read when she was only four years old.

2 Her father was a professor of science. The instruments that he kept in a glass case fascinated Marie. She dreamed of becoming a scientist, but that would not be easy. Her family became very poor, and at the age of 18, Marie became a governess. She helped pay for her sister to study in Paris. Later, her sister helped Marie with her education.

3 In those days, there were no universities for girls in Poland. So, in 1891, Marie went to the Sorbonne University in Paris. She was so poor that she ate only bread and butter and drank tea. She wore old clothes she had brought with her from Warsaw.

4 Every day, she would study in the library until 10:00 p.m., then go to her cold little room and read until 2 or 3 o'clock in the morning.

5 After four years at the Sorbonne, Marie married Pierre Curie, a well-known physicist. (A physicist studies the physical nature of the world—what things are made of and why they do what they do.)

6 Together the Curies began looking for new elements. They took uranium ore, ground it up, and boiled it. They treated it with acids and other chemicals. Finally, after four years of hard work and tons of ore, they had one-tenth of a gram of pure radium. They had discovered the first radioactive element!

7 In 1903, Marie, Pierre, and another scientist, Henry Becquerel, were awarded the Nobel Prize in Physics for their discovery of radium and their study of radioactivity. Marie Curie was the first woman to win a Nobel Prize in Physics. Later, she won a second Nobel Prize, in Chemistry.

8 During World War I, Marie worked to develop X-rays in order to help people. She believed they could help treat diseases like cancer as well as help doctors on the battlefield.

The Nobel Prize

Alfred Nobel was a successful inventor and businessman who lived between 1833 and 1896. Nobel explained how he wanted his great fortune to be used after he died. He decided to give awards to people doing excellent work that helped others. He wanted the prizes to be given each year for work in physics, chemistry, medicine, literature, and peace. A prize for economics was added in 1968.

Timeline of Marie Curie

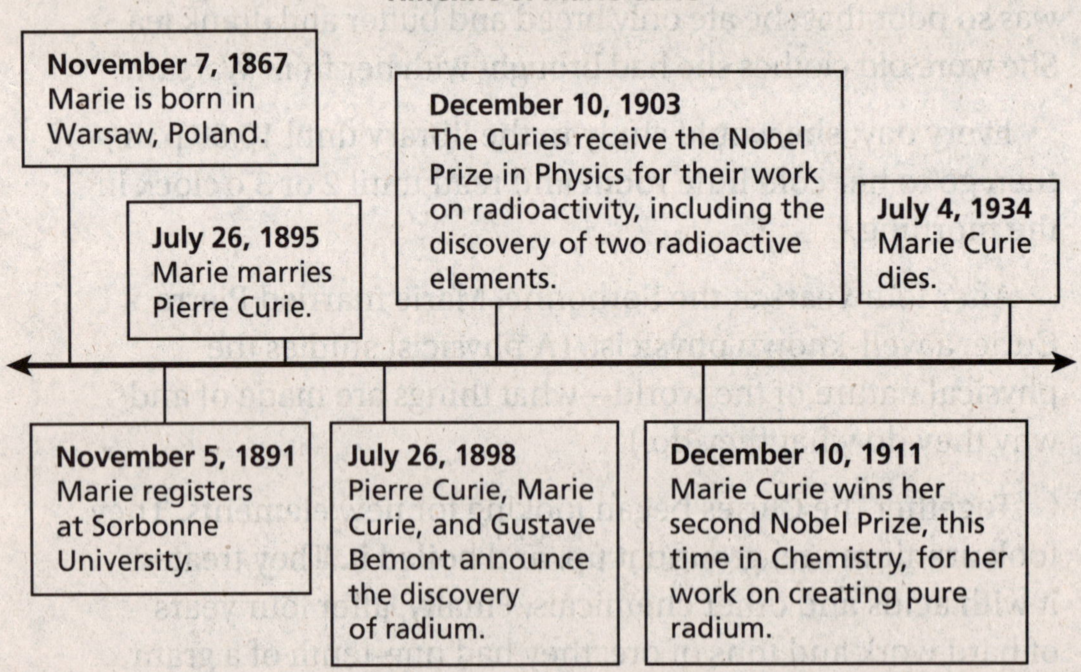

36

How does the timeline aid the reader's understanding of the article?

Ⓐ It shows why Marie Curie's success happened.

Ⓑ It shows what discoveries Marie Curie made.

Ⓒ It shows how Marie Curie's discoveries were made.

Ⓓ It shows when events occurred in Marie Curie's life.

37

Which key detail **best** supports the main idea of the article?

Ⓐ Marie Curie married a well-known physicist.

Ⓑ Marie Curie studied at a university in Paris.

Ⓒ Marie Curie was honored with two Nobel Prizes.

Ⓓ Marie Curie was interested in science instruments.

38

Which sentence from the article **best** supports the idea that Marie Curie loved science?

Ⓐ "She learned to read when she was only four years old."

Ⓑ "As a child, she amazed people with her great memory."

Ⓒ "Her family became very poor, and at the age of 18, Marie became a governess."

Ⓓ "Every day, she would study in the library until 10:00 p.m., then go to her cold little room and read until 2 or 3 o'clock in the morning."

39

What is the meaning of the word physicist as it is used in this sentence?

(A physicist studies the physical nature of the world—what things are made of and why they do what they do.) (paragraph 5)

Ⓐ someone who wins a Nobel Prize in science

Ⓑ someone who has an interest in nature

Ⓒ someone who studies different world cultures

Ⓓ someone who specializes in physics research

40

Underline the sentence that **best** shows that Marie Curie's family supported her.

2 Her father was a professor of science. The instruments that he kept in a glass case fascinated Marie. She dreamed of becoming a scientist, but that would not be easy. Her family became very poor, and at the age of 18, Marie became a governess. She helped pay for her sister to study in Paris. Later, her sister helped Marie with her education.

41

Based on the information in the text box, why did Marie Curie receive the Nobel Prize?

Ⓐ Her research and discoveries helped many people.

Ⓑ She made several discoveries in physics and chemistry.

Ⓒ She was successful throughout her career as a scientist and researcher.

Ⓓ Her research began during the time period the first Nobel prizes were awarded.

42

How does the author support the idea that Marie Curie wanted to help others? Use details from the passage in your answer.

Write your answer in the space provided.

Editing Task

The underlined parts of the passage show words, phrases, or sentences that may be incorrect. After you read the passage, you will answer questions about the underlined text.

My Favorite Activity

My favorite activity is playing soccer. My favorite part of playing soccer is playing goalie. I am the starting goalie for our team, the Scorpions. I think that the goalie is the most importint member of the team. The goalie is the player who has to stop the ball from going into the net and stop the other team from scoring.

Some people think being goalie is boring. Well, it's not boring. You have to be alert all the time when you're guarding the goal. You have to be watching the game no matter where the ball is. When your the goalie, a shot can come at you from any place at any time. It can come from the center the right, or the left, and you have to be ready.

Penalty kicks are the scariest moments for a goalie. It's just you against the kicker. With no other defenders helping. Stopping a penalty kick is the best feeling for a goalie. My teammates and I celebrate when that happens.

43

Read these sentences from the passage.

> <u>My favorite activity is playing soccer. My favorite part of playing soccer is playing goalie.</u>

What is the **best** way to combine the sentences?

Ⓐ My favorite activity is playing soccer, or my favorite part of playing soccer is playing goalie.

Ⓑ My favorite activity is playing soccer, my favorite part of playing soccer is playing goalie.

Ⓒ My favorite activity is playing soccer my favorite part of playing soccer is playing goalie.

Ⓓ My favorite activity is playing soccer, and my favorite part of playing soccer is playing goalie.

44

Read this sentence from the passage.

> I think that the goalie is the most <u>importint</u> member of the team.

Which of these corrects the underlined word?

Ⓐ inportant

Ⓑ importent

Ⓒ important

Ⓓ The word is correct as written.

45

Read this sentence from the passage.

> When <u>your</u> the goalie, a shot can come at you from any place at any time.

Write the correct spelling of the underlined word on the line below.

____

46

Read this sentence from the passage.

> <u>It can come from the center the right, or the left, and you have to be ready.</u>

Write this sentence using correct punctuation on the lines below.

____

____

____

____

47

Read these sentences from the passage.

> It's just you against the kicker. With no other defenders helping.

What is the **best** way to revise these sentences?

Ⓐ It's just you. Against the kicker. With no other defenders helping.

Ⓑ It's just you. Against the kicker with no other defenders helping.

Ⓒ It's just you against the kicker with no other defenders helping.

Ⓓ The sentences are correct as written.

Editing Task

The underlined parts of the passage show words, phrases, or sentences that may be incorrect. After you read the passage, you will answer questions about the underlined text.

The Amazing Bowerbird

Many creatures are builders besides human beings. Beavers build dams birds build nests. One of the most amazing builders is the bowerbird. It lives in Australia and New Guinea. Bowerbirds build the nests that they call home. They can also make special buildings called bowers. The males build bowers two attract females.

The bowers are usually built of sticks or grass. They actually look like tiny buildings. The birds decorate their bowers with pebbles, berries, feathers, flowers, and shells. Bowerbirds like brightly colored decorations.

Different kinds of bowerbirds build different kinds of bowers. Some are tall and some are short. Some are in the shape of a pyramid. One species makes a green big lawn around its bower. One species paints its bower blue. It paints it blue with a mixture of spit and natural color.

Bowerbirds are related to birds of paradise. Birds of paradise have brightly colored feathers while bowerbirds are plain. However, I think bowerbirds make up for it by painting these colorful bowers.

48

Read this sentence from the passage.

Beavers build dams birds build nests.

Correct this run-on sentence on the lines below.

49

Read this sentence from the passage.

Bowerbirds build the nests that they call home.

Which of these corrects the underlined word?

Ⓐ who

Ⓑ whom

Ⓒ which

Ⓓ The word is correct as written.

50

Read this sentence from the passage.

> **The males build bowers two attract females**

Which of the following should replace the word two?

Ⓐ to

Ⓑ tu

Ⓒ too

Ⓓ The word is correct as written.

51

Read this sentence from the passage.

> **One species makes a green big lawn around its bower.**

Which of these corrects the order of the underlined words?

Ⓐ a lawn green big

Ⓑ a big lawn green

Ⓒ a big green lawn

Ⓓ The words are correct as written.

PRACTICE TEST 1

52

Read this sentence from the passage.

> Birds of paradise have brightly colored feathers while bowerbirds are plain.

Write this sentence using correct punctuation on the lines below.

STOP

Listening

Listen to the presentation. Then answer the questions. You may use the space below to take notes.

Breads from Around the World

53

What is the main idea of the presentation?

Ⓐ Ancient civilizations started growing wheat, so it became a popular part of people's diets.

Ⓑ Although it comes in many different forms, bread is a main part of people's diets all over the world.

Ⓒ When people started baking wheat paste, bread became important.

Ⓓ The differences in types of bread found around the world have to do with how the bread is cooked.

54

According to the presentation, which statement identifies how Egyptian bread was different from other early breads?

Ⓐ It used flour to make wheat.

Ⓑ It used water to make dough.

Ⓒ Egyptian bread was baked.

Ⓓ Egyptian bread was leavened.

55

Read the sentence from the presentation.

> **Bread has been a <u>staple</u> of people's diets for centuries.**

What does <u>staple</u> mean as used in the presentation?

Ⓐ fastener to hold things together

Ⓑ special ingredient

Ⓒ main part

Ⓓ type of bread

56

According to the speaker, why are there so many types of bread available in American supermarkets? Use details from the presentation to support your answer.

Write your answer in the space provided.

57

How does the speaker support the idea that bread has been an important part of people's diets for a long time? Use details from the presentation to support your answer.

Write your answer in the space provided.

58

Write the letter for each statement in the correct locations on the graphic organizer to show how bread changed over time.

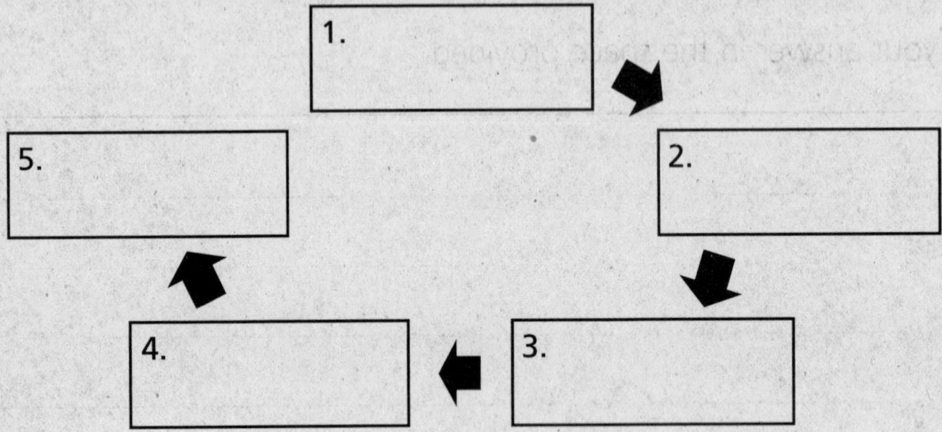

Ⓐ Bread becomes available in all forms, shapes, and sizes in bakeries and stores across the United States.

Ⓑ People grind wheat and add water to make a form of wheat paste to eat.

Ⓒ Leavened bread becomes popular.

Ⓓ Ancient cultures start planting and growing wheat to use for food.

Ⓔ People learn that they can bake bread to make it more inviting to eat.

STOP

Read the passages, and respond to the Writing Prompt that follows.

Hang Gliders Sail the Sky

Humans tried for centuries to unlock the secret of flying like the birds. For a long time, this was possible only in mythology and fantasy. In the twentieth century, however, people finally found a way to take to the sky without a motor, using only simple wings. Hang gliders, at last, allowed humans to soar with the birds.

History

The creation of the modern hang glider began in the 1960s as a part of the space industry. Francis Rogallo, a NASA engineer, developed a light, flexible wing to help return spacecraft to Earth. Other developers who were interested in non-motorized flight studied Rogallo's wing. In the late 1960s, Australian inventor John Dickenson and Australian builders Bill Moyes and Bill Bennett collaborated to develop the first hang glider that could be launched by foot.

Hang Glider Design

The hang glider is a simple aircraft. Its main feature is a large triangle-shaped wing. This wing is made of a lightweight, flexible material that is attached to a frame made of aluminum tubes. The control bar, a small triangle-shaped tube that the pilot uses to guide the glider, is attached to the frame. The frame is hinged so that the glider can be easily folded. A harness is attached to the very center of the hang glider, right below the control bar. The harness holds the pilot and allows for free movement.

How It Works

To launch a glider, the pilot runs down a slope. Lift happens when the air is moving about fifteen to twenty-five miles per hour over the wing. Lift is a force that works against gravity, causing the glider to rise. Once the glider is flying, gravity once again begins to exert its force. This pulls the glider back down toward Earth, which forces it to move forward. The forward movement causes air to continue to flow over the wing, which keeps the glider flying.

Another force, drag, helps the glider fly. Drag is created when air crashes against the wing. The faster the glider goes, the more drag it creates. It is the balance of the three forces—lift, drag, and gravity—that determines how high and how fast the glider can fly. To change direction while flying, the pilot shifts his or her weight.

Hang gliders do not have a motor. The wind moves the glider.

Safety

Hang glider pilots must wear helmets to protect themselves in case of crashes. Most pilots also wear goggles to protect their eyes from the moving air and glare from the sun. For flights that climb to higher altitudes (usually several thousand feet up), the pilots bring along reserve parachutes.

A Newer Kind of Chute

Paragliding is closely related to hang gliding. The main difference is the equipment. Paragliders do not have frames or triangular-shaped wings. Instead, paragliders are basically flattened, oval-shaped parachutes. Because of the different structure, paragliders take off and fly differently from hang gliders.

History

During World War I, members of the navy first used parachutes for something other than slowing a person's fall to Earth. Men attached to parachutes were towed behind submarines to get better views of what was on the surface of the ocean around them. That was just the beginning. People were fascinated by the possibility of flying without using motors. American Domina Jalbert invented the first gliding parachute in 1952. In 1965, David Barish, working with NASA, flew using his "Sail Wing," which was an early prototype for the paraglider. Finally, in June 1978, a group of three friends in France brought it all together and made the first successful paraglider flight.

Paraglider Design

A paraglider can be thought of as an inflatable wing. This wing, known as a "ram-air airfoil," is made of two layers of strong fabric. The two layers are joined in places to form a series of cells. The cells are open in the middle, and they fill with air when the paraglider takes off. When the oval-shaped parachute inflates, it lifts off the ground. The pilot is buckled

Although the paraglider looks like a parachute, its operator has the ability to control the chute and launch from the ground!

into a harness that hangs below the wing, much like a person hangs below a parachute. A network of lines connects the harness to the wing, and the harness supports the pilot.

Flying

Pilots open regular parachutes as they approach the ground. For example, a pilot will pull a cord to open a parachute after jumping out of an airplane. Unlike parachutes, paragliders are completely opened while still on the ground. To launch a paraglider, the pilot walks or runs forward, pulling on the wing. This increases air pressure and fills the cells with air. Once the wing is inflated, airflow causes the glider to slowly lift up from the ground. The lift generated by air, wind, and temperature allows the paraglider to fly higher and maintain his or her distance from the ground.

Some paragliders have small, foot-controlled speed bars. The pilots can use these to change the angles of their wings and control speed. Hand controls also allow the pilots to control speed and direction.

Although paragliding is a form of recreation, it has also become a competitive sport. A number of leagues have formed around the world. Pilots compete based on distances, altitudes, and speeds. There are also trick pilots who specialize in stunt flying.

Safety

Training and proper equipment are the most important safeguards for paraglider pilots. Safety equipment, such as helmets and eye goggles, is also necessary. Many pilots also carry spare parachutes in case of emergencies.

Writing Prompt

> **The readings discuss the history of and science behind hang gliding and paragliding. Write an informative essay explaining the differences between the two sports. Use information from the passages in your essay.**

Manage your time carefully so that you can

- plan your essay;
- write your essay; and
- revise and edit your essay.

Be sure to include

- an introduction;
- support for your opinion using information from the sources; and
- a conclusion that is related to your opinion.

Your writing should be in the form of a well-organized, multiparagraph essay.

Write your essay on the following pages.

Write your answer in the space provided.

AzMERIT Practice Test 2

Directions

This Practice Test is designed to help you prepare for tests that you will take on the computer. It includes new types of questions that have been adapted to work in a paper-and-pencil format. Some questions have direction lines that will tell you how to complete the question and indicate your answer. Always read the directions carefully. You will mark your answers and write your responses directly into the Practice Test book.

This Practice Test includes two main parts:

1. English Language Arts
2. Writing Task

The English Language Arts part of the test contains reading, editing, and listening sections. After completing the reading and editing sections, stop and wait for your teacher to give you instructions on taking the listening section of the Practice Test. Your teacher will give you instructions on when and how to complete the Writing Task.

Read the stories, and answer the questions that follow.

Text A

The Fog

a Maine tall tale

1 I've heard that people in England are always bragging about how their fogs are the thickest in the world. I'm telling you, though, that the English fogs are nothing compared to the fogs on the Bay of Fundy right here in Maine. Our fogs spread for miles and are so thick you could cut them with a knife. Why, you could stick a nail in one of them and hang your coat on it! That's how thick *our* fogs are. I'm going to tell you a story that proves it.

2 A few years back, a fog as thick and as <u>massive</u> as a mountain rolled in across the bay. It was so bad that my neighbor, Claude, couldn't go out on his fishing boat. Claude's a fisherman. He makes his living by going out on the bay, loading up his boat with fish, bringing them back, and selling them. Well, he wasn't going out on the water that day. He couldn't even see his hand in front of him because the fog was so thick. Instead, he decided to do some chores around the house.

3 "Going up to the roof, hon'," he told his wife, Maud. "Need to see to those loose shingles."

4 "Not in this weather, dear," Maud said, a load of worry in her voice. "I don't want you to hurt yourself. You can't see a thing in this fog."

5 "Don't need to see much," Claude replied, as he struggled into his coat and grabbed his tools. "I know that roof from one end to the other. I'll have those new shingles on it in no time."

6 Claude started repairing the roof around 7 a.m., just after breakfast. Hours passed, and Claude still wasn't back. He missed lunch, and as dinnertime approached, Maud got worried.

7 Just as she was ready to go outside into the cold and damp of that old fog, Maud heard the door open. "Claude, is that you?" she called from the kitchen.

8 "Yup," Claude replied as he walked in the door and removed his wet coat.

9 "Did you finish the roof?" Maud called out.

10 Claude walked into the kitchen and nodded.

11 "What took you so long?" Maud asked as she carried the baked beans to the table.

12 Claude looked at her and shook his head. "I knew our house was big, but that roof just seemed to go on forever. I didn't think I was ever going to finish."

13 No one knew the size of their house better than Maud. She'd cleaned it often enough. She didn't say a word, though, because her husband was clearly tired from all his hard work. As soon as the dinner dishes were washed and put away, Claude and Maud headed upstairs to bed.

14 When Claude woke up early the next morning, he pulled on his pants over his long johns, slipped on his shoes, and grabbed his coat. Claude opened the front door and stepped outside to see if the fog had lifted enough for him to take the boat out. Maud was right behind him. The fog was still there, strong and thick, but as they turned around, they could at least see the outline of the house.

15 "Let's take a look at that big old roof you spent all that time fixing yesterday," Maud said. Claude nodded.

16 They both looked and couldn't believe their eyes. My neighbor Claude had shingled the roof all right. But that wasn't all. As far as the eye could see, Claude had shingled the fog as well. That's right. Claude had nailed shingle after shingle on top of that big old fog. Now that's what I call a *thick* fog!

Text B

Adapted from

The Old House

by Hans Christian Andersen

1 A long time ago, in a small village filled with clean and modern houses, there stood a very old house. While the house was large, and probably grand in its day, it was now falling apart. Along the front of the house were fancy carvings—lion heads with gaping mouths, dragons and angels, flowers and curlicues. No doubt these carvings were once magnificent, but time had not been kind to them. Chips and holes were everywhere, and moss and ivy covered much of the house.

2 Across from this old house, in a nice, well-kept modern house, lived a little boy and his parents. The boy often looked out the window at the old house, wondering if anyone lived there. One day, the boy heard his parents talking about the owner of the house. "Poor old man," Mother said.

3 "He must be very lonely, living there alone," Father responded.

4 Feeling sad for his neighbor, the boy went to his toy chest and took out two tin soldiers. He loved those soldiers, but he took one of them and put it in a little box. He then took it across the street and knocked on the door of the old house. A tall man in a butler's suit opened the door and looked down at the boy.

5 "May I help you?" the butler asked.

6 "I have a gift for the man who lives here," the boy replied.

7 "I will take it to him, young man. Thank you. Good-bye," the butler said as he shut the door.

8 A few weeks later came an invitation for the boy to visit the man who lived in the old house. His parents agreed that he could go.

9 The following weekend, the boy knocked on the door of the house and was shown in by the butler. The house inside was much like the house outside. The walls, the drapes, the lamps, and the furniture were once very grand in style, but age had left them worn.

10 Sitting by a warm fire was a tiny, old man with frizzled, white hair. He was wearing funny, old-fashioned clothes. "Come in," he said, smiling, and waved the boy over to a chair.

11 The boy and the old man had a nice visit, sharing tea and candies. The man told the boy tales from his youth, about dear friends and loving family. Instead of sad and lonely, the old man seemed content to spend his time with his happy memories.

12 The boy continued to visit with his neighbor over the years. After one of the boy's visits, the little tin soldier whom the boy had given his friend could take it no longer.

PRACTICE TEST 2

13 "That man may be happy," the tin soldier said, "but I'm miserable. I don't have any happy memories here. It's empty and lonely for me. Take me back, please!"

14 The boy shook his head. "I'm sorry, but you were a gift. I can't take you back."

15 The little tin soldier was so upset that he jumped off the shelf and fell through a wide crack in the rotting wooden floor. He landed beneath the house, and no one could find him.

16 As the years passed, the boy became a man and married. The old man across the street eventually passed away. Someone bought the old house and tore it down to build a nice modern one. One day as the boy, now a man, and his wife walked past the place where the house once stood, they spotted a small, shiny object.

17 "It's the tin soldier!" the man cried. He told his wife how he had taken the tin soldier as a gift to the old man across the street. He talked about their wonderful visits and how seeing the tin soldier reminded him that a simple gesture had turned into a special friendship. He spoke of how sad he was when the soldier was lost.

18 "We must take him home," the wife said, cleaning off the soldier.

19 As the tin soldier headed home with his new owners, he thought about how nice it was to be remembered after all. Now he looked forward to making his own memories.

1

Which statement **best** summarizes what happens in Text A?

Ⓐ Although the fog is thick, a man finally goes out and does not come back for hours. His wife is worried, but he returns at last, safe and sound.

Ⓑ Because of a thick fog, a fisherman decides to do chores at home. It takes a long time for him to fix the shingles on the roof. In the morning, he and his wife discover that he has shingled over the thick fog.

Ⓒ A fisherman goes out on his boat but ends up heading back home because of the thick fog. He goes up on his roof and fixes some missing shingles and then comes back in to have dinner with his wife.

Ⓓ The Maine fog is so thick that even fogs in England are not as bad. A fisherman sets out to prove that the Maine fog is thick. He fixes some shingles on his roof and keeps going until he puts a roof on the thick fog.

2

Which phrases **best** describe the character of Claude in Text A? Select **three** phrases from the choices below.

A. ☐ easily frightened by bad weather

B. ☐ a hardworking man

C. ☐ not very helpful to his wife

D. ☐ not very talkative

E. ☐ willing to see a job to the end

PRACTICE TEST 2

3

This question has two parts. First, answer part A. Then, answer part B.

Part A

Read the sentence from Text A.

> A few years back, a fog as thick and as <u>massive</u> as a mountain rolled in across the bay. (paragraph 2)

Which word is a synonym for the word <u>massive</u> as it is used in the sentence?

Ⓐ giant

Ⓑ rocky

Ⓒ moist

Ⓓ beautiful

Part B

Which detail from Text A helps you identify the meaning of the word <u>massive</u>?

Ⓐ "spread for miles"

Ⓑ "see his hand in front of him"

Ⓒ "hang your coat on it"

Ⓓ "cut them with a knife"

4

Which sentence **best** describes the old house in Text B?

Ⓐ It is magnificent with modern details and in perfect shape.

Ⓑ It was impressive in its day, but time and neglect have allowed it to fall apart.

Ⓒ It is still grand, but it does not fit in with the modern houses.

Ⓓ It is dangerous and rundown, so it does not fit in with the grand houses.

5

Summarize what happens in Text B. Use details from the story in your answer.

Write your answer in the space below.

PRACTICE TEST 2

6

This question has two parts. First, answer part A. Then, answer part B.

Part A

Which phrases **best** describe the boy in Text B? Choose **all** that apply.

A. ☐ lonely and discouraged

B. ☐ friendly and concerned for other people

C. ☐ generous with things that he cares about

D. ☐ willing to take chances to do the right thing

E. ☐ afraid of things that are different from what he knows

Part B

Write **two** details from Text B that support your response to Part A.

Write your answer in the space below.

How are Text A and Text B similar?

Ⓐ Both tales tell how a man learns about what is really important in life.

Ⓑ Both tales tell about a relationship between a husband and a wife.

Ⓒ Both tales are mainly about events that could happen in real life.

Ⓓ Both tales are a mix of ordinary life and imaginary events.

8

In the boxes below, write the letters of the sentences that describe the point of view of each story.

"The Fog"	**"The Old House"**

A. The story is told from a third-person point of view by an all-knowing narrator.

B. The story is told from a first-person point of view by a neighbor.

C. The narrator tells the story in a humorous way and wants us to be entertained by the story.

D. The narrator tells the story in a serious way and wants readers to learn a lesson.

PRACTICE TEST 2

Read the article, and answer the questions that follow.

Telling Stories with Light and Shadow

1 Legend has it that a magician in China created shadow puppets to cheer up a sad emperor after his wife died. The magician used leather and sticks to make a life-sized figure of the emperor's wife. The magician then brought the puppet "to life" by making it dance between the light from a fire and a screen on which the shadow appeared. The emperor was pleased, and a new art form was born.

2 Shadow puppets are used for many reasons. They help to preserve a culture's history, explain religious beliefs, and entertain people. Telling stories through shadow puppets dates back hundreds of years. Shadow puppets are used in many cultures, including those of Southeast Asia, Turkey, Greece, and France.

3 Historically, puppeteers learned about local problems and issues while they traveled. They then took those stories and created plays. The puppet characters included kings, queens, spirits, famous people, and ordinary people. Shadow puppet plays were a way of sharing stories and connecting people who lived far from each other. In some ways, shadow puppetry was like an early form of television.

4 Shadow puppets used to be flat and made from leather. The puppet makers cut holes in the leather to add details like eyes and mouths. Cuts in the material let light shine through. Today, shadow puppets can be made from a variety of materials, such as plastic, cloth, paper, or wood. Puppet makers also use wires, feathers, and even dried flowers to make shadow puppets.

5 To produce a shadow puppet show, a puppeteer shines a light behind the puppets, projecting their images onto a <u>translucent</u> screen. This lets the audience see the puppets' shadows. The puppeteer moves the puppets' arms and legs using bamboo sticks. The audience, sitting on the other side of the screen, watches the puppets' shadows act out the play. Sometimes, the play is accompanied by a collection of musical instruments called a gamelan. This group of instruments can include flutes, strings, and gongs.

6 Specific details of the plays vary from culture to culture. In traditional Chinese shadow puppet plays, the audience can tell whether the characters are good or bad based on the puppets' outfits. In Indonesia, the plays tell stories that weave together Hindu, Buddhist, and Muslim beliefs. Shadow puppet plays in India keep alive ancient tales that are part of the oral tradition. Although there are many differences in form and style, all of the shadow puppet plays continue to entertain viewers—old and young alike.

9

Which of these **best** describes how paragraph 1 is structured?

Ⓐ by compare and contrast

Ⓑ by cause and effect

Ⓒ by comparison

Ⓓ by chronology

10

Which sentence **best** explains how the audience sees shadow puppet characters?

Ⓐ The puppeteer cuts holes in leather to create details and uses bamboo sticks to make the puppets move in the light.

Ⓑ The light streams through the holes in the leather, providing details that help the audience determine whether the puppet is a king or an ordinary person.

Ⓒ A light behind the puppet creates a shadow on a screen, which can be seen from the other side.

Ⓓ A light is projected from behind the audience and lights up the puppets as they act out the story.

11

Which sentence from the article **best** helps explain what the historical shadow puppets looked like?

Ⓐ "In some ways, shadow puppetry was like an early form of television."

Ⓑ "The puppet makers cut holes in the leather to add details like eyes and mouths."

Ⓒ "They then took those stories and created plays."

Ⓓ "Sometimes, the play is accompanied by a collection of musical instruments called a gamelan."

12

This question has two parts. First, answer part A. Then, answer part B.

Part A

Which statement **best** describes the main idea of the article?

Ⓐ Ancient shadow puppets were made of leather, but contemporary shadow puppets can be made from all kinds of different materials.

Ⓑ Shadow puppet shows involve puppeteers, puppets, lights, a screen, and music.

Ⓒ Shadow puppet plays often reflect local problems and issues.

Ⓓ The tradition of shadow puppetry has lasted for hundreds of years and is used to share cultural history, to tell stories, and to entertain.

Part B

Which paragraph in the article **best** supports your answer in part A?

Ⓐ paragraph 1

Ⓑ paragraph 2

Ⓒ paragraph 3

Ⓓ paragraph 4

PRACTICE TEST 2

13

What is the meaning of the word <u>translucent</u> as it is used in this sentence?

> **To produce a shadow puppet show, a puppeteer shines a light behind the puppets, projecting their images onto a <u>translucent</u> screen. (paragraph 5)**

Ⓐ clear enough for light to shine through

Ⓑ see-through, like a window

Ⓒ reflective, like a mirror

Ⓓ solid white so you can see an image on it

14

How are shadow puppets used to "preserve a culture's history" (paragraph 2)? Use details from the article to support your answer.

Write your answer in the space provided.

15

In paragraph 3, the author claims that "[i]n some ways, shadow puppetry was like an early form of television." How does the author support this statement? Use details from the passage to support your answer.

Write your answer in the space provided.

PRACTICE TEST 2

Reading

Read the story, and answer the questions that follow.

Excerpted from

Emily's Bluebird

1 It was a sunny afternoon in May, and Emily was searching her backyard for signs of spring. She ran to an old, dead tree where woodpeckers had made a nest hole. Sometimes other birds use old woodpecker holes for their nests, and she listened eagerly for the "peep peep" of baby birds. If she were lucky, she might even see a parent bird fly up with food for its hungry chicks.

2 Just as Emily reached the old tree, she saw something moving in the grass under the woodpecker hole. It was a baby bird!

3 It didn't fly away when Emily got closer. Maybe it was too young to fly.

4 "I'll take you home, little bird," she said to the chick. "Mom will show me how to take care of you. Mom knows all about nature."

5 Emily's mother did not seem thrilled when her daughter plopped a baby bird onto the kitchen table.

6 "Emmie, it's perfectly normal for babies to jump out of the nest a few days before they can fly. Nests are dangerous places. They're easy for predators like squirrels and snakes to find, and after a couple of weeks, a nest full of chicks can get pretty dirty. Most songbird chicks leave as soon as they're old enough to hop and climb, but before their feathers have grown enough to fly."

7 "This is a bluebird chick, and it looks healthy to me," said Emily's mom. "Bluebirds eat bugs and worms. We can't take care of it nearly as well as its mother and father. They don't need our help, so let's put it back before the parents get too worried. Help me find a good, safe place."

8 Emily followed her mother into the backyard, carrying the bluebird chick. Near the old tree, Emily saw a bush with lots of branches and leaves.

9 "How about here, Mom?" she said.

10 "That will be perfect, Emmie," said her mother. "The chick will be safer than on the ground, and the parents should find it quickly."

11 With a boost from her mother, Emily put the chick on a small branch, out of reach of cats. As soon as they backed away, the hungry little bird began peeping. Emily's mother explained that chicks peep so their parents can keep track of them. Sure enough, an adult bluebird arrived a minute later with a juicy caterpillar and poked it into the chick's mouth. Yum!

12 Emily was a little disappointed that she wouldn't have a baby bird to take care of, but she was happy that the chick was safe and the parents weren't worried about it. But she wasn't prepared for what happened next: three more bluebird chicks climbed out of the nest hole, looked around at their new world, and fluttered right into the same bush! The nest was empty, and all the babies were safe. Emily was glad she hadn't <u>interfered</u> too much with nature.

13 That night, a big storm arrived. The next morning, Emily saw that the old nest tree had been blown down by the storm's strong winds. She wondered, what will the bluebirds do now?

14 Emily decided to look on the Internet for more information about bluebirds. Emily asked her father to help her make a bluebird nest box to replace the woodpecker hole in the old tree.

15 They bought the materials, and together they built the nest box in her father's basement workshop. It was easy, and fun. Emily's father fastened the new box to another tree in the backyard, not far from the old one that blew down.

16 Emily watched the nest box every day. After only a week, she saw a pair of bluebirds checking out the box, and soon another nest was underway.

17 Were they the same bluebirds? Could be!

16

At the beginning of the story, how is Emily's view of the baby bluebird different from her mother's view?

Ⓐ Emily is concerned about the bird's safety, but her mother thinks Emily should have left the bird in the yard.

Ⓑ Emily is disappointed about finding the bird, but her mother thinks the bird will make a nice new pet.

Ⓒ Emily is excited to have a new pet, but her mother is worried about how the cat will react to the bird.

Ⓓ Emily doesn't want to take care of any new pets, but her mother promises to help build a box that can be used as a nest.

17

What does the word <u>interfered</u> mean as used in the sentence?

> Emily was glad she hadn't <u>interfered</u> too much with nature. (paragraph 12).

Ⓐ cooperated

Ⓑ meddled

Ⓒ cared for

Ⓓ argued

18

Which statement **best** expresses the theme of the story?

Ⓐ Mother birds care for babies until the chicks leave their nests.

Ⓑ Nest boxes provide a safer home for birds than regular nests.

Ⓒ Animals must have help from people to survive in nature.

Ⓓ People can harm animals in nature while trying to help.

PRACTICE TEST 2

19

Which sentences from the story **best** show that Emily is fascinated by nature? Select **two** sentences from the choices below.

A. ☐ "If she were lucky, she might even see a parent bird fly up with food for its hungry chicks."

B. ☐ "Emily's mother did not seem thrilled when her daughter plopped a baby bird onto the kitchen table."

C. ☐ "As soon as they backed away, the hungry little bird began peeping."

D. ☐ "That night, a big storm arrived."

E. ☐ "Emily's father fastened the new box to another tree in the backyard, not far from the old one that blew down."

F. ☐ "Emily watched the nest box every day."

20

Which sentence from the story **best** supports the idea that the nest box was designed to meet the needs of bluebirds?

Ⓐ "The next morning, Emily saw that the old nest tree had been blown down by the storm's strong winds."

Ⓑ "Emily asked her father to help her make a bluebird nest box to replace the woodpecker hole in the old tree."

Ⓒ "They bought the materials, and together they built the nest box in her father's basement workshop."

Ⓓ "After only a week, she saw a pair of bluebirds checking out the box, and soon another nest was underway."

21

Which of the following **best** summarizes the story?

Ⓐ Emily discovers a baby bluebird that has fallen out of a woodpecker hole in her backyard. She wants to keep the bird, but her mother convinces her to return the bird to its nest.

Ⓑ Emily learns not to interfere with nature after she discovers a baby bluebird in her backyard. She and her father find another way to help by building a nest box for the birds.

Ⓒ Emily and her mother nurse a baby bluebird back to health after it falls out of its nest. Emily and her father then build a new nest box for the chick to live in where it will be safe.

Ⓓ Emily finds a small bird on the ground with a broken wing. She and her mother decide the safest place for the bird is on a small bush in the backyard.

22

How might the passage be different if it were written in the first person, from the mother's point of view? Use details from the passage to support your answer.

Write your answer in the space below.

PRACTICE TEST 2

Read the passage, and answer the questions that follow.

Adapted from

Village Life in America

by Caroline Cowles Richards

Caroline Cowles Richards grew up in Canandaigua, New York, during the 1800s. Richards started a journal about her life when she was ten years old. She wrote the following passages in April 1865 as the Civil War was coming to an end.

1 *Monday morning, April 10.*—"Whether I am in the body, or out of the body, I know not, but one thing I know," Lee[1] has surrendered! All the people seem crazy as a result. The bells are ringing. Boys, girls, men, and women are running through the streets wild with excitement. The flags are all flying, one from the top of our church.

2 We were quietly eating our breakfast this morning about 7 o'clock when our church bell started to ring. Then the Methodist bell started to ring, and now all the bells in town are ringing. Mr. Noah T. Clarke ran by, all excitement. I don't believe he knew where he was. No school today. I saw Capt. Aldrich passing, so I rushed to the window. He waved his hat. I raised the window and asked him what was the matter? He came to the front door where I met him. He almost shook my hand off and said, "The war is over. We have Lee's surrender, with his own name signed."

3 I am going downtown now. I want to see for myself what is going on.

[1]**Lee:** Robert E. Lee, the general who led the Confederate army in the Civil War

4 *Later*—I have returned from town now. I never saw such performances in my life. Every man has a bell or a horn, and every girl a flag and a little bell, and every one is tied with red, white, and blue ribbons. I am going downtown again now, with my flag in one hand and bell in the other to make all the noise I can.

5 Mr. Noah T. Clarke and other leading citizens are riding around on a cart with great bells in their hands. They are ringing the bells as hard as they can. Dr. Cook beat upon an old gong. The latest musical instrument invented is called the "Jerusalem fiddle." Some boys put a dry goods box upon a cart, put some rosin on the edge of the box, and pulled a piece of timber back and forth across it. It made the most unearthly sounds. They drove through all the streets, Ed Lampman riding on the horse and driving it.

6 *Monday evening, April 10.*—I have been out walking for the last hour and a half, looking at the brilliant decorations. I don't believe I was ever so tired in my life. The bells have not stopped ringing more than five minutes all day. Everyone is glad to see Canandaigua startled out of its proper manners!

7 Every yard of red, white, and blue ribbon in the stores has been sold. Every candle and every flag has been sold as well. One society worked hard all the afternoon making transparencies. But then there were no candles to put in to light them. They will be ready for the next celebration when peace is proclaimed.

8 The Court House, Atwater Block, and hotel have about two dozen candles in each window. They also have flags and mottoes of every description. It is certainly the best sudden display ever gotten up in this town. "Victory is Granted" is in large red, white, and blue letters in front of Atwater Block.

9 The speeches on the square this morning were all very good. Dr. Daggett started with a prayer. I wish all could have heard it. Hon. Francis Granger, E. G. Lapham, Judge Smith,

Alexander Howell, Noah T. Clarke, and others made speeches. We sang "Old Hundred" at the end. Then Rev. Dr. Hibbard dismissed us with the benediction.

10 I shook hands with Mr. Noah T. Clarke. He told me to be careful and not hurt him, for he blistered his hands today ringing that bell. He says he is going to keep the bell for his grandchildren. Between the speeches on the square this morning a song was called for. Gus Coleman started "John Brown." Everyone joined in the chorus, "Glory, Hallelujah."

11 This has been a never-to-be-forgotten day.

12 *April 15.*—The news came this morning that our dear President, Abraham Lincoln, was assassinated yesterday. It was the day we were going to celebrate thanksgiving for Union victories. I have felt sick over it all day. So has everyone that I have seen. All seem to feel as though they had lost a personal friend. Tears flow plenteously.

13 How soon has sorrow followed upon the heels of joy! One week ago tonight we were celebrating our victories with loud mirth and good cheer. Now everyone is silent and sad. The earth and heavens seem clothed in sackcloth. The bells have been tolling this afternoon. The flags are all at half-mast, draped with mourning.

14 On every store and home some sign of the nation's loss is visible. Just after breakfast this morning, I looked out of the window and saw a group of men listening to the reading of a morning paper. I feared from their silent, motionless interest that something dreadful had happened. I was not prepared to hear of the cowardly murder of our President. And William H. Seward[2], too, I suppose cannot survive his wounds. Oh, how horrible it is!

[2]**William H. Seward:** secretary of state under President Lincoln, who was wounded in an assassination attempt on the same night that Lincoln was killed

23

In paragraph 1, Richards writes that "people seem crazy as a result" of Lee's surrender. Which details in the passage support this statement? Choose **all** that apply.

A. ▢ They are flying flags.

B. ▢ They are running through the streets.

C. ▢ They are ringing bells as loudly as they can.

D. ▢ They are decorating things in red, white, and blue.

E. ▢ They are giving and listening to speeches.

24

Why does Noah T. Clarke **most likely** plan to keep his bell for his grandchildren? Use details from the passage to support your answer.

Write your answer in the space provided.

PRACTICE TEST 2

25

This question has two parts. First, answer part A. Then, answer part B.

Part A

Read this sentence from the passage.

> **How soon has sorrow followed upon the heels of joy! (paragraph 13)**

What kind of figurative language does the author use here?

Ⓐ simile

Ⓑ metaphor

Ⓒ personification

Ⓓ idiom

Part B

What is the meaning of the figurative language used above?

Ⓐ Sorrow came immediately after joy.

Ⓑ Sorrow inspired the same behavior as joy.

Ⓒ Sorrow lasted as briefly as joy did.

Ⓓ Sorrow was just as exciting as joy.

26

How did the author know that something bad had happened even before she learned that President Lincoln was assassinated?

Ⓐ She felt sick all day.

Ⓑ She saw that flags were flying at half-mast.

Ⓒ She noticed the serious faces of the men hearing the news.

Ⓓ She knew that William H. Seward was wounded.

27

This question has two parts. First, answer part A. Then, answer part B.

Part A

Which of the following **best** describes the text structure of the passage?

Ⓐ chronological

Ⓑ cause and effect

Ⓒ problem and solution

Ⓓ compare and contrast

Part B

Write **three** details from the passage that support your answer to part A.

Write your answer in the space provided.

28

Read the following description from *History of the Civil War, 1861–1865*, in which the author describes how the people of the North rejoiced when Lee surrendered.

> **Cannons fired, bells rang, flags floated, houses and shops were gay with the red, white, and blue.**

Which sentence from "Village Life in America" best supports this description?

Ⓐ "Every yard of red, white, and blue ribbon in the stores has been sold."

Ⓑ "The speeches on the square this morning were all very good."

Ⓒ "The earth and heavens seem clothed in sackcloth."

Ⓓ "On every store and home some sign of the nation's loss is visible."

Read the play, and answer the questions that follow.

A New Beginning

CAST OF CHARACTERS
PAPA
MAMA
MARY
ROSA
PRESIDENT ROOSEVELT (*heard over the radio*)

SCENE 1

1 (*PAPA, MAMA, and MARY are traveling in a car covered in dirt.*)

2 PAPA: (*sighs*) It's sad we're leaving the farm, but we had to get away from those dust storms.

3 MARY: Can you see the road, Papa?

4 PAPA: Not very well, Mary. Those dark dust clouds have blocked the sun. It's like driving in a black fog.

5 MARY: Will we go back to Oklahoma when the dust storms are gone?

6 MAMA: I don't know, Mary. We'll find a new place to live in California. We could be so happy there that we may never want to return.

7 MARY: Oh, but Mama, I already miss the farm. I can't imagine living anywhere else.

SCENE 2

8 (*MARY has dropped her books in the schoolyard. ROSA is helping her collect them.*)

9 MARY: Thanks so much for helping me. My name is Mary.

10 ROSA: I'm Rosa. Are you new here?

11 MARY: We just moved here from Oklahoma.

12 ROSA: I moved here, too! But that was two years ago. Why did you move?

13 MARY: Last year there was a drought. The rain never came. Then there were dust storms, and our farm was ruined. At night, I slept with a towel over my face to keep the dust off! We had to leave everything behind. It was scary.

14 ROSA: We're farmers, too. We left Mexico to come here. At first, I was sad. Now I'm happier. I like my new school and my new friends.

15 MARY: I wish I were still in Oklahoma. I miss our old farm. Everything here is so different, and I don't know anyone.

16 ROSA: I know what you mean. It was strange at first. But then I made new friends. And I went to the ocean and saw the mountains on the coast.

17 MARY: Oh! The ocean! I've never seen it. And mountains! Oklahoma is so flat.

18 ROSA: There is a lot to see in California.

19 MARY: Maybe it won't be so bad here.

20 ROSA: Just wait until you get settled. You'll see.

21 MARY: Thanks, Rosa. You really helped me feel better.

SCENE 3

22 (*MARY's family and ROSA are gathered around a radio in MARY's new home.*)

23 PRESIDENT ROOSEVELT: (*over the radio*) The test of our progress is not whether we add more to the abundance of those who have much; it is whether we provide enough for those who have too little.

24 MARY: I don't understand what the president means. What is "abundance"?

25 MAMA: Remember the days when we had a big harvest? We enjoyed abundance then. We had everything we needed and more. So the president is saying that we will become a better country if we help people who do not have everything they need, like our neighbors who are still in Oklahoma.

26 ROSA: I'm sure glad you left when you did.

27 PAPA: I agree, Rosa. I was lucky to find work here, and Mary seems happy in her new school. Many of our friends back in Oklahoma aren't so lucky. They lost a lot. They didn't leave in time, like we did. Where they live is now called the Dust Bowl.

28 MAMA: You know, President Roosevelt is going to help our friends. Soon, the land will get better. Then people will be back at work on their farms.

29 MARY: (*interrupting excitedly*) Yes! Then we can go visit, but not to stay. There's so much to see here!

30 ROSA: I can't wait to go with you to the ocean!

29

How do you know that *A New Beginning* is a play? Choose **all** that apply.

A. ☐ It is mostly dialogue.

B. ☐ It includes several characters.

C. ☐ It is mostly description.

D. ☐ It has stage directions.

E. ☐ It tells about the past.

F. ☐ It is split into scenes.

30

This question has two parts. First, answer part A. Then, answer part B.

Part A

Which word means the **opposite** of <u>drought</u>?

Ⓐ flood

Ⓑ harvest

Ⓒ farm

Ⓓ dust

Part B

Underline the **two** clues that help you understand the meaning of the word <u>drought</u> in the excerpt below.

13 MARY: Last year there was a <u>drought</u>. The rain never came. Then there were dust storms, and our farm was ruined. At night, I slept with a towel over my face to keep the dust off! We had to leave everything behind. It was scary.

31

What is **one** difference between California and Oklahoma that is important to the play?

Ⓐ Oklahoma has farms, but California does not.

Ⓑ Oklahoma had a drought, but California had dust storms.

Ⓒ California is near the ocean, but Oklahoma is far away from any ocean.

Ⓓ California has schools, but Oklahoma does not.

32

Which word means the same as <u>provide</u> as it is used in this sentence?

> 23 **PRESIDENT ROOSEVELT: (*over the radio*) The test of our progress is not whether we add more to the abundance of those who have much; it is whether we <u>provide</u> enough for those who have too little. (paragraph 23)**

Ⓐ improve

Ⓑ subtract

Ⓒ hunger

Ⓓ supply

33

Read Mary's dialogue from the play.

> **Then we can go visit, but not to stay. There's so much to see here! (paragraph 29)**

What can you conclude about Mary from these sentences? Use details from the play to support your answer.

Write your answer on the lines provided.

34

Write a summary of the play in the space provided.

35

Which of the following sets would be used in a staged version of this play? Choose **all** that apply.

A. ☐ a dusty country road

B. ☐ a schoolyard

C. ☐ a farm in Oklahoma

D. ☐ a California beach

E. ☐ a room in a house

Reading

Read the article, and answer the questions that follow.

Make Your Own Invisible Ink

1 Whether you're a spy or a kid just wanting to have fun, invisible ink can come in handy. Invisible ink is easy to make and fun to use.

2 Making invisible ink isn't just fun and games, however. It involves real science and chemical reactions. It's all about how certain substances react with oxygen when heated. Try making some invisible ink to see for yourself.

3 Here are two different ways to make invisible ink:

1. Use lemon juice. For this process, you'll need lemon juice, a thin paintbrush, a piece of paper, and a lamp with a lightbulb. (Caution: Do not use a halogen light. It will be too hot.) First, dip the paintbrush in lemon juice, and write your message on the paper. Then, let the message dry until it becomes invisible. To read the message, turn on the lamp and hold the paper close (but not too close) to the lightbulb. Your message will slowly appear on the page. The chemicals in the lemon juice change from the heat of the lightbulb, which makes your message brown.
2. Use milk. This process is the same as the lemon juice process, but you use milk instead. First, dip the paintbrush in milk, and write your message on the piece of paper. Let it dry until your message disappears. To read your message, hold the paper close to the lightbulb. The milk, like the lemon juice, will react to the heat and turn brown. Your message will appear.

PRACTICE TEST 2

4 Making invisible ink is just one way to use simple science activities to entertain yourself. In the case of invisible ink, you've learned how some everyday items react when they are used together. The next time you're stuck inside on a rainy day, you might want to find some other simple—and safe—science activities that you can do on your own or with a friend. You never know what you might learn!

36

Which of the following is **not** used to make invisible ink as described in this passage?

Ⓐ juice or milk

Ⓑ a thin paintbrush

Ⓒ a halogen light

Ⓓ a piece of paper

37

Show the correct order of steps for making invisible ink using lemon juice. Write the letter for each step in the correct locations on the graphic organizer.

Ⓐ Hold the paper to the lightbulb.

Ⓑ Dip the paintbrush in lemon juice.

Ⓒ Let the message dry.

Ⓓ Write the message.

38

Which word is the **best** synonym for <u>substances</u> as it is used in the sentence?

> It's all about how certain <u>substances</u> react with oxygen when heated. (paragraph 2)

Ⓐ materials

Ⓑ waters

Ⓒ papers

Ⓓ inks

39

Which statement **best** expresses the author's main idea in the passage?

Ⓐ Making invisible ink with lemon juice is fun.

Ⓑ Spies and kids have used invisible ink for centuries.

Ⓒ You can always find some science activity to do on a rainy day.

Ⓓ Making invisible ink is one of the many fun science activities you can do.

40

Milk, like lemon juice, contains acid. What information in the article allows readers to know this fact?

Ⓐ Both need to dry to disappear.

Ⓑ Both eventually turn brown when heated.

Ⓒ Both can be read in front of a lightbulb.

Ⓓ Both look invisible on paper.

PRACTICE TEST 2

41

This question has two parts. First, answer part A. Then, answer part B.

Part A

What inference can you make based on details in step 1 of the article?

Ⓐ Using halogen light will not cause a chemical reaction.

Ⓑ If you hold the paper too close to the light, the message will not appear.

Ⓒ The paper might catch on fire if you don't follow the instructions carefully.

Ⓓ A halogen light only works with milk, not lemon juice.

Part B

Underline **two** details that support your inference in part A.

1. Use lemon juice. For this process, you'll need lemon juice, a thin paintbrush, a piece of paper, and a lamp with a lightbulb. (Caution: Do not use a halogen light. It will be too hot.) First, dip the paintbrush in lemon juice, and write your message on the paper. Then, let the message dry until it becomes invisible. To read the message, turn on the lamp and hold the paper close (but not too close) to the lightbulb. Your message will slowly appear on the page. The chemicals in the lemon juice change from the heat of the lightbulb, which makes your message brown.

42

What is the author's purpose for writing this article? Use details from the article to support your answer.

Write your answer on the lines below.

PRACTICE TEST 2

Editing Task

The underlined parts of the passage show words, phrases, or sentences that may be incorrect. After you read the passage, you will answer questions about the underlined text.

Jason's Choice

Jason was hanging around the fence at recess with nothing to do. He had just had a fight with his best friend Charles, and they didn't want to play together anymore. Jason will be looking down at the ground and kicking pebbles. All of a sudden, he saw something lying there on the ground. It was a watch. He knew it was his friend Charles's watch once it had the stretchy strap and the big black numbers. Charles liked that watch more than anything else he owned.

Jason picked up the watch. He wished it was his. It could be his if he didn't tell Charles he found it. As soon as he thought that, Jason started to feel bad about not being honest.

He wondered Should I tell Charles that I just found his watch?" Finally, he decided. He picked up the watch, he walked over to his friend. Charles was standing at the other end of the playground, by the fence, looking down and kicking pebbles.

"Look what I found," Jason said.

"Hey, thanks!" Charles said.

From that moment on, Jason and Charles were friends again. They began playing together right away. Jason was glad he gave the watch back to Charles.

43

Read this sentence from the passage.

> **Jason <u>will be looking</u> down at the ground and kicking pebbles.**

Which of these corrects the underlined words?

Ⓐ looked

Ⓑ looking

Ⓒ was looking

Ⓓ The words are correct as written.

44

Read this sentence from the passage.

> **He knew it was his friend Charles's watch <u>once</u> it had the stretchy strap and the big black numbers.**

Which of these should replace the underlined word?

Ⓐ because

Ⓑ even though

Ⓒ before

Ⓓ The word is correct as written.

45

Read this sentence from the passage.

> <u>He wondered Should I tell Charles that I just found his watch?"</u>

Write this sentence using correct punctuation on the lines below.

46

Read this sentence from the passage.

> **He picked up the <u>watch, he walked</u> over to his friend.**

Which of these corrects the underlined words?

Ⓐ watch he walked

Ⓑ watch. And he walked

Ⓒ watch and walked

Ⓓ The words are correct as written.

47

Read this sentence from the passage.

They began playing together right away.

Which of these corrects the underlined words?

Ⓐ rite

Ⓑ write

Ⓒ wright

Ⓓ The word is correct as written.

Editing Task

The underlined parts of the passage show words, phrases, or sentences that may be incorrect. After you read the passage, you will answer questions about the underlined text.

Jerry's First Day

"Hey, where am I?" Jerry thought when he was born. He was confused but happy. He stumbled and fell over the African grassland. Then, he felt something soft and warm nuzzling him. It was his mother's tongue. With her long head, she was pushing Jerry onto his feet. After a while, he was able to walk nicely.

"Wow. The view from up here is pretty good!" Jerry thought. He was six feet tall and weighed 150 pounds. Standing around him were creatures which looked like he did but were much taller. They had very long necks and four long legs. They had dark brown squarish spots separated by light brown lines. Their ears were long, and two knobby horns topped their heads. Their faces were long triangals with big, dark eyes and long lashes. They were beautiful!

Jerry noticed that some of the spotted tall animals were stretching their necks upward to nibble at the leaves of trees. Others were stretching their necks downward to sip at a small stream that flowed beneath the trees.

"It's so nice to drink water once in a while," one of the creatures said. "I'm tired of getting almost all my water from leaves."

"What am I, Mommy?" Jerry asked.

His mother bent her long neck to come close to him. "We're giraffes, honey" she said in a tiny voice "and you're a giraffe too."

48

Read this sentence from the passage.

He stumbled and fell <u>over</u> the African grassland.

Which of these corrects the underlined word?

Ⓐ onto

Ⓑ under

Ⓒ within

Ⓓ The word is correct as written.

49

Read this sentence from the passage.

Standing around him were creatures <u>which</u> looked like he did but were much taller.

Which of these corrects the underlined word?

Ⓐ whose

Ⓑ they

Ⓒ who

Ⓓ whom

50

Read this sentence from the passage.

> **Jerry noticed that some of the spotted tall animals were stretching their necks upward to nibble at the leaves of trees.**

Which of these corrects the underlined words?

Ⓐ spotted, tall

Ⓑ tall, spotted

Ⓒ tall spotted

Ⓓ The words are correct as written.

51

Read this sentence from the passage.

> **Their faces were long triangals with big, dark eyes and long lashes.**

Write the correct spelling of the underlined word on the line below.

52

Read this sentence from the passage.

> <u>"We're giraffes, honey" she said in a tiny voice "and you're a giraffe too."</u>

Write this sentence using correct punctuation on the lines below.

STOP

Listen to the presentation. Then answer the questions. You may use the space below to take notes.

Ballad of the Jelly-Cake

53

Read these lines from the poem.

> **A little boy whose name was Tim**
> **Once ate some jelly-cake for tea—**
> **Which cake did not agree with him,**
> **As by the sequel you shall see.**

What does the phrase did not agree with him **most likely** mean?

Ⓐ argued with him

Ⓑ did not go well with the tea

Ⓒ did not taste like cake

Ⓓ made him feel sick

54

Which sentence **best** describes the character of Mrs. Nightmare?

Ⓐ She's worried about young Tim.

Ⓑ She enjoys causing the young boy pain.

Ⓒ She is eager to warn children about jelly-cake.

Ⓓ She loves to sing, dance, and tell stories.

PRACTICE TEST 2

55

Read these lines from the poem.

> "Good gracious! what can ail the child!"
> His agitated mother said.

Which word **best** explains the meaning of the word agitated?

Ⓐ hopeful

Ⓑ sick

Ⓒ thankful

Ⓓ upset

56

Summarize "Ballad of the Jelly-Cake." Use details from the presentation to support your answer.

Write your answer in the space provided.

57

Based on information in the poem, which of the following words and phrases describe Tim? Choose **all** that apply.

A. ▢ foolish

B. ▢ greedy

C. ▢ careful

D. ▢ sorry for what he's done

E. ▢ mean to others

F. ▢ scared of Mrs. Nightmare

58

Think about how the poem was read aloud and what it sounded like. How would the poem be different if it were written as a story? Use details to support your answer.

Write your answer in the space below.

PRACTICE TEST 2

STOP

Writing Task

Read the passages, and respond to the Writing Prompt that follows.

Kids Should Do Chores

How do kids learn the skills they will need as adults? According to many people, helping with chores at home plays an important part in learning these skills. Housework is real. It needs to be done. It isn't something that is the responsibility of only one person. Everyone who lives in the house should share the responsibility and the work.

One of the most important skills kids learn from doing chores is a sense of responsibility. As kids and as adults, we must know how to assume responsibility. We're responsible for doing our work in school. Others depend on us to do our parts in projects. We're responsible for doing our school assignments so that we can learn what we need to become successful adults. Later in life, at our adult jobs, others will depend on us to do our work. Our employers will expect us to be responsible for doing our parts to make the companies successful. We also have responsibilities to others in all of our personal relationships.

Sharing chores with other members of the family builds teamwork. You learn to work with and depend on others as they work with and depend on you. Everyone learns to do his or her part. Teamwork is an important part of school, extracurricular activities, and work for the rest of your lives. Knowing how to be a team member helps make you a better coworker.

One part of being responsible and independent is being able to do practical things for yourself. Skills such as cooking, doing laundry, and cleaning are crucial in college and in adult life. Learning to do them as a child prepares you to take care of yourself later.

Doing household chores can also help kids develop a number of other traits that help them become successful students and adults. The successful completion of tasks raises self-esteem. It empowers kids to have confidence in their ability to take care of themselves. It teaches patience and the capacity to stick with a task until it's finished, even if it isn't much fun. By working with others, including parents, kids develop a work ethic that will help them in school and in life.

Not only do family members learn a number of valuable skills by sharing chores, they also make more time to enjoy themselves. Sharing household chores means the chores get done faster. Parents have more time to spend with their children doing things that are fun. By working together, a family can also make time to play together.

Kids Shouldn't Do Chores

Should kids be expected to do chores at home? Some people think they should not. There are several reasons given for kids not being expected to do housework. Safety is one reason cited for not doing chores. Many household items and appliances can be dangerous. For example, vacuum cleaners can be heavy and difficult to operate. Improper use can put children at risk for injuries. Many appliances are electrical, and children might not have the ability to operate or clean them properly. This can be a risk. Young people might not have the skills or strength to perform some tasks properly, such as washing dishes. There is a risk of spreading germs because of improper washing. Glassware breaks easily, and broken glass is a risk. It is also dangerous for children to handle sharp knives and other types of kitchen tools.

PRACTICE TEST 2

There are also some health risks involved in household chores. Many children suffer from allergies or asthma. These conditions can be made worse by the dust from sweeping—even if a vacuum cleaner is used. Many household cleaners are toxic, and young people should not come into contact with them.

Health and safety are just the tip of the iceberg, however. School and homework put serious demands on children's time and energy. Education must be a priority for children. Therefore, students must have time to complete homework and study at home. They must also get adequate rest so they can perform well at school. Chores and housework take away from the time kids should be studying or sleeping.

Kids also need time to develop socially. They need time for activities with their friends. Not only are these relationships and activities important for social development, they also provide stress relief. Kids need to unwind and relax. They need to play and enjoy the outdoors. They need to just be kids. The lack of these outlets could result in mental and physical distress for children.

Learning responsibility is vital to becoming a successful person. Kids can learn responsibility at school, in the clubs and activities they join, and with their friends. They don't need to be burdened with household chores in order to learn responsibility.

Writing Prompt

The readings discuss whether or not kids should be responsible for doing chores in their homes. Write an essay in which you give your opinion: should children do household chores? Use the information from the passages in your essay.

Manage your time carefully so that you can

- plan your essay;
- write your essay; and
- revise and edit your essay.

Be sure to include

- an introduction;
- support for your opinion using information from the sources; and
- a conclusion that is related to your opinion.

Your writing should be in the form of a well-organized, multiparagraph essay.

Write your essay on the following pages.

Write your answer in the space provided.

PRACTICE TEST 2

Informative-Explanatory Essay Writing Guide

Purpose, Focus, and Organization	Evidence and Elaboration
The response is fully sustained and consistently focused within the purpose, audience, and task; and it has a clearly stated controlling idea and effective organizational structure creating coherence and completeness. The response includes most of the following: • Strongly maintained controlling idea with little or no loosely related material • Skillful use of a variety of transitional strategies to clarify the relationships between and among ideas • Logical progression of ideas from beginning to end, including a satisfying introduction and conclusion	The response provides thorough and convincing support/evidence for the controlling idea or main idea that includes the effective use of sources, facts, and details. The response includes most of the following: • Relevant evidence integrated smoothly and thoroughly with references to sources • Effective use of a variety of elaborative techniques (including but not limited to definitions, quotations, and examples), demonstrating an understanding of the topic and text • Clear and effective expression of ideas, using precise language • Academic and domain-specific vocabulary clearly appropriate for the audience and purpose • Varied sentence structure, demonstrating language facility

Conventions
The response demonstrates an adequate command of basic conventions. The response may include the following: • Some minor errors in usage, but no patterns of errors • Adequate use of punctuation, capitalization, sentence formation, and spelling

Credit: Arizona Department of Education, AzMerit Student Writing Guide. September 2015.

Opinion Essay Writing Guide

Purpose, Focus, and Organization	Evidence and Elaboration
The response is fully sustained and consistently focused within the purpose, audience, and task; and it has a clearly stated opinion and effective organizational structure creating coherence and completeness. The response includes most of the following: • Strongly maintained opinion with little or no loosely related material • Skillful use of a variety of transitional strategies to clarify the relationships between and among ideas • Logical progression of ideas from beginning to end with a satisfying introduction and conclusion	The response provides thorough and convincing support/evidence for the writer's opinion that includes the effective use of sources, facts, and details. The response includes most of the following: • Relevant evidence integrated smoothly and thoroughly with references to sources • Effective use of a variety of elaborative techniques, demonstrating understanding of the topic and text • Clear and effective expression of ideas, using precise language • Academic and domain-specific vocabulary clearly appropriate for the audience and purpose • Varied sentence structure, demonstrating language facility
Conventions	
The response demonstrates an adequate command of basic conventions. The response may include the following: • Some minor errors in usage, but no patterns of errors • Adequate use of punctuation, capitalization, sentence formation, and spelling	

Credit: Arizona Department of Education, AzMerit Student Writing Guide. September 2015.

NOTES

NOTES

NOTES

NOTES

NOTES

NOTES